praise for barry friedman and his books

"No one I know of has honored a father as gallantly as has Barry Friedman, animating 'the oddities and wonders of Jack Friedman' for readers whose misfortune was never to have met him. Jack's enormous success was to have raised a son who loved him so faithfully, so drolly, and—our reward—so memorably."

> Mark Singer, author of *Funny Money* and staff writer for *The New Yorker*

"You can't go on the road with standup comedian Barry Friedman, which is probably good for your health and sanity. But you can feel what it felt like, through this funny, gritty, wondrously detailed and scarily honest book I really am enjoying it."

> Dave Barry, author, recipient of the Pulitzer Prize and the Walter Cronkite Award for Excellence in Journalism (about *The Joke Was on Me*)

"From the Baby O! Lounge in Hastings, Nebraska to the Elks Lodge in Seminole, Oklahoma, it's Barry Friedman! Let's give him a big hand, folks. He's written a book with all the wisdom and humanity of Alexis de Tocqueville's Democracy in America, but with way better jokes and twice as many clitoral piercings."

> John H. Richardson (about *The Joke Was On Me*)

"This masterpieces would blow away the competition, if there were competition for such a masterpiece, which there is not."

Shane Gericke, bestselling author of *The Fury* (about *Jacob Fishman's Marraiges*)

"Seeing the broken yet still beautiful work through Barry's eyes is cathartic"

Jennifer Taub, author of *Big Dirty Money* (about *Jacob Fishman's Marriages*)

"I knew this book would be special after reading the first sentence — 'You died today.' I was right. In *Four Days and a Year Later*, every single word counts. Barry Friedman invites readers to bear witness as he opens his heart and soul and pulls no punches in telling a story of loss and survival that is both tragic and inspirational. This book is simply incredible. What a gift Friedman has created for us."

Michael Wallis, author, *The Best Land Under Heaven: The Donner Party in the Age of Manifest Destiny*

"I haven't been able to get five pages in without having to catch my breath. You're a brave writer, my brother."

Charles P. Pierce, *Esquire* (about *Four Days and a Year Later*)

"[*Four Days and a Year Later*] is a shattering memoir about love and parenthood and all the ways you can love too much and still lose everything. For anyone struggling to understand the current drug crisis and anyone trying to imagine the outer edges of family this book will both sear and hold you. Powerful, brutally self aware, Barry Friedman is a flashlight through loss and redemption"

Dahlia Lithwick, Senior Editor, *Slate*

jack sh*t 3

jack sh*t 3
I'm the Father

Barry Friedman

Copyright © 2025 by Barry Friedman

eBook ISBN: 978-1-964832-35-7

Paperback ISBN: 978-1-964832-37-1

Hardcover ISBN: 978-1-964832-36-4

First edition by Babylon Books

All rights reserved under the International and Pan-American Copyright Conventions.

No part of this book may be reproduced or transmitted in any form or by any means, electronic or mechanical, including photocopying, recording, or by any information storage and retrieval system, without permission in writing from the publisher.

To Susan . . .
Daughter, Sister, "Woman from Long Island"

foreword

Previously . . .

It was the beginning of 2018.

My father, Jack Friedman, who had turned ninety-one the prior October, was preparing to move into a one-bedroom apartment at the Tulsa Jewish Retirement & Health Center, courtesy of "the Big Guy," which was what he called Jim Jakubovitz, its CEO—not because Jim was big, but because Jim was bigger than my father and my father couldn't remember his name. My father couldn't remember names, or, most likely, didn't feel it was important enough to remember them, including, maddeningly, his own daughter's—my sister, Susan. He called most women he'd see, or meet, regardless of age, nationality, understanding of English (and this included the Vietnamese women who gave him pedicures) "Miss America." Men were "Mr. America." He couldn't remember names of places, either. Old School Bagel Cafe, where we spent most Saturday mornings, was "Owl Head," and the Tulsa Jewish Retirement & Health Center, later renamed Zarrow Pointe, was "the Hebrew Home" or simply "the Hotel."

"What kind of bill am I running up here?"

"It's all included, Dad. Nothing."

"What do you mean 'nothing'?"

"It's nothing."

"How can it be nothing?"

"Because it's all included in the rent—the meals, the security, all of it."

"C'mon, give me a figure."

"There's no figure!"

"Why do I ask you anything?"

He had moved from Las Vegas years earlier—dragged to Tulsa by me, according to what he told everyone—and had been living at Tulsa's Mansion House Apartments, which he called, simply, "the Mansion," as if Tulsa had just one and he was in it before coming to the Hebrew Home. A few weeks before the move, we were at NYC Pizza, a place run by a guy named Kenny, who came to Tulsa from the Bronx. We were sitting under a framed photo of the 1962 New York Yankees. Kenny, who liked my father, as did most people, had just brought our pizza and told us about yet another relative of his who'd just died.

"He just dropped dead and died," Kenny said of some cousin. "And that was after his brother died *and* the sister had cancer. I got this thing now with my gut, so what are you going to do?"

"This guy with his stories," my father said, after Kenny walked away. "Wow-wee-wow! By him, everyone dies or has got some disease. This guy is Dr. Death."

Back to the photo.

My father, who was thirty-six in 1962, grew up in Brooklyn but was a Yankees fan.

"Look at that!" he said, staring at it. "Look at that," he repeated. "Mantle, Maris, Berra, Whitey Ford, Skowron. What a team that was."

He knew all their names.

"How do you know their names and can't remember your daughter's, which is Susan, by the way?"

"This was, like, a million years ago. Where the hell did the guy get this picture?"

"Probably bought it."

"Why?"

"I don't know why. He liked it. How should I know, though? Kenny's from New York, the Bronx—his whole family is—so it makes sense."

"What are you talking about?"

"The name of the restaurant: NYC Pizza."

"Yeah, yeah, I know. What's your point?"

"That's why they have the picture."

"What do you mean?"

"The Yankees, the Bronx. These guys are from the Bronx."

"All right, don't get so shook up."

His attention then returned to the picture. I watched him disappear into the Jack Friedman of fifty-six years ago.

What was he thinking?

"Say, Ba, let me ask you something," he said. "Any Jews on that team?"

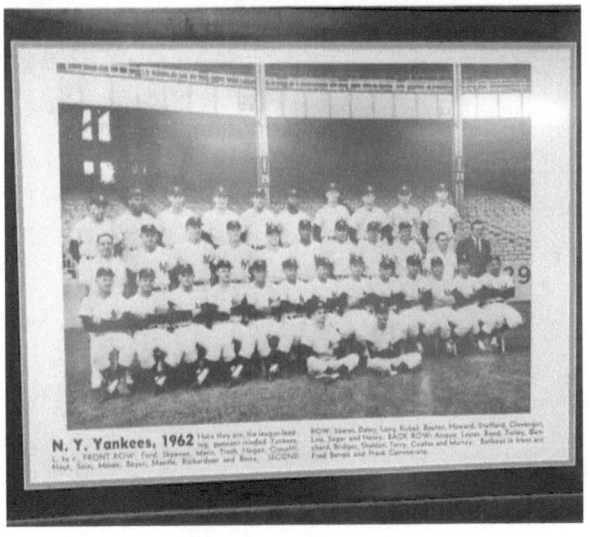

one
2018

FEBRUARY

3 FEBRUARY

We are at 61 Nails in Tulsa for pedicures. The last time we were here, my father told the two Vietnamese women, Diane and her mother, Amy, who were both working on his feet, that what they were doing "was better than sex." Today they had Diane's brother, Amy's son, work on his nails.

"Hello, Mr. America," my father says to him, even though it's obvious he knows no English. "You know why you can't cut that one?" my father asks, pointing to the nail on his big toe. "Because of the war. This was before your time."

Soon my father is telling him the Purple Heart story.

The guy is probably 19 and appears to know less English than his mother and sister.

"Why," my father asks the guy, "are my nails so hard and not glossy? Is it because I'm ninety-one? Is it circulation or what?"

The guy smiles.

"Hey, Ba," my father mouths to me—I am sitting next to him —"they take charge cards here?"

"Yeah."

"Say, is that toe warped?" my father asks the guy, now

masked. "I think the toe's deformed, I really do. You know, in the war, I had a piece of metal sticking out of it. That's why I got the Purple Heart. But it feels very good. No joke. It's better than sex."

It's a good punchline.

"I don't think that guy speaks English," my father says on the drive home. "I keep talking. He says nothing. Don't misunderstand me, he does a fabulous job on feet. But say something, for crying out loud."

* * *

7 February

My father is unhappy with the Yankef-Leibisch Family Circle financial management. He received a letter from Ida, Family Circle president, informing him that his $8/year dues is late. The letter went on to say that if dues weren't paid promptly, it might put his burial plot at risk and he would no longer receive the Yankef-Leibisch Family Circle newsletter.

"I called Pitsy," my father says about one of two in the family named Pitsy.

"Why'd you call Pitsy? Ida's the problem."

"Ida doesn't know from nothing. Did you know Pitsy married Jerry Parker?"

"I'm aware. Why do you call her 'Pitsy,' anyway?"

"Why?"

"Why?"

"Why."

"Yes, why?"

"She's Pitsy. It means 'small.' *Pitseleh*. It's Jewish."

"You mean Yiddish?"

"What'd I say?"

"Close enough."

"But back to Ida."

"Last time, she had me speak to the collector."

"The family circle has a collector?"

"You know what I mean."

"I actually have no idea what you mean."

"She wasn't home. I spoke to Ida's husband. What's his name? Or maybe they're not married. Who can keep track? Ida always has a fella. Anyway, the guy, the collector, said I didn't owe any money and not to worry about it. They moved to New Rochelle."

"Ida didn't move to New Rochelle."

"No, not Ida. Jerry and Selma."

"Who's Selma?"

"That's Pitsy. We call Selma 'Pitsy.'"

"Which Pitsy?"

"Pitsy! I pay every year. You know you and Wayne and Susan can be buried there."

"Yes."

"But not Melissa, because she's not Jewish."

"I know. But it's not like anyone's going to ask."

"Those things are not cheap, those plots. No joke."

"I know."

"You know how many people are buried there?"

"The exact number? No."

"The whole family's there. I mean the dead ones."

"Right."

We drive by St. Francis Hospital. After seeing the statue of St. Peter and the gigantic cross on the ground, my father asks, "These are the Catholics?"

"Yeah."

"Wow-wee-wow! What's the matter, Jews couldn't build a hospital in Tulsa?"

* * *

11 February

David Blatt and Patty Hipsher, dear friends of mine, join us at Owl Head Bagels.

"So the bridge fell on my toe. This was 1945," he tells them.

Again.

"I got a Purple Heart, but no joke, it fell on my toe. Went to the hospital. This was before your time. It was, like, seventy years ago."

"How does it feel now?" David asks.

* * *

16 February

"Ba, why can't I hear you?" he asks on the phone.

"Why? I don't know why."

"Are you on your phone?"

"Yes, I'm on my phone. We're talking."

"So maybe I need to get a phone-to-phone thing."

"A phone-to-phone thing?"

"You know, when people call."

"That's called a phone."

"What do you mean?"

"They have a phone. You do. You talk back and forth."

"I know, I know. So, what's up, sweetheart?"

* * *

17 February

At Owl Head, once again, with David and Patty.

"Barry's mother is from Oklahoma," my father tells David.

"No, she wasn't," I say. "She was born in New York, in Brooklyn, like you."

"What are you talking about?"

"She wasn't born in Oklahoma."

"I was born in Brooklyn."

"So was she."
"Then her parents were born here."
"They were not. They were born in Poland and Russia."
"Then why was your mother here?"
"She left you."
"Left me?"
"Yeah, remember, for about a year?"
"Oh, that's right. So who was born here?"
"Nobody in the family."
"Then what the hell am I doing here?"

* * *

18 February

We're at Owl Head, yet again, and Joe, one of the owners, surprises my father with a beautiful plate of pancakes and eggs.

"What is this?" my father asks as Joe puts the plate in front of him.

"Pancakes and eggs."

"I'm getting this and the egg and soft roll?"

"No, no, just this," Joe says. "Enjoy."

"Who ordered this?" my father asks after Joe leaves.

"Nobody. He just thought you'd like it."

"Who the hell can eat all this?"

"This is where the 'thank you' goes."

"Who made this?"

"Joe."

"You mean the Big Guy? Not Owen?"

"Aaron."

"Aaron. Why do I think his name is Owen?"

"God only knows. But they're partners."

"Take some," he says, sliding eggs over to my plate.

"I don't want any. You want syrup?"

"Yes, a little. Put it over here," he says, pointing to an empty place on his plate.

I pour the syrup, which quickly mingles with the pancake and, horror of horrors, the egg.

"Ach," he says, "you got it on the egg."

"Is that a problem?"

"Well, you put syrup on pancakes, not eggs. It's all right, though. No big deal."

After breakfast, sitting in the car in front of his apartment at the Mansion, he says, "Thanks for everything you're doing with the move. You need dough?"

"No, I'm good."

"You need money for gas?"

"No."

"Oh, that's right, you drive an electric."

"Right."

"You don't need dough?"

"I don't need dough."

"Let me give you a couple of hundred."

"No, I'm fine."

"All right, thank you again for everything. I'd kiss you, but I'm achy."

* * *

22 February

"What do you got there?" he asks as I enter his apartment at the Mansion.

"Boxes."

"Boxes?"

"Boxes."

"What kind of boxes?"

"They're boxes."

"I know, but . . . what? For packing?"

"Yes, for packing."

"That's all you brought?"

"That's all I could carry."

"You should have gotten them bigger."
"Go watch TV."
"Don't get so shook up."
"Don't talk to me. I got shit to do."
"All right, I won't ask questions. What are you packing, though?"
"Why are you talking to me?"
"All right, I won't talk to you."
Moments later, I enter the room with pictures from the bedroom.
"What are you doing with the pictures?"
"Packing them."
"What are they? Pictures?"
"Yes."
"Mine? Of what?"
"People, things."
"Let me see. Ba, question: At the new place, the Hebrew Home, what kind of garbage do they have? A chute or a room?"
"I don't know."
"I just wanted to know if it's a chute or a room."
"I don't know."
"It's probably a chute. Do you know anyone who lives there?"
"Yeah."
"Who do you know?"
"I know people there."
"Who?"
"Does it matter? People."
"Do you know if they have a chute?"
"If they have a chute, you have a chute, and, no, I don't know."
"I just didn't know, that's all. So when can we move in?"
"This weekend."
"You mean, what, Saturday, Sunday?"
"Yeah, the weekend."
"Friday?"

"Sure, Friday."

"But you don't know what kind of garbage they have? Because we have a chute here. Ah, Ba, I hate moving. How am I going to find everything?"

"They'll be in boxes."

"I'm going back to Vegas."

"I'll help you pack."

"You're knocking your brains out."

"Wayne will be here Saturday. He'll help."

"I hate for Wayne to come. He works, he's got responsibilities. He's a busy guy."

* * *

23 February

When I arrive this morning at the Mansion, he is opening a box.

"What are you doing?" I ask.

"You packed something I needed. I couldn't find it this morning."

"What was it?"

"It was in one of the boxes."

"What was it?"

"What I needed?"

"What did you need?"

"I couldn't remember. But I couldn't find it."

"So how do you know I packed it, or that you even need it?"

"I don't. But you must have."

"But you didn't know what you were looking for."

"It's not a big deal. I just couldn't find it, that's all."

* * *

25 February

At dinner, Melissa, my girlfriend, whom I've mentioned in

the previous volumes, says, "You know, Jack, you're a good-looking man. Why don't you just take off the toupee?"

And he does.

Just like that.

At the kitchen table, he holds it in his hand and, as Hamlet spoke to Yorick's skull, says to his hairpiece (I think this one was named Caroline), "You're going into the closet. It's all over. You've had a short life, but it's been a nice one. I'll see you around. [*Strokes it.*] Keep yourself nice because if you don't, nobody's gonna take you."

* * *

26 February

The Big Guy invites us to dinner at the Hebrew Home. Malyn, one of the activity coordinators, stop by.

"Hi, Barry."

"You know her?" my father asks.

"Yes."

"That's my son," he says to her, pointing to me.

"I know," she says.

"I'm the father."

"She knows, Dad."

"She knows?"

"She knows."

"How does she know?"

"She knows."
"*Voudriez-vous vous promener sur les Champs Elysées?*"
"I don't speak French," she says.
"You're uncivilized. Where you from?"
"America."
"No, I mean your family."
"They're from Germany."
"There's a lot of that going around."

MARCH

1 March

Tonight, at the Hebrew Home, Jack Friedman enjoys his first dinner as an official resident. Decked out in his new blue hat from Target, upon his now-toupee-less head, he is approached by Jim—not "Big Guy" Jim, another Jim—the restaurant manager, a sweet guy, who, after welcoming us, has some bad news.

"Mr. Friedman, I hate to ask you this, but we don't permit hats in the dining room."

"Jim, can I talk to you a moment? Dad, I'll be right back."

I get up. We walk to the kitchen.

"You have to do me a favor," I say. "That man over there"—I point to my father—"has worn a toupee for forty-four years. It's been off for three days. He's not ready. Can you make an exception on this one?"

"I would," he said, "but some people complain about hats. It's policy."

"I'm begging you. If he goes back to the toupee, and he will, it'll be on your head, please excuse the pun, and then . . . well, you want to hear people complain, just wait."

"Is it that serious?"

"Imagine taking a hypodermic away from a heroin addict."

"How much time do you need?"

"A week."

"All right, you got it."

* * *

3 March

"The Home here gives you thirty meals a month?" my father asks.

"Yes."

"But what about those months when there are thirty-one days?"

"I think they include thirty-one meals that month."

"You sure?"

"Pretty sure."

"Did you ask?"

"No."

"I'll just skip one meal. No big deal."

"You don't have to skip a meal."

"Nah, I don't have much of an appetite anymore after I stopped playing tennis."

"You stopped playing tennis ten years ago."

"You know what I mean."

* * *

4 March

This morning, I'm in the lobby of the Hebrew Home and I hear another man, not my father, say to a woman sitting on one of the sofas, "Hello, Miss America."

Guy's stealing my father's act.

"Bad news, bad news," my father says when I see him. "My adding-machine tape broke. I need my computer."

"Why don't I just bring you more adding-machine tape? And a computer, what does that have to—"

"—because I need my computer for the . . . you know, I have a lot of tax stuff. I should never have given up the computer."

"You did the returns by hand."

"You don't know. I did a lot on computers. Let me come over to your house and work on your computer."

"I don't have tax programs on my computer."

"What are you talking about? I don't need those. What is that, anyway?"

"This is my point."

"And now my adding-machine tape goes out. Ach, I give up! What do they want from my life? I need this like a hole in the head."

"Dad, I'll bring you paper for the adding machine."

"What do you mean?"

"I'll bring you paper."

"You know what paper I need. It's for the—"

"—adding machine."

"Where you going to get it?"

"I have some."

"You have some?"

"I have some."

"What do you mean?"

"I have adding-machine paper."

"Why do you have adding-machine paper?"

"Because I have an adding machine."

"So why don't I have paper?"

"You had it and then ran out. I didn't. Life is like that sometimes."

"Can I get some of yours?"

"Yes. I'll bring some over."

"You know what I need. The white that's in the, you know, a circle."

"A spool."

"A what?"

"Never mind."

"All right, tell you what. You bring over the adding-machine paper and I'll put it in my machine, or you can. I don't know how these things work anymore."

"Great idea."

* * *

8 March

"Ba, a guy called me from downstairs and wanted to know what I wanted for dinner tonight."

"Did you tell him?"

"I didn't know what to tell him."

"What do you want for dinner?"

"I don't know."

"Did he give you options?"

"Yeah."

"What sounded good?"

"I think the chicken."

"So call him back and tell him you want the chicken."

"Okay. You mean, call him now?"

"Yeah."

A minute later, the phone rings.

"I'm not calling. I'm going down to tell them I want the chicken."

"You're right. This is no job for the phone."

Five minutes later, the phone rings.

"Okay, I went down there and told him. I have to tell him every day?"

"No. It's probably because you're new."

"I don't mind telling them. I just don't know what to say. But they got a good chicken, you know."

* * *

9 March

We're on meal eleven out of the allotted thirty—I have been there for two of them. Shabbat dinner counts for two meals, but you get a better cut of meat, the challah, matzoh-ball soup, and homemade dessert. Adding to the mathematical woes on the horizon, on Sunday Melissa, Gregory, her son, who's 13 and lives with us, and I are joining my father for dinner, which will add three to the monthly tally. My father will get "back" three meals at the end of the month because he'll be in New York with Susan, and he'll save three more by going to the "Hot Rod" Casino—explanation just below!—for its buffet for the next three weeks. These are things that occupy my thoughts these days.

* * *

13 March

LeAnna at the Hard Rock Hotel and Casino—which my father, you might remember, calls the Hot Rod Casino—took my father out to dinner last night. At dinner tonight at the buffet, she tells me their server was nonbinary.

"Oh, dear," I say. "How did that go?"

LeAnna quoted my father: "'I don't know who he or she was supposed to be,' she reported. 'Don't get me wrong . . . very nice. But I didn't see any bosoms? Did you see any bosoms?'"

"LeAnna, I don't know what to tell you . . . but did you?"

Later, on the way back to the Hebrew Home: "Dad, you comfortable at the new place?"

"Very much so. I eat dinner with these two guys. One's older than me, but the other one, he's in . . . the carriage, the machine."

"The carriage . . . the machine? You mean a walker?"

"No, no, you walk with the thing and you push it. There's, like, four hundred of them at the place."

"The walker. He's got a walker."

"Anyway, these two guys. One of them is falling apart. They eat the salad, but they never eat the dinner. Well, last time they ate the dinner. I wonder why one day they eat the dinner, the main course, and then one day they don't. Anyway, they both have these people, I don't know why. What do you call them?"

"Helpers."

"Helpers?"

"Yeah, personal aides."

"Why do they have aides? Do I need an aide?"

"You have an aide."

"Who?"

"Me."

"Oh, yeah, that's right. Anyway, they have these aides. I joke around with the black aide. He's very nice. I think he's from Poland or Russia."

* * *

24 March

"They all make big bucks up there," my father says of his daughter, my sister, Susan, in anticipation of his trip to New York. "Big bucks! Even Emily, the girl, makes money, and she takes me to the movies twice a week. And Chris, he fell into this computer thing, and he's making big money. Probably forty grand a year."

"He's making more than that."

"No."

"Yeah."

"No."

"I'm telling you."

"Your sister works hard. They all go to work. Every morning. There's, like, seven cars in the driveway. Even Jesse, who wants to be a pastor—and where did that come from?—is making money. And Noah, the biggest one, has the smallest room. He's making money at the airport. What does he do there, again?"

"He—"

"—anyway, I almost never pick up a check when I'm there. You know how much that would be? There are five big eaters there. They're enormous. I'd go broke. Susan says I can stay as long as I want."

"Good."

"And Leo Meltzer died in his sleep? How does that happen? You wake up, choke, and then die? I don't get that."

* * *

27 March

Jim, "the Big Guy," tells me that my father asked one of the teenage girls serving at the Hebrew Home to sit on his lap.

"You want me to talk to him about it?" I ask.

"He won't remember, but, yeah, mention it."

I relay the story to my father.

"What do I say?" he says. "They don't know what they're talking about. I was joking. Ach, I want to go back to Vegas."

We arrive at the Hot Rod buffet minutes later, and LeAnna, as she usually does, seats my father early. When I arrive at the table, I hear this: "So, tell me," my father asks her, "have you gained weight since you started working here? Because who the hell can eat like this every night?"

* * *

30 March

My father calls to tell me, "So, I was at dinner last night, and I asked for another piece of chicken, and the one waitress said to the other one, 'Give him what he wants. He's the father of the famous son.'"

"Nice."

"'No,'" my father says he told her. "'What do you mean? Me? I'm not famous.'"

"I don't think they were talking about you."

"Then who were they talking about?"

"How many sons do you have in Tulsa?"

"You? They were talking about you? No, no, they said the famous son. They were talking about me."

"Dad, you're the father, remember?"

"I know that. Wait. How do they know you, then?"

"I don't know who they are, but apparently they know who I am. You told me the story."

"How do they know you?"

"I don't know!"

"I thought they were talking about the Big Guy."

"But Jim's not your son."

"Who?"

"Never mind."

"No, no, they said I had a famous son. They said it to ME. And I thought, 'I have a famous son?'"

"Most importantly, did you get the chicken?"

APRIL

3 April

As mentioned, my father has gone to Mastic Beach, New York, on Long Island, while I work in the Bahamas before returning to Tulsa for a prostatectomy, something I decided not to tell him. I cannot imagine how that conversation would go and just how many times I would have to say the word "prostatectomy." As it turns out, doctors got all the cancer, and I'm not in any danger of dying, which is good, because I promised my father I wouldn't.

MAY

4 May

Susan calls to tell me our father gave her ten bucks for her birthday at dinner the other night.

"What did you get Barry?" she says she asked him.

"What did I get him? I came here for six weeks. That was my gift to him."

* * *

9 May

My father is still doing accounting work for clients of his in New York.

I call him at my sister's. "Dad, you got a check from the guy Marc, the limo driver."

"How much?"

"Fourteen hundred."

"Great. Take half, since you did the work on his whatchamacallit."

"Thank you for that."

"No, you deserve it. Really, take a third."

"You just said half."

"I thought you didn't want half."

"Why would you think that?"

"You just said you didn't want half."

"I didn't say that."

"Okay, I thought you said that, that's all. No, take—what do you want to take?"

"This is hilarious. I'll owe you pretty soon."

"No, take half, you deserve it."

"Thanks."

"Yeah, so put it in the bank and take, what'd we say, a third, a half, I don't remember. Tell you what: Take four hundred dollars."

"Sounds good."

* * *

18 May

My father, home from New York, walks into my house—Susan and her daughter, my niece Emily, flew home with him—and sees Melissa on the floor, on her foam roller, stretching her back.

"What are you doing on the floor?" my father asks.

"Stretching."

"Stretching? What's the matter? You not feeling well?"

"I'm not, actually."

"Yeah, because you look terrible."

* * *

20 May

My father is watching television with his reading glasses. It's eighty-two degrees.

"Just the man I wanted to see," he says. "I can't see anything with these glasses."

"That's because you're watching television with your reading glasses."

"No, I'm not. These are for reading. The others are for watching television."

"That's my point."

"Oh, yeah. Why do I have these on? Where are my other glasses?"

"I just got here."

"Where the hell did I put them?"

"Probably on the table."

"You're not going to find them. I looked everywhere."

I see them on the table. "They're right here."

"Where'd you find them?"

"On the table."

I hand them to him.

"Where were they?"

"On the table."

"I looked there."

"That's where they were."

"I'm watching this movie, *Troy*, and it's too dark and they're mumbling and I can't hear anything. It's a jerky picture anyway. It's like they're talking in Spanish. Put on the show for me . . . the nurses show. Have you seen the show? Another thing. Why is it so goddamn hot in here?"

I look at the thermostat. "You turned the heat on."

"I turned the heat on? I didn't touch it."

"You must have done something."

"I didn't do anything. I pushed a couple of buttons. That's all."

"That's touching it."

"You know what I mean. I was just checking the thing out and it's not very clear. They got, like, eighteen buttons. Why do they have so many buttons? Ach, I give up! What do they want from my life?"

"I don't know, but, look, I set it to seventy-six and the A/C. Don't touch it, okay?"

"I never do. I don't go near it. Hey, did you know the woman across the hall is not Jewish?"

"I did not know that."

"No joke. She's not Jewish. The one right across the hall! She wears a . . . you know . . . a thing."

"A crucifix?"

"Yeah. It's a Jewish place, right?"

"Yeah, but you don't have to be Jewish to live here."

"Does she know she's surrounded by Jews?"

"Surrounded? I don't know, but we should ask. But let's break it to her gently."

"What?"

"Nothing. You want to go to lunch?"

"Yeah. By the way, what time does the mail get here? I mean here, where I live?"

* * *

25 May

"This is my son. I'm the father," my father says to Mort and Sherman at dinner. "That's what's-his-name and this . . . is—"

"—Hi, Mort, hi, Sherman," I say.

"He's a tailor," my father says. "He learned at Auschwitz."

"That's how I survived," Sherman says, dipping his spoon into some matzoh-ball soup. "Ach!"

"What's the matter, Sherman?" I ask.

"There's no flavor to this soup."

"Really?"

"No taste."

"None?"

"Not like my lady used to make."

"She made good soup, did she?"

"Yeah, but she was a compulsive gambler."

He goes on. "I mean, it's okay now, but when the place first opened, it was all Jewish, so you had blintzes—Jewish food. But now, they opened it up to everyone, so they have to serve different kinds of food. And the gentiles, you know. They'll eat anything."

* * *

29 May

My father calls. "Tonight, Ba, when we go to the buffet, I think Leonora—"

"—LeAnna."

"What'd I say?"

"You were close. LeAnna!"

"Anyway, I think she wants to comp us. I mean, she didn't say anything, but I think—"

"Dad, I don't think she does. I don't think she can."

"No, no, I'm not suggesting she will, but I think she wants to. She's never said anything, but I think she does anyway, so when we get there and she sees us, she may tell us to come in. So let's hang around and I think she'll, you know . . . I mean, I don't know. I didn't ask."

"Dad, she's not going to comp us. This isn't Vegas. It doesn't work like that. She just can't walk two people into the buffet. She's the restaurant manager, but trust me, she's not doing that."

"Well, not you. Just me."

"You think she wants to comp just you?"

"Well, you know, we're running together."

JUNE

3 June

"So, Dad, the dinner was good last night?"

"Oh, yeah, very good, very elaborate. Lots of desserts. And we had, oh, what the hell was it? Anyway. No, they don't fool around with dinner at this place. I wonder what it's costing me."

"Nothing. It's included."

"What do you mean?"

"It's all part of the same charge every month. I take care of it. Don't worry."

"But some of the guys don't eat. They eat the salad and that's it. Why do they do that?"

"Maybe they're not hungry."

"Nah, c'mon!"

"All right, I don't know why. They don't want to eat. Why is that your business?"

"They come to dinner, they don't eat. I don't understand that. What's the matter with these people?"

* * *

6 June

LeAnna, with more patience than Gandhi had with British rule over India, comes over to the table to say hello at the Hot Rod Tuesday-night buffet. My father sees her name tag.

"LeAnna?" he asks. "I thought it was Elena."

"No," she says, "it's LeAnna."

"I thought it was LeOna," he replies.

"Nope."

"All right," he says, "give me a kiss and a hug. What the hell?" He stands and she hugs him. He sits.

"So, do you eat the food here?" he asks.

"Sometimes."

"What did you weigh when you started?"

She smiles, taps his shoulder, and walks to another table, laughing to herself.

"You do all right," he calls to her, then turns his attention to me. "You know, I run around with her a little. She's off Mondays."

* * *

8 June

"Ba, that chicken and cheese you bought the other day is the best thing ever," he says to me in the kitchen of his apartment at the Hebrew Home.

"Really?"

"Fantastic. Where'd you get it?"

"A deli counter."

"Like a grocery store?"

"Yeah. One with a deli counter."

"Outstanding. The best thing you've ever done."

"The best?"

"Well, you know what I mean."

"I have yearned for years for your approval."

"What?"

"Nothing. But you like? Good."

"Out of this world. Sometimes I don't even use the bread. I just take the chicken and put it between two pieces of cheese and eat it like that."

"Then what do you do with all the bread you have?"

"I freeze it for when I need it."

* * *

12 June

On the way to the Hot Rod, we see a billboard for a weight-reduction clinic in which a woman is pictured, smiling, with the caption "I lost 142 pounds and I feel fantastic."

"C'mon, nobody loses that kind of weight and feels good," my father says as we drive by. "You know how much weight that is?"

"I'm thinking 142 pounds."

"You can't lose that kind of weight and feel okay. You'd be lethargic. The body would be . . . blah. It's not normal. She's lying."

* * *

17 June

"So the bank charges three dollars and fifty cents," my father says today at Panera, "just to check a balance?"

"Well, the casino does. The bank then sometimes charges another two fifty."

"The miserable bastards. The nerve of them. That's all. I'm finished with banks."

"Good plan."

"You know, I was dizzy earlier."

"You didn't tell me."

"It's softening up. I don't mean dizzy, I mean, you know, unsteady."

"That's dizzy."

"I had to sit down, that's all."

"That's dizzy."

"Ach, dizzy. I don't know if I was dizzy."

"You were dizzy. Did you eat anything today?"

"No, I didn't. That's probably it."

"You didn't eat anything? You didn't have your cereal this morning?"

"You know I combine the Frosted Flakes and the Rice Krispies. Great combination. Every morning I have it."

"I'm aware. And you didn't eat any this morning?"

"No, I did."

"You just said you didn't."

"I did. But I didn't have that much."

* * *

20 June

"So I hear the casino doesn't pay when the dealer busts on twenty-two in blackjack," my father says to me on Interstate 244, on the way to the Hot Rod.

"That's not true."

"No, it is. I saw it."

"Maybe you miscounted the dealer's hand."

"Well, I wasn't playing. It's possible. I was just walking by the table, and the dealer went like this"—he swipes his hand in midair, indicating a push. "But it's what I saw."

"But it's not. When the dealer busts with twenty-two, the house pays."

"Maybe. But the nerve of them to do that."

"But they don't do that."

"No, I saw. It happened. Not tonight, but before."

"But you just said you weren't playing at that table and maybe you were mistaken."

"Well, still, imagine—they do that!"

"But they don't do that."

"Vegas doesn't do that."

"They don't do it here, either!"

"Maybe Vegas does it now too."

"Dad, the casino pays when the dealer busts."

"So you're saying they get to not pay on twenty-two, but I lose on twenty-two?"

"No. You lose on twenty-two and they lose on twenty-two. But if they hit twenty-two and you're still playing, they lose."

"What kind of cockamamie state is this? They allow that? Is this an Indian thing?"

"They don't allow that! The house pays when the dealer busts on twenty-two."

"I'm telling you, I saw the dealer had a twenty-two and he didn't pay. He went like this." And, again, he swipes his hand through the air.

"Dad, listen to me, they pay when they bust on twenty-two."

"Why don't you check when we get there?"

"I checked."

"And what did they say?"

"They pay when a dealer busts on twenty-two."

"Who did you talk to?"

"A dealer."

"Which one?"

"I don't know which one."

"You have to talk to a boss. The dealers don't know."

"The dealers don't know? Of course the dealers know."

"I gotta find out. You don't pay on twenty-two. How do you not pay on twenty-two?"

"They pay on twenty-two!"

"Ach, Oklahoma!"
"Dad, one more time. When a dealer busts, they pay."
"No. Somebody told me they don't."
"Somebody?"
"Yeah, somebody. A guy."

A friend sent me a message today:

"Had a strange encounter with your father today at the gym. I did my workout and got into the shower. Seeing something odd about one of the soap dispensers, I looked closer and found a pair of hearing aids, which I took back to my locker while dressing. Jack appeared and said he had lost his 'ear plugs.'

"I said, 'Do you mean hearing aids?' and handed him what I had found. He was most appreciative and asked my name, which he immediately forgot, but before leaving, he said, 'If you need a woman or something, just ask.'"

* * *

26 June

"This soccer," my father says this morning at Owl Head, "all they do is run. What kind of sport is that? It's only with the feet."

JULY

3 July

"Dad, where are the hearing aids?" I ask as he gets in the car.
"You mean the plugs? I don't need them today."
"Today?"
"What?"
"Today you don't need them?"
"No, no. I know where they are. I was watching television, and I didn't put them in, that's all."

"I should get them."

"Where?"

"In your apartment."

"I know where they are."

"I'll get them."

"I don't need them. I hear fine. I had the TV on all day and heard every word."

"Dad, you sit five feet away from it and you have the closed captioning on."

"The what?"

"The script."

"Yeah. I put that on the TV."

"I know."

"You have to show me how to put that on the TV."

"But it's on there."

"I mean, in case you're not around."

"Where would I be?"

We get to the Hot Rod for the buffet and LeAnna ushers us into the dining room.

"We are swamped today," she says. "The hotel is giving away pool floaties. None of these people"—she scans the array of people here for the Tuesday buffet—"have pools, so I don't get it. Besides, you can get them at Walmart for $4.95. I swear. They could give a roll of toilet paper away and people would line up."

My father rolls up his sweatpants leg to his knee.

"Look," he says to LeAnna. "Look."

"What am I looking at?" she asks.

"My leg."

"I see that. What about it?"

"Huh?"

"Jack. What do you want me to do?"

"You see it?"

"I see it."

"You want to touch it?"

"I'll pass."

"C'mon, it's a dollar a touch."

She laughs and leaves.

"Hey," he calls after her, loud enough for those who have been squirreling away floaties, "I'll call you Monday."

"She's such a nice girl," he says as he turns back to me. "You know she's full Indian."

"You told me."

"How many tribes you got here? In Oklahoma, I mean."

"I don't know."

"They all got casinos?"

"I don't think so."

"The Apaches here?"

"I don't think so."

"They were the fighters."

"If you say so."

"She's Creek, I think, LeOna."

"LeAnna."

"What?"

"Nothing."

"Cherokee. I don't know. One of them. She's very nice, though."

* * *

7 July

We're at Owl Head this morning when Michael Wright, a writing instructor at the University of Tulsa, comes by carrying a copy of Steinbeck's *The Grapes of Wrath*.

"What are you reading?" asks my father.

Michael shows him.

"*The Grapes of Wrath*? *The Grapes of Wrath*? That's, like, a thousand years old. You're just now reading it?"

"I'm rereading it," says Michael.

"When did that come out?" my father asks.

"1939."

"1939?"

"1939."

"What printing is that?"

What printing is that? "Dad, have you read it?"

"Well, you know, I, uh . . . I saw the movie. Is he still alive?"

"Steinbeck? No," I say.

"When did he die?"

"I don't know."

"What's the book about?" he asks Michael. "I mean, the story."

"It's about the Dust Bowl, the banks, people getting screwed."

"He's probably a Republican."

"Actually, he was a socialist," says Michael.

"Well, there's a lot of that going around. So he died?"

"Steinbeck? Yeah."

"I didn't know he died."

"He died."

"You know what we should do?" my father asks. "We should go back to the beginning, before anything bad happened, and this way we can avoid all the bad stuff. Like, when Hitler was born. When he was a baby, we should have killed him right there. That's all."

* * *

8 July

"Why doesn't God take me already?" my father asks this morning at iHop. "What does he want from my life? But I'll tell you what, Ba. You can have the clients. Hey, no joke. It's good money. Don't forget. Jovanovic, the doctor, has a big carry-forward loss. He's on extension. What the hell did we order, anyway?"

* * *

10 July

A woman at the Hebrew Home approached me yesterday and said, "I just had the nicest talk with your daddy. He told me about his entire life. How he was in the Philippines and your mom, who was a dancer in Las Vegas."

"That pretty much covers it."

"No. He's so proud of your mom. A dancer! In Las Vegas. It's so sweet the way he talked about her."

"Yeah, really is. If only it were true."

"Your mom wasn't a dancer?"

"Maybe around the house, but not in Vegas."

"I wonder why he said that."

"He's Jack Friedman, that's why."

"He's very proud of you."

"He is?"

"Oh, yeah. He said you were the best son who dragged him to Tulsa."

"Perfect."

"He said you meant well."

My father and I then head to the Hot Rod buffet.

Let me back up a little. LeAnna called late last week to tell me her boyfriend was back in her life and they were getting married. She was worried, though, how my father would take the news because, well, they were "running together." She thought he might be developing a crush on her.

"He is," I said.

I told her we'd come by.

We arrive.

We sit down at the buffet, and she puts her hand on the table, her engagement ring visible.

He sees it.

"What, are you married?" my father asks.

"Actually," she says, "that's what I wanted to tell you. I just got engaged."

"Engaged?" he asks. "Engaged?"

"Yes."

He does not then say, "Congratulations." He does not say, "I'm happy for you."

Jack Friedman, ninety-one years old, asks LeAnna, who's in her early fifties and now engaged, "Does he know about me?"

* * *

14 July

We're headed to Owl Head.

"Ba, how did Bernie die?"

Bernie Newman—and this is important to the story—was his cousin. They grew up across the street from each other in Brooklyn. This has been (and will be) an ongoing conversation.

"Again with this? He died. Old age."

"He was six months older than me."

"People die at your age, and he didn't just die."

"What? Didn't he just die?"

"No. He's been dead for years."

"And Lylah died. How did she die?"

"I don't know Lylah."

"She was married to Bernie."

"I didn't know Bernie."

"How could you not know Bernie? He was my cousin growing up. Oh, yeah, that's right. You weren't born yet. I gotta call Pitsy and find out how he died."

"He died, Dad, years ago."

"They called you?"

"No. They didn't call me."

"He's in that picture. Have you seen the picture? That picture I have."

"Yes."

"They're all dead. All the old-timers."

"The picture was taken in 1936. Some of those people were

sixty then. It would make them, like, 140 now. Yes, they're going to all be dead."

"I'm the only one left. Well, Pitsy's alive. She married Jerry Parker. Who knew that was going to happen?"

"I don't know."

"They had a big fight with Mel. Pitsy was Mel's girl."

"Last time in Florida, they told us this wasn't true."

"Ach! I give up. So they ran back to New York and now live in, you know, upstate. New Brunswick. Mel's in California. He takes naps."

"New Rochelle."

"Something with his foot. Leo's dead, too. Morris, Miltie. These were friends. They're all dead. Your mother's dead. She's not in that picture that I have with all the old timers. And Red dies in his sleep, next to Ida. He's holding the flag in the picture."

"The flag? What flag?"

"The flag. The Family Circle had a flag."

"The Yankef-Leibisch Family Circle had a flag?"

"Yes. And Red was holding it. And then he died."

"I'm sure there were other things that happened in his life between him holding the flag and dying."

"But Bernie Newman died? Not good, Ba. Not good."

"He died a long time ago. Besides, how long had it been since you talked to him?"

"Who knows. Lylah was impossible. Forty years, maybe. But still. Make a phone call."

We arrive at Owl Head, and as we walk toward the entrance my father sees the "Old School Bagel Cafe" sign—the real name of the place.

"'Old School Bagel Cafe'"? he asks. "I didn't know they called it that. Old School? Why Old School? Why not New School?"

* * *

17 July

"So she's getting married to this guy," my father says as we walk into the Hot Rod Casino before seeing LeAnna. "Do you know? She's got a ring. I saw it. He gave her a ring?"

"I was there."

"What do you mean, you were there?"

"I was there when LeAnna told you."

"Told me?"

"That she was getting married."

"Yeah, I know. She told me. Anyway, he gives her a ring?"

"That's what guys do sometimes."

"He's in his sixties. She knows him, I guess. I don't know. So what does she want with me?"

"I don't think she wants anything from you. She likes going to dinner with you."

"Well, we go to dinner and he knows about me. She told him."

"He's a secure man."

"What?"

"Nothing."

"You know Leonora is a full Indian."

"LeAnna."

"What?"

"LeAnna!"

"That's what I said."

"Okay."

"Let me ask you. Do Indians have last names? I never noticed."

"Yeah."

"Does LeOna have one?"

"LeA—never mind. Yes, Dad. She does."

"It's Bennett or something."

"Barnardo."

"What'd I say?"

"Close enough."

"You know, I saw her for lunch. She picked me up because I don't have a car. It was nice, very nice. It's just lunch, dinner. You know. There's no physical interchange."

* * *

18 July

Good friend Walter Lipman from New York has arrived in town.

"So when do you fly?" my father asks about his travel plans back to New York.

"Thursday."

"In an airplane or a zeppelin?"

"An airplane."

"I wonder how fast a zeppelin goes."

"About thirty miles per hour," Walter replies, because Walter knows such things.

"Yeah, no joke? I thought it was more."

* * *

25 July

"Where you from, dear?" my father asks Mai, a nurse at Dr. Schumann's office.

"Thailand."

"Thailand? I was in Tokyo."

"That's in Japan," Mai says.

"Well, that was during the war."

* * *

27 July

"So, Dad, you still eat dinner with the same two guys every night?" I ask him.

"Dinner? What are you talking about?"

"The guys who sit at your table during dinner."

"Guys at my table? What guys at my table?"

"The two guys at your table where you live with whom you have dinner every night."

"I don't eat dinner with two guys."

"Dad, yes, you do. Dinner at your place, where you live. You sit with two guys."

"Two guys?"

"Yeah, the two guys."

"Oh, you mean the guys I have dinner with? I thought you meant something else."

"What . . . never mind. Those two guys."

"What about them?"

"Do you still have dinner with them? Are they still at your table?"

"Oh, those guys. Yeah, yeah, they're fine. One doesn't talk much, though. He's, like, 107."

"He's not 107."

"He's ninety, at least. The other one, I don't know. He eats, he doesn't eat. They have great meals at the place, though, I'm telling you. They don't fool around. Tonight they had roast beef. Some had it wet."

"Wet?"

"You know, with the juice on top."

"Juice? You mean gravy?"

"No. I don't like gravy. I had it dry."

* * *

28 July

"Ba, I need some flakes," he says to me at Owl Head. "I'm out. I need them. You know which ones I mean?"

"Yes."

"The sugar ones."

"Okay."

"I want the double box."

"Double box?"

"It comes, you know, with the tape between the boxes so you get two."

"Well, if they don't have the double, I'll get you two single boxes."

"Why wouldn't they have the double boxes? You know what I'm talking about?"

"Yes, but some stores don't have double boxes—"

"—It comes with the tape."

"I know, I'm just saying."

"Well, I like the two boxes because you get more than the one box."

"Really?"

"Yeah, because I eat a lot of it. So, you'll get me the double box?"

"If they have. If not, I'll get you two single boxes."

"I don't know why they wouldn't have the double box. It comes with the—"

"—the tape, I know."

"Make sure it's the flakes with the sugar, not the regular ones. It's all I eat. Every morning, I eat the flakes and coffee, so get me the double box. Oh, that reminds me. I need milk. Get me the double quart."

"A half gallon?"

"No, no, the double quart. I use a lot of it."

"Dad, a double quart is a half gallon."

"What are you talking about?"

"Two quarts is a half gallon."

"I know. So get me a double quart."

"Okay. You want two individual quarts . . . or one half gallon?"

"You don't understand. I'll get it myself."

"Dad, you want a half gallon of milk, I got it."

"No, get me the double quart. Two of them."

"So you want four quarts, then? A gallon."

"No. You know what I mean—a double quart. Two of them. I'll tell you what. I already have a double quart, or what's left of it, so don't get me two. Get me one double quart."

"A half gallon?"

"Whatever you think."

"Okay. Anything else?"

"No."

"You sure?"

"All right, get me some cookies, but not too many. And last time you got me ice cream sandwiches, and they were very good. They came six in a box."

"However many come in the box, I'll get you ice cream sandwiches."

"I'm sure it was six. Anyway, take a look. If it's four, it's four, but, you know, the sandwich with the ice cream in the middle."

"Anything else?"

"A bottle of soda."

"Any specific kind?"

"No, doesn't matter. Root beer or orange."

"Okay."

"But no cans. I don't like the cans."

While my father napped in the car, I went into Reasor's, our local grocery store, and got him a half gallon of milk, a half gallon of orange juice, two boxes of Frosted Flakes, a large chocolate bar, a box of dark-chocolate-covered marshmallows, and a four-pack of ice cream sandwiches with vanilla ice cream inside two chocolate chip cookies with M&Ms. When he'd call and say, "I need the world," this is what he meant. When we got back to his apartment at the Hebrew Home, he seemed worn out. I gave him a piece of chocolate and told him I'd check in with him later.

I call.

"How you feeling?"

"Much better. I was falling apart earlier. I don't sleep because I don't exercise."

"But you're feeling all right now?"

"Yes, yes. So what's new, sweetheart?"

"Did you like the ice cream sandwiches?"

"Oh, yeah. Very much. I had one. I had the chicken and cheese, the ice cream sandwich, a piece of your chocolate—I have to keep it out because it gets too hard in the refrigerator—and one of those chocolate marshmallow things. Great with coffee. You know, I don't eat lunch, just breakfast and the dinner, so this was a nice bridge."

* * *

31 July

"So," my father says, getting in the car, "Cynthia's gone, Normie is gone. He doesn't have a stone, but he's there in the cemetery. He never got a stone. Nu? He was blind, too. But Pitsy married Jerry Parker. Where did that come from? I wonder if Mel is still alive. I mean, I know he takes naps. Mel and Pitsy had a thing and then something happened and she wound up with Jerry. Was a bad scene. So they ran to Florida. Now they're in New York somewhere."

"Yeah, New Rochelle," I say.

"No. It's upstate. Right above New York. I think New Rochelle."

"That's probably it."

"Jerry had something with his foot. Anyway, Gene Tanner is

gone, Bucky Simons is gone, Morris and Miltie are gone, George Topperoff is gone. Marvin is gone. You met him. Did you meet him?"

"I met him."

"He died. These are the guys I grew up with. I'm the only one left. And you know who died? Bernie's younger brother."

"I never met him."

"He was Bernie's brother."

"I never met Bernie."

"What are you talking about?"

"I never met him."

"Anyway, Bernie's brother was a colonel in the Army. He died. And Red Meltzer died in his sleep, but Ida is still in Florida. She's hanging in there. What about your friends? Any of them dead?"

AUGUST

5 August

"Dad, how are you? I'm in Dallas."

"Good. You still in Dallas?"

"Yeah."

"Dallas? What's in Dallas? Anyway, how is Dallas?"

"Good, we have some friends—"

"Get me a souvenir that says, 'I've been to Dallas.'"

"Okay."

"You know, a souvenir."

"Yeah."

"Like a T-shirt."

"Okay."

"You know, something. A souvenir."

"Got it."

"Doesn't have to be much."

"Okay."
"Is it a nice city?"
"Yeah."
"I heard it was big."
"It's a good size—"
"—You don't have to rush back. I've got plenty of food."

* * *

11 August

"Ba, I need a sled," he says, getting into the car before we go to Owl Head.

"A sled?"

"You know, a sled."

"A sled? You mean a walker?"

"No, no, not a walker. A thing you push yourself with . . . the rolling thing. They all have them. You know, a walker."

"A walker."

"Yeah, yeah, a walker. You know, a cart."

"Why do you want one?"

"Because I was downstairs talking to a woman. I know her. I mean, I don't know who she is, but I know her face, and she asked how old I was. I told her ninety-one, and she said, 'Ninety-one?' and then she got hysterical. 'Where's your walker?' she asked. It seems like ninety-five percent of the people there have walkers. Am I the only one who doesn't have one?"

"No, there are others."

"Is it because I played a lot of tennis in Vegas?"

"Maybe that was part of it. Good genes. Who knows?"

"Anyway, what's new, sweetheart?"

"Nothing."

"So, you know, Jovanovic has a carry-forward loss. Did you call him? He's on extension."

"No. Why would I call him? He's your client."

"I've gotta call him. When's Wayne coming?"

"In two weeks."

"You think I should have the egg today or the cheese?"

"The egg."

"Right. The cheese is fattening."

We eat. It's rather uneventful. On the way out of the parking lot, we see Aaron, one of the owners—everyone calls him "Q"—coming in. My father calls him "Owen."

I lower the window.

"What are you doing?" my father asks him from the passenger side, "taking the day off?"

Aaron/Q/Owen smiles.

"So are you married?"

My father asks him this every time he sees him.

"You married, have kids, divorced, what's going on?"

"Jesus!" he says. "You sure ask a lot of questions."

"No, seriously, how goes your life?"

We arrive at the Hebrew Home. I drop him off. He walks a few steps and then comes to the driver's-side window. I open it.

"You need a couple of bucks, sweetheart?"

* * *

12 August

"Say, Ba, I just spoke to Jovanovic. He said he spoke to you."

"Yeah, he called to tell me you weren't answering your phone."

"This stupid phone. I don't know how it works. It rings, it doesn't ring. Well, anyway, he told me you sounded very intelligent."

"That's nice. Probably had me confused with someone else."

"No, no joke. He said, 'Your son sounds so intelligent.' I said to him, 'My son Barry? Barry sounds intelligent?' I didn't know you sounded that way."

He comes over for dinner. I made pizza.

"Ba, it's a good pie. It's wet."

"Wet?"

"No joke. A lot of pies you get are hard and dry, but this one is moist and loose."

* * *

14 August

"You have that much trouble breathing?" my father asks LeAnna.

She's now wearing an oxygen tank and a breathing mask. She has lung cancer. She didn't tell my dad.

"A little. It's getting better, though."

"So what happened? What is it, the breathing?"

"Lung problems."

"You gotta walk around with that thing?"

"Yeah. It's not so bad, though."

"Well, walk slow."

"Okay."

"No, I mean it. Walk slow."

"I will."

"Is it from the smoking?" my father asks.

"I'm sure that didn't help," she says.

"And did the doctor mention your weight?"

"Dad!"

"What?"

"I can't believe you just asked that."

"I'm just curious."

"Jack, it's inappropriate," says LeAnna.

"I just meant because of the breathing. The weight puts a strain on the lungs, that's all."

* * *

18 August

"Ba, not good. I fell."

"What happened?"

"Well, I fell. I mean, I didn't fall, but, you know . . . I was going to the bathroom and my legs gave out. It's like they weren't there."

"Are you hurt?"

"No, no, but what the hell happened?"

"You lost your balance, I imagine, and that's why you fell."

"I didn't fall. No, it wasn't a fall, but I went down. Boom! Maybe my leg fell asleep, that's all."

"As long as you're okay."

"Yeah, I don't know. It's never happened before."

"Not important, but it has. Usually when you get up from a chair."

"When did that happen? I don't remember. I fell? I didn't fall."

"It has, but, again, not important. A lot of guys your age use the walkers—"

"You mean—"

"Yeah, the sleds. But maybe a cane just to help you get up from chairs and the bed. To balance yourself."

"A cane? I don't need a cane. I mean, this has never happened before. I've stumbled, I went down before, but not like this. This was a fall."

We head to Owl Head, where, as usual, I get him the toasted croissant with egg and where, as usual, he sits while I get him his decaf with four Sweet'N Lows and four mocha-, chocolate-, vanilla-, and caramel-flavored Half and Half mini containers.

"They make great coffee here, you know?" he says, before sticking his spoon in my Diet Dr. Pepper to get an ice cube. "Why do they make the coffee so goddamn hot here?"

"Would you keep your spoon out of my drink?"

"I'm trying to cool down the coffee, that's all."

On the way out, he sees one of the guys who works at Owl Head changing the liner on the garbage pail.

"It's just like putting on a rubber," he says.

* * *

21 August

On the way to the Hod Rod tonight, he says, "I couldn't for the life of me remember your name the other day."

"What happened?"

"A woman asked me how I got to Tulsa, and I told her my son dragged me from Vegas."

"Sounds about right so far."

"Wait. So she asks, 'What's his name?' and I tell her, 'Oh, you know him. He's, uh, you know. He's around. We have the same last name—Friedman.'"

"And?"

"She doesn't know who I'm talking about."

"Imagine that."

"So all I can think is your name is Enis."

"Enis?"

"I mean, I know it's not Enis, but it has the 's' sound, and I know that rhymes."

"My name doesn't have an 's' sound."

"But 'Dallas' does."

"But my name isn't Dallas."

"I know. But you were in Dallas a few weeks ago, remember? And that's how I remembered. 'Barry was in Dallas.' So what's new, sweetheart?"

* * *

23 August

"I'm dying, Ba. I'm dying, Ba," he tells me.

"You're not dying."

"I'm not?"

"You're not."

"How much longer I got?"

"Six years."

"Six? Six?" He looks up. "What does HE want from my life?" Then he looks to me. "Your mother is waiting. She's wondering, 'Jack, where the hell are you already?' And where the hell is my copy machine? I want to make copies. I can't make copies. Ach! I give up."

* * *

28 August

"You want to do my apartment next?" my father asks one of the cleaning people who make the rounds at the Hebrew Home.

"*No habla inglés.*"

"No, I'm saying: Do you want to do my apartment next?"

The woman smiles.

"Dad," says Wayne, who's here visiting from California. Wayne, my brother, is two years older than me.

"Dad," I say.

"She knows I'm joking. May you never know the horrors of stretch marks."

The woman continues smiling.

"Dad!" says Wayne. "Let her work."

"I'm just saying—"

"Dad," I say, "she doesn't speak English."

"What do you mean?"

"The act's not going to work," Wayne tells him.

* * *

29 August

Melissa mentions she wants another tattoo—this will be her seventh.

My father points to both of her breasts and says, "I know. Have them say 'Sweet' and 'Sour.'"

Then he asks her, "How old were you during the war?"

"I wasn't born."

"What do you mean?"

"I wasn't born. My parents weren't even born. My grandmother was three."

"Three? Did she tell you about the war?"

"She was three!" I say.

"She didn't tell you?"

"You're mad at my grandmother for not telling me about the war?"

"I have a Purple Heart, you know. Have you seen it?"

"Yes. You shouldn't have stolen it," I say.

"What stolen? I went to the bathroom and when I came back it was lying on the bed."

"But you don't remember if it was your bed. And there's no record of you getting it."

"Well, on the other medal I got, they spelled my name wrong. But this one wasn't engraved."

"Why is that?" I ask.

"It was being engraved, but then the bombs started dropping and the guy, the engraver, had to stop engraving."

SEPTEMBER

6 September

The Social Security Administration sent a letter to Petar, my father's eighty-four-year-old Yugoslavian doctor who's also his client, a delightful man. He forwarded it to my father, a ninety-one-year-old accountant who shouldn't be doing this anymore.

"Petar, what? What?" my father asks. "Speak up! This stupid phone."

"Dad, put it on speaker."

He does.

"Jack, I got something—"

"—Speak up, Petar."

"I got—"

"Petar, what?"

"Jack, listen, I got a form and—"

"What's with this stupid phone?"

"I got a—"

"—What did you get?"

"A—"

"What? Form? Well, what kind of—"

"It's a form."

"Oh."

"Jack, from the—"

"—What from who? A form?"

This goes on for about thirty minutes until I take the phone and tell Petar to send me the form.

"So what's going on, Ba?" my father asks.

"I'm having Petar send us the form."

"That's what I told him to do."

* * *

7 September

Upon meeting Lucy, Melissa's new dog, my father asks, "Male or female?"

"Female," says Melissa.

"So she's going to get pregnant? Oh, boy, you better watch out."

"No, she's not," says Melissa.

Then, making a circle with his thumb and index finger from one hand, he begins to stick the other index finger in the opening. Then he stops and asks, "So, you're going to get her closed?"

* * *

10 September

We're at dinner at the Hebrew Home.

"Dad, Susan and Noah may be coming for a visit."

"No, I don't want soup. It fills me up and then I can't eat the chicken."

"No, no. Susan and Noah may come for a visit in the next few weeks."

"Susan? You mean Susan?"

"Yeah. Susan. And Noah."

"Noah. You mean the big one?"

"Yeah. The big one."
"Now?"
"Not now."
"What did you order?"
"The salmon."
"You know a lot of people here are not Jewish?"
"I know."
"Does the chicken come with mashed?"
"I don't know."
"They make a great mashed. What am I drinking here?"
"Water."
"It's not water."
"It looks like water."
"It's not water."
"Okay, it's not water. Maybe it's 7-Up. What did you order?"
"You talked to Susan?"
"Yeah."
"I think I need a car. I have no wheels."

* * *

20 September

Today the Hebrew Home took its van and participating residents—five in all, I think—to River Silk (River Spirit Casino, if you're just joining us), for a morning of gambling, followed by lunch, which was how the problem started.

My father got lost.

Malcolm, my urologist's father—it's a small Jewish world here in Tulsa, what can I tell you?—a resident who was on the trip, called to tell me that when the group couldn't find my father, he asked a security guard to page him.

They don't page at River Silk.

"So the security guard asked what your father looked like," Malcolm said. "I didn't know what to tell him. I said, 'He's short, he's got a great personality.'"

"That about covers it," I said.

The chaperone of the trip also called to say she hoped I wasn't worried, as she has never lost one resident yet. Next time I saw Jim, the CEO, "the Big Guy," I thanked him for having such a great staff.

"We don't have any control over quantity of life," he said, "but if we can add a little quality, we are all over it. But I told them, in the future, should it happen again, just to leave him there."

"Perfect."

* * *

27 September

During a dinner of Swedish meatballs and pasta at the Hebrew Home, my friend Peggy Cadenhead, 93, comes over to discuss today's impeachment hearings against Trump in Washington, for trying to strong-arm Ukraine's Zelensky.

"Barry, did you watch today?"

"Oh, Peggy—Jack Friedman."

"I'm the father."

"I know, Jack."

"How do you know?"

"I know who you are, Jack."

"I spent eight years in Vegas."

"Dad, she knows. You've met before. Don't you remember? And, yeah, Peggy, I watched. I need a drink."

"I already had one. I don't like this guy at all."

After she leaves, my father asks me, "Who's that?"

"Peggy."

"Peggy?"

"Peggy."

"You know her?"

"I know her."

"How do you know her?"

"How do I know her? I know her!"
"So did you meet her here?"
"Her husband was my political-science professor forty years ago at the University of Tulsa."
"When did you meet her?"
"I don't remember."
"But you know her?"
"I know her."
"From here?"
"Maybe from here."
"You didn't know her then?"
"I didn't."
"But you know her now?"
"Yeah."
"Does she know I'm your father?"
"She knows."
"You told her?"
"YOU told her."
"Is she a customer of yours?"

* * *

30 September

"Did you go to the movie last night at the home?" I ask on the phone.

"No. I mean, yeah. I went, I went."

"What did you see?"

"Some English picture. What's-his-name was in it. You know."

"Any good?"

"Eh. I don't know. The guy is playing with this young girl. And then he gets older and she kills herself."

OCTOBER

3 October

"You know," he says, "I looked at my legs today. I have nice legs. I should have worn shorts."

* * *

5 October

"You know, Ba," he says on the phone, "Melissa is a very pretty girl. I've been meaning to tell you. Gorgeous. No joke. That's a good-looking girl you got there. I don't know why they turn to you all the time. I'm very serious. Tell her I said so and that if she wasn't attached to you, I'd run after her. Well, I'd walk fast after her."

* * *

14 October

"Hey, Dad, more than three hundred people wished you a happy birthday on Facebook."

"Where?"

"Facebook."

"Three hundred?"

"Three hundred."

"What'd they say?"

"'Happy birthday.'"

"How do they know me?"

"They know you, believe me."

"How?"

"I write about you, I talk about you. They know me."

"They know you? What do you say?"

"I quote you."

"Me?"

"Yes, you."

"What do I say? Well, that's very nice. So then why did I lose at the casino tonight?"

* * *

16 October

"How old is the oldest person ever?" my father asks.

"I think someone made it to 113."

"What are you talking about? I read in the paper someone was 139."

"Nobody lived to 139."

"I'm telling you, she was 139. Maybe more."

"She was not in her 140s."

"I knew I should have cut it out of the paper."

"Dad—"

"—I'm telling you. She was 139, 149 . . . something. She was in a chair, though."

* * *

19 October

I come over with a double quart of milk this morning. When I arrive, he's watching a crime show about an elderly handicapped man who keeps his young wife a sex slave. She is slithering on a pool table when I sit. I turn off the TV.

"What's up, Dad?"

"So, Mendel dies and then what's-her-name brought the little girl back to Canada. You remember them?

"Who?"

"Mendel! Mendel!"

"Mendel who?"

"Mendel! She married what's-his-name."

"This was before my time."

"You don't know Mendel?"

"I don't."

"Mendel!"
"Stop saying 'Mendel.'"
"So what happened to Leo Sturm?"
"I don't know who that is."
"He married the girl—oh, you know, what's-her-name? And they're both gone. And my father's brother, Sam B. Friedman, went to Hollywood and provided the furs. He's gone, too. They're all gone. We have to travel, Barry. We have to travel before it's too late."

* * *

23 October

"So, Dad, what'd you do today?" I ask on the way to the Hot Rod Casino.

"Oh, today, I went to a lecture downstairs at the hotel."

"You don't live in a hotel."

"Well, you know what I mean. The home."

"Great. What was the lecture about?"

"Who can remember? It was a guy and he was talking about, I don't know, Jews, I think, and then non-Jews. And how we get along and then how we don't get along. Very interesting, though."

* * *

25 October

I take my father out to dinner on what would have been his and my mother's 65th wedding anniversary.

"Why are we going to dinner again?" he asks, getting into the car.

"Today's your anniversary, remember?"

"Oh, yeah, yeah. You know my birthday was the 14th?"

"I'm aware."

"So what is it with God and breasts?" he asks.

"Oh, this should be good. What do you mean?"

"What? He gives women breasts and then he puts cancer in the breasts. Why does he do that?"

"That's actually a very good question."

"I mean, like, how many women are there in the country?"

"Probably 150, 160 million."

"And of course they all have breasts, right? So what I'm wondering is why is there so much cancer in them?"

"Dad, cancer attacks every part of the body."

"Yeah, I know, but the breasts—there's so much of it. Is it because, uh, the skin is so fleshy there?"

NOVEMBER

2 November

A tax client of my father's emails me today to tell me to alert my father that his accounting services have been terminated immediately.

"Hey, Dad, you were fired today."

"Fired? What do you mean, 'fired'?"

"Fired."

"Fired? By who?"

"Mark."

"Who the hell is that?"

"You know, the guy who owns the limo service, your client."

"Who?"

"See, this could be the reason."

"Why did he fire me? He fired me?"

"He fired you."

"I'll be a son of a gun."

"You haven't been doing much of a job lately."

"Yeah, I know. But that miserable son of a bitch. So does this mean I don't have to finish the work I was doing?"

"That's right."

"I was tired of it anyway. I'm just going to throw his shit out. If he wants it, he can call me. You know how many years I've had him?"

"No, I don't."

"Actually, I don't know either. Long time, though. Oh, it goes back years."

* * *

3 November

"I remember this place," my father says at 61 Nails. "They're Native American, Indians, if I remember."

"Vietnamese."

"That's what I meant."

"You do hair here?" he wants to know, sitting in one of the chairs. "And why is that one toe darker than the other? Was that from the bomb?"

Amy, the mother of the owner, or maybe she owns it too, smiles.

"I'm ninety-three—should I be ninety-three?"

Amy smiles and starts using a pumice stone on his heel.

"Oh, that feels good. Had I known you were going to do that, I would have taken off all my clothes. It's better than sex."

Amy smiles.

"You know, my feet feel great," he says on the way back to the home. "Those girls are from Vietnam, not the Philippines."

He goes on. "I got a couple of local clients—"

"—What local clients?"

"Here at the home."

"This is not good."

"What? They asked me."

"Who asked you?"

"Well, nobody asked me, but, you know. Someone was talking about taxes and I said I'm a CPA."

"But you're not a CPA."

"I was."

"No, you weren't."

"Anyway, he said he was doing his taxes and he was talking to me and I was talking back."

"So you're not really doing his taxes?"

"No. But if he asks—what should I charge him? I'm not suggesting he's going to ask. That's all. What am I doing taxes for, anyway? I'm pushing ninety-three."

"You just turned ninety-two."

"Say, Ba," he says, looking out the window, "how many Walgreens are there? So many stores they have. I think they're bigger than CVS."

* * *

6 November

"Ba," he says on the way to the Hot Rod, "I feel really good. Oh, I gotta get rid of this gut, so tomorrow morning, I think I'm going to take a trot."

"A trot?"

"I'm going to trot around. What? No good?"

"You want to trot, trot."

"I'll trot. What the hell, right?"

* * *

11 November

"Dad, it's cold out, so if we're going to the casino tonight, you should put socks on."

"What do you mean?"

"Socks."

"I got socks."

"I know you have socks. You should put them on."

"I got plenty of socks. White ones, black ones."

"Good. Go get a pair."
"Why?"
"Because it's cold out."
"I had them on earlier."
"And you took them off?"
"I don't wear them in the house."
"So you put them on and then took them off?"
"Well, you know what I mean."
"Dad, we're leaving the house. You should get some socks."
"Socks."
"Yeah, socks."
"I don't need socks."
"It's cold. You really will."
"But I was just wearing them."
"Not since I've been here."
"Not today. The other day."
"You had socks on the other day?"
"Yeah."

* * *

17 November

"Ba, this soup at Panera is delicious. I love the soup."
"Good."
"What kind of soup is it?"
"Chicken noodle."
"Ah, delicious. It's got the chicken and the noodles. Perfect."
"It's why they call it chicken noodle soup."
"Yeah, and the broth. It's very good. They give you a good couple of pieces of chicken, too. Very good. What are you eating?"
"Just some bread."
"You don't want soup?"
"No."
"Why don't you want soup?"

"I don't want soup."

"You like soup."

"But I don't want it now."

"So how did Marilyn die?"

"Heart attack."

"So sudden."

"Well, she was ninety-three, so, you know, there really isn't 'sudden' at that age."

"Yeah, I guess you're right. So, how much longer I got?"

"You'll live to ninety-seven."

"Why not ninety-eight?"

"Okay, ninety-eight."

"Ach, I give up. Everything hurts. Everything hurts. And I'm gaining weight because of you."

"Me?"

"Yeah, you buy the cookies and what-not. But you get the chicken and cheese—that's good. It's a good nosh. But you buy too much cheese. I'm putting on weight."

"Would you stop bitching?"

"Why? I'm entitled. I'm ninety-three."

"You're ninety-two."

"Wait till you're ninety-two."

"I'll probably be sitting here with you," I say. "Look, your life is good. Enjoy yourself. Eat what you want."

"But I can't button my suit."

"You don't wear suits."

"What if I get married again?"

"I'll get you a suit."

"You know the guy I sit with at dinner made suits for Hitler."

"No, no. He was in concentration camps. He was a tailor and made uniforms for German soldiers—not Hitler. That's how he survived."

"Yeah, I know, and the other guy, what's-his-name, at the table. He doesn't like the meat they serve. I don't understand. He eats it and then he doesn't eat it. Why doesn't he like it?"

"I don't know."
"They make a good meal there, no joke."
"Wonderful."
"This is great soup, I tell you."
"You mentioned it."
"You gotta bring me this soup."
"Or we could just come back."
"Yeah, but if you ever want to bring me food. That's all. It's really terrific soup. Just right."

* * *

20 November

"What kind of traffic is this?" he asks on the way to the Hot Rod.
"What kind?"
"Yeah. They going to the casino or going home from work?"
"Work."
"I don't know. Maybe they called the wife and said, 'I'm not coming home for dinner,' and decided to go to the casino. I betcha that happened. Say, Ba, what kind of work do these people do?"
"In these cars? I don't know. Construction, office, all kinds."
"I mean, is Tulsa a big work town?"
"A big work town? I guess. People work."
"Still an oil town?"
"Yeah. Oil services, mostly."
"How much oil you got left in the ground? A lot?"
"I don't know."
"Texas has oil and the ranches, yes?"
"Yeah."
We pass a QT sign advertising diesel ($2.95) and regular ($2.05), with the diesel price on top.
"Why is diesel so much more?"
"I don't know."

"And why is the $2.95 on top?"
"I don't know."
"Wouldn't it make sense to put the lower price up there? It's cheaper."
"Well—"
"I know why. Truckers sit higher. But why do they use diesel?"
"Diesel engines."
"What makes it a diesel engine?"
"I don't know."
"Can they use regular gas?"
"If they have a regular gas engine."
"How many of them are there?"
"Gas truck engines? I don't know."
"I'd still put the lower price on top."

We take the exit to the casino and see a homeless man with a sign, but as we make the light, we can't read it.

"What does that sign say?"
"I don't know."
"What does he want?"
"I don't know. Probably money."
"So why doesn't he write a novel?"
"I don't know."
"You think he eats at the buffet?"
"Probably not."
"You think he knows you can get in half-price tonight?"
"Don't know."
"You know I love Panera?"
"I do."
"I ate at my first one in Long Island."
"No, you didn't. You were in Las Vegas."
"Well, that's what I meant. You know, Long Island has the 'Long' in it and Las Vegas has the 'Las,' so I got them confused. That's all."
"It happens."

***

24 November

Had a lovely breakfast today at Owl Head with my friend Tamara Piety, a law professor at the University of Tulsa who follows my father's story closely, her mother, Pat, and my father. Upon learning that there were three Piety children, all girls, he asks about their sex lives.

"So," he asks Pat, "when did they all get destroyed?"

"Destroyed?" we reply simultaneously.

"You know," he says, "when did they lose their virginity?"

Pat then tells us a joke.

"Donald Trump gets in an elevator with an absolutely gorgeous woman. It's just the two of them. At some point, she hits the 'Stop' button, bringing the elevator car to a stop, and says, 'Mr. Trump, I have admired you for years, all that you've accomplished. You are such a turn-on to me. What I would really like to do is blow you right now, right here. It's what I really want.'

"Trump replies: 'What's in it for me?'"

***

28 November

"Now, remember, when I die," he tells me at lunch today at Doug's Cafe at the Hebrew Home, "you get me up to your mother. There's a plot next to her. It's reserved for me."

"Don't worry."

"What if they put someone else in there?"

"They didn't."

"But what if they did, by mistake?"

"They won't."

"All right, but if they do, you get me a stone anyway."

"You want me to put a stone up even if someone else is buried there?"

"Yes! Put it there. Take the other guy's stone away. I don't care. Bury him somewhere else."

DECEMBER

2 December

Lately, to help my father with his memory, I have been testing him on the names of the people in his life. Tonight at dinner, we had a session.

"Here we go. What are the names of your children?"

"Wayne and Susan."

"And?"

"Uh, you."

"Good. What were your parents' names?"

"Samuel and Riva."

"Well done. Your wife's name?"

"Ralph—Florence, I know, I know."

"Wayne's daughter's name?"

"Frankie."

"Very good. Susan's kids?"

"Emily, that's the girl. There's Christopher, Noah, and . . . the other one."

"Jesse."

"Jesse. I knew that."

"My girlfriend's name?"

"Misha."

"Melissa."

"Melissa."

"What's my daughter's name?"

"Which one?"

"I only have one."

"Uh, let's see. Don't tell me. Penelope."

"Penelope? Where the hell did you get that?"

"Not Penelope? You sure?"
"Yeah."
"Okay. Pat?"
"No."
"Patricia?"
"I would have given it to you on Pat. No."
"Uh..."
"Nina."
"I meant Nina."
"Sure you did."
"You know Bernie Newman had a daughter."
"He did?"
"He died, you know."

* * *

6 December

We're at Panera, where "they have great soup," talking again about the stone at the cemetery.

"You better get me there."
"I'll get you there, I promise."
"You promise?"
"You or your ashes, yes."
"Doesn't matter, as long as you get the stone."
"Promise."
"What are you going to put on the stone?"
"What do you want on the stone?"
"I'll leave it to you."
"How about, 'I'm going back to Vegas'?"
"Oooh, I like that. Very good. Now, how the hell did Bernie Newman die?"
"Again."
"What? I've never asked you."
"Dad, I don't know how Bernie died. I never met Bernie."
"He was my cousin. What do you mean, you never met him?"

"I never met him."

"We grew up together."

"I know, but I wasn't born yet."

"What are you getting shook up about? I wasn't asking you."

"You weren't?"

"No. I was just wondering if you knew how he died."

"That sounds like the same thing."

"Wait, I know. I'll ask Ida. She'll know."

"Good idea."

"But I won't come right out and ask. I'll call and say, 'Hi, Ida, it's Jack. Blah, blah, blah. Do you know how Bernie died?'"

"Very clever."

"You know Bernie's wife died too."

"I've heard. Very sad."

"How the hell did she die? You know Red died in his sleep?"

"I know."

"How the hell do you die in your sleep?"

"You just do."

"Don't you thrash around, start choking? How do you not wake up the person next to you?"

"How do you know this is what happens when you die in your sleep, Dad?"

"I don't know. I'm just guessing."

* * *

9 December

On the way to Owl Head . . .

"Oh, I broke my glasses," he tells me.

"What happened?"

"I didn't do anything. They just came apart. Here, here's the piece that came off." He hands me the broken arm. "So we need to get some cellophane."

"Cellophane? You mean tape."

"Yeah, cellophane. What did I say?"

"We'll just get them fixed."

"Fixed?"

"Yeah, fixed."

"What are they going to charge for that?"

"Not much. They just have to reattach the arm."

"Nah, we'll just get some cellophane."

"Dad, it's no big deal. You can't put cellophane on them."

"Why not? I do it all the time."

"No, you don't."

"I did once."

"We'll get them fixed."

"It's going to be thousands of dollars."

"No, it's not. Why would you think that?"

"I mean, I don't know."

"So why would you think it's going to be thousands of dollars?"

"What, you think they're going to replace the broken piece just because you tell them to? No, they're going to want to fix the whole thing."

"If you tell them you want them to fix the broken arm, they'll fix the broken arm."

"You got a guy?"

"Yeah, I got a guy."

"What's his name?"

"Why do you care what his name is?"

"What does he do?"

"He's an optometrist. What does he do? He sells cars. What do you think he does?"

"You know him?"

"You know him. You've been to him."

"I have?"

"Yeah."

"I don't remember."

"Don't worry about this. It's no big deal."

"And why am I gaining weight? I eat one meal a day."

"We're done with the glasses, yes?"

"Yeah, yeah! I don't know. Do what you want. I'm not spending a thousand dollars. I can just get some cellophane. That's all he's going to do anyway."

"He's not going to put cellophane on your glasses."

"What do you think? They actually replace it?"

"Yes, I'm sure of it."

"Ach. I give up."

"They're glasses. We'll fix them."

"All right, all right. Do what you want. How's Melissa? Does she still get the headaches?"

* * *

11 December

My father and I arrive at the front of the line at the Hot Rod, and LeAnna, recently married, meets us. As she is hosting, she is holding a number of straws in her hand, to be placed on tables as dinner guests are seated. That's key to the story.

"So, how you been?" I ask, referring to the cancer and her diabetes.

"You got straws?" my father asks. "Why?"

Since it's a question that doesn't need immediate attention, we ignore it.

"Better, much better," she says to me.

"Good. So you're feeling OK?"

"How many straws you got there, anyway?" asks my father again.

Since this is the same question and also doesn't need attention, we ignore it again.

The diabetes, LeAnna tells me, due to the insulin being injected into the midsection, has the effect of extending it in a condition known as insulin hypertrophy, I believe.

"And your neck and lungs?"

"Also good, better," she asks.

"How much soda are you going to drink, anyway?" my father asks, still spying the straws.

Again it is ignored, but I see LeAnna holding in a laugh.

"And, Barry, you good?" she wants to know.

"Yeah, everything worked out well for me with my hip surgery."

"How the hell can you drink all that soda?" my father asks again. "All those straws. How many you drink a night? It's probably what's putting on the weight."

And then LeAnna asks the question that so many of us have wanted to ask my father since I started keeping this little blog.

"Jack, what the hell are you talking about?"

LeAnna then makes the tactical mistake of explaining to my father about insulin hypertrophy and its side effects.

"So is that why your stomach is inflated? It looks inflated. I've noticed. Do you eat a lot here? Are you pregnant? Or has all this happened since you got married?"

* * *

16 December

"Hey, Dad, what's up?"

"What?"

"Turn the TV down."

"What?"

"Turn the—"

"—I just did."

"No, you didn't. I can still hear it."

"Okay, I just turned it off."

"Good. How are you?"

"Barry, I just figured out something. When I get older, I'm going to die."

"Yes, you are."

"Ach! I give up. My fingers. Why do my fingers hurt?"

"It's arthritis."

"But why my fingers?"
"Why not your fingers?"
"Ach! What do they want from my life?"
"It's normal to have some arthritis at your age. You're still alive, you woke up. It's a good day."
"Yeah, but my fingers. I don't understand."
"It's arthritis."
"But I don't get it. I've never had it before."
"You were never ninety-two before."
"I can't close my hand tight. You know what I mean?"
"Yeah."
"I mean, I don't think I can even grab a tennis racket."
"That works out. You're not playing tennis anymore."
"So what else would I need to make a fist? Grab a baseball bat?"
"Again, I think you're good."
Later . . .
He gets in the car outside the Hebrew Home.
"The women at this hotel, Ba—"
"You don't live at a hotel."
"You know what I mean. She asked me if I was married and I told her I was but my wife died, and then she sidled up next to me and I said, 'I don't remember anything about sex.'"
"Smooth."
"No. It's very nice. I tell them the jokes. You know, the one-liners, and they get hysterical."

* * *

24 December

Apparently, because he has not run the dishwasher since he moved into the Hebrew Home last March, my father has caused something of a flood due to excess water buildup. That, anyway, was his recounting of the conversation he had with the facility's employee who discovered the flood. My father was told to run the dishwasher once a week.

Call One:

"Ba, I was just told I had to run the dishwasher. How the hell do I do that?"

"I'll come up. Don't do anything."

"You'll come up?"

"I'll come up."

"I give up. I never use it. Put an 'on' switch on this thing, for crying out loud. I have one plate. And now it floods. What kind of cockamamie thing is this?"

Call Two (three minutes later):

"All right, don't worry about it. I turned the oven on."

"Why did you turn the oven on?"

"They told me to turn the oven on."

"The dishwasher, not the oven."

"Which one's the dishwasher?"

"By the sink."

"So why did they tell me to turn the oven on?"

"They didn't. They told you to turn the dishwasher on."

"Wait a minute. Back up. Which one's the dishwasher?"

"Turn the oven off, first thing."

"How do I do that?"

"Did you turn on the oven or the stove?"

"I didn't do anything. No, wait! Okay, I turned it off. I think."

"You sure?"

"Yeah, yeah. Where's the dishwasher, again?"

"By the sink."

(I call the front desk to alert them they might want to get someone to my father's apartment in the next, oh, fifteen minutes or so, or else the entire place might be in flames.)

Call Three (six minutes later):

"Someone was just here."

"I know. I told them to come up."

"Why did you do that?"

"Wanted to make sure the oven was off."

"I didn't have the oven on. My mistake. I turned the dishwasher on. I said it was the oven. It was the dishwasher. You know what I'm saying?"

"No."

"See, I turned on the top part. Water dribbled out. The dishes and glasses were moist."

"Are you sure?"

"Yeah, yeah. They were wet."

"So the oven wasn't on?"

"Why would the oven be on? I don't cook."

"You told me you turned it on."

"I meant the dishwasher. But just the top. My mistake."

"Dad, you can't just turn on—never mind. So, everything is off in the kitchen now?"

"Yes."

"Grab some cookies, walk out of the kitchen, and don't go back in . . . ever."

"Let me ask you something: They make technology so if you don't use it, it floods the place?"

* * *

25 December

To Hot Rod Casino on Christmas.

"Where are all the people? Isn't this a workday?" he asks on I-244.

"It's Christmas."

"Oh, right, so they're home with the presents. Is the casino even open?"

"Open? It'll be packed."

"You mean with Jews?"

"Not just Jews."

"Question: How come the Christians get to gamble on their holidays and the Jews can't?"

"What do you mean, we can't gamble?"
"We're not supposed to, but the goyim are allowed?"
"We can gamble too, you know."
"I'm not saying we can't. You know I live in a Jewish place?"
"I know."
"But it's not all Jewish. There's one woman who wears the, you know, the uh . . ."
"The cross—"
"—No. The cross around her neck."
"The cross. That's what I said."
"So, she wears the cross. She also has the tank."
"The walker."
"Yeah. The thing she pushes. I don't want a tank. They sit. They have a seat. Did you ever? Anyway, you think she knows it's a Jewish place?"
"I'm sure she has an idea."
"They do the prayers on Friday night, so I guess she just doesn't pay attention—or maybe she doesn't eat on Fridays."

* * *

27 December

"So the guy at the home, one of the guys," he tells me, "he chews his food and spits it out like he doesn't like it. Why does he do that?"
"Maybe he doesn't like it."
"You know which guy I'm talking about? That one guy. Not the guy, but the other guy."
"Yeah, I know. The other guy."
"Anyway, I don't understand. He puts it in his mouth, takes a few bites"—at which point my father illustrates how one would take a few bites—"and then spits it out. Very funny. He doesn't eat the meat. You think he gets any nourishment from it? I mean, I guess it would depend how long it's in his mouth."

"I think you have to chew and digest the meat to get any protein."

"Oh, by the way, don't buy me any more roast beef. It gets hard and old, but the chicken, or turkey, whatever you get, is delicious. It's soft and moist and goes with the cheese you buy. I make a sandwich, sometimes with the bread, sometimes I put the chicken around the cheese and the chicken acts like the bread. You know what I'm saying?"

"Yeah."

"So no roast beef. You know, I only eat the chicken at the dinner too."

"Don't you want to try something else?"

"Nah, I like the chicken. I . . . I just don't get involved with the other meats."

* * *

28 December

"Ach, I give up. This finger hurts," he says, bringing up the finger in question to my face as we sit in Panera. "I mean, it doesn't hurt. It's annoying. It's like a dull pain. Not an *oww-oww* pain. I can barely make a fist. If I was hanging from a pole with two hands, I don't think I could pull myself up. Or even hold myself up."

He then puts both hands above his head to show me the pose he would strike.

"Why would you be hanging from a pole?"

"I'm not suggesting I would, but I just know that I couldn't. This goddamn finger won't bend."

"You would never be hanging from a pole."

"But what if you're not around?"

"What does my having to be around have to do with anything? Are you ever in a position where you have to hang from a pole and can't pull yourself up?"

"No. But you know what I mean. What if I am?"

"That's not going to happen, believe me."

"Why did they give me the pain there?"

"They? Who they?"

"They! You know. Why the fingers? Nu? The fingers. What do they want from my life? Ach! How much longer do I got, Barry, anyway? How much longer?"

"Six years."

"Why six?"

"Why not six? It gets you to ninety-eight. It's a good life."

"All right, I'm not going to go until my fingers feel better, though."

"That's the spirit."

two
2019

JANUARY

2 January

"Pick me up something in Spain, would you?" he asks me. I'm headed over there to see a dying friend. "Something Spanish. You know what I mean? Like a decal for the car."

"You want a decal for the car?"

"Yeah, you know. For the windshield or bumper."

"You don't have a car, remember?"

"Oh, that's right. Remember that time we went to Italy, and they ran out of spaghetti?"

"Well, that restaurant did. I don't think the whole country did."

"They spoke Italian."

"Seems about right."

"I don't know why I thought they'd speak Jewish."

"Hard to know."

* * *

8 January

I return from Spain with a coffee mug.

"Why'd you buy this?"

"You drink coffee."

"Oh, yeah, that's right."

We go to the buffet tonight at the Hot Rod. LeAnna introduces us to her friend Billie, who starts singing "It Had to Be You."

"Jack," she says, "I was married for sixty-eight years to a doctor. But he died."

"What kind of doctor?" he asks.

"Well, he was a psychiatrist in New York."

"I went to Columbia," he says.

He didn't.

"I'm a widow now," says Billie.

"I got a Purple Heart for running the wrong way after the bomb hit."

"My husband was in Normandy," says Billie. "He was on the front lines. Very dangerous."

"So the sergeant said, 'Drop what you're doing and run,'" my father adds, "and the last thing I heard is 'You're running the wrong way.' Boom!"

"I love to dance," says Billie. "And sing."

"Well, let me show you a picture of my wife. Here"—he offers one—"is one . . . and here is the other one"—he flips it over—"where she's not wearing makeup."

"Very lovely," says Billie.

"So is your husband still practicing?"

"No," Billie says, "they don't let you practice after you've been cremated."

* * *

13 January

"Dad, how are you?" I ask on the phone. "I'm coming over with food for you."

"Food?"

"Food."

"Food? What kind of food? I don't need food. I eat every night here at the hotel."

"It's not a hot . . . never mind. This is for the rest of the day. You need anything?"

"Oh, yeah. I don't know. Yeah, maybe. I feel good, nothing hurts, but then I think the world is going to cave in. I don't know. I'm just not activated enough."

"Activated?"

"You know—active. I used to play tennis and ball."

"Ball? You played ball? Yeah."

"You don't know."

"Anyway, you're plenty active."

"I love that steam room."

"Good. You got chicken and cheese?"

"I eat it for lunch. It's a great snack."

"I know. You need any?"

"I'm down to one slice of chicken. The cheese is totally gone. So why am I so achy?"

"You're ninety-two."

"I get up from a chair and sometimes I don't get up right so I have to sit back down and do it again."

"Good thing you have plenty of time during the day."

"Oh, you know what I need? The soaps."

"The soaps?"

"For the washer."

"They do your laundry."

"She doesn't come."

"She comes on Tuesdays."

"Yeah, I know."

"So you don't need the soaps."

"I was just wondering, that's all. But I feel good. Nothing hurts."

* * *

15 January

We don't go to Hot Rod tonight. We head to the home dining room.

"Where you been?" Sherman asks me.

"That's my son," my father says.

"I know him," says Sherman.

"How do you know him?"

"From here."

"Here?"

"Here."

"When?"

"Every time he comes to dinner."

"I didn't know," my father says. "So where's the Sprite?"

"Dad, you want a Sprite?"

"It's not that I want one, it's just they always bring me one."

"Well, do you want one?"

"It's not a question if I want one."

"Actually, that is the question. I'll get you a Sprite."

"Where you going to get a Sprite?"

"I'll ask the waiter."

"He's not going to bring it."

"Of course he's going to bring it."

"Nah, he brought the water. You think he's going to bring a Sprite now. But usually he brings the Sprite."

"He probably just forgot. I'll get you a Sprite."

"Nah, I fill up on them."

"You fill up on them? I'll get you a Sprite!"

(I ask the waiter to bring my father a Sprite, which he does, and it's set in front of my father.)

"Did you get me this?" my father asks me.

"Yeah."

"Why?"

"You wanted one."

"I don't know if I wanted one. All right, leave it."

The meal progresses. Sherman likes absolutely nothing. The chicken is too cold, the fries are too spicy, the cake is too dry. He talks of great blintzes he's had and his time in Auschwitz. Meal over, I get the car to head to "River Silk" Casino. My father gets in.

"That Sherman likes you."

"I like him."

"He kept saying, 'I like your boy, I like your boy.'"

"That's nice."

"I don't know why he likes you so much."

"Beats me."

"No joke. He kept saying, 'Why don't you bring him around more?' 'Why didn't you tell me he was so smart?' 'I like your boy, Jack.'"

"Nu," my father adds, "I have to listen to this?"

* * *

19 January

"I swear to God, Ba, this is the best thing I've ever owned," my father says about a three-foot shoehorn he got from that woman from Long Island.

* * *

20 January

"Maybe, Barry, I should have got married."

"To whom?"

"You know, what's-her-name? When I was in Vegas."

"Jeannette?"

"Jeannette?"

"Jeannette."

"Jeannette? No, not Jeannette. Wait. Which one was Jeannette?"

"Remember, she was the one who buried two husbands who lived in the mobile home. She was in the bowling league with you."

"Oh, her! Not her. Well, yeah, she wanted to marry me too. I'm talking about the other one."

"There was no other one."

"You don't know. This was the woman, you know, the psychologist who had a house."

"A psychologist who had a house? You didn't know anybody like that."

"Yes, yes. She was short and plump and had a house and customers used to come see her."

"A short and plump psychologist who had customers who came to her house?"

"Yes! What was her name? Oh, she wanted to marry me. Move in. There was room for an office. Why didn't I marry her?"

"Because she didn't exist?"

* * *

22 January

When I come over today, my father asks, "So why doesn't Normy have a stone at the cemetery?" Norm Blumstein, his nephew, was married to Cynthia. "There's a sign but no stone. You know he was blind. Was he out of money?"

"I don't know, Dad. You haven't been there in years. He may have a stone now."

"Nah. He doesn't have one."

"He might. How do you know?"

"You know his wife—what's-her-name died, too."

"I know."

"How did she die, anyway?"

"I don't know."

"She was a sickly girl, Susan."

"Cynthia, not Susan."

"She's buried next to my mother."

"Your sister."

"My what?"

"Your sister, Vivian, her mother. Cynthia is buried next to her."

"Who's Susan?"

"Your daughter."

"I know that."

"Of course you do."

"They're all gone. Gene Tanner, a good-looking guy, and Billy Stein. They died. Marvin Kraftchin died. I'm the only one left. And Mel takes naps and Jerry wound up with Pitsy. Pitsy? It was a bad scene with Jerry and Mel. Pitsy was Mel's girl. And then Jerry and Pitsy had two girls."

"They got married in their seventies. They didn't have two girls."

"You know what I mean."

"Rarely."

"Who am I thinking of?"

"Tough to know."

"And Bernie Newman died."

"I can't do this again."

"And his wife died too. Nu?"

"Husbands and wives die. Did you even like them?"

"You remember that time we went to their house and she—Lylah, Lylah was her name, did you know Lylah?—wouldn't come out to say hello?"

"I wasn't there."

"What do you mean, you weren't there? Oh, that's right. It was your mother who was there. There was a fight about the card game and she wouldn't come out."

"I know this story. I heard you cheated at pinochle—and it's a different Bernie. Not Newman, but Metz."

"I cheated?"

"That's what I heard."

"I didn't cheat."

"It's okay with me if you did."

"Anyway, who knew she died?"

* * *

24 January

Upon arriving at his apartment, I notice my father has

purposefully taken a scissor to his jeans—he calls them "dungarees"—for two-inch vertical cuts from the waist down along the belt loop on both sides to make room for his expanding stomach.

"What are you doing with your jeans?" I ask. "You cutting them?"

"Cutting them?"

"Yeah, you cut them."

"I didn't cut them. I opened them up. I'm gaining weight because I'm not playing tennis anymore. I'm inactive, so I cut them to make room. What the hell am I eating, anyway? I eat one meal a day."

"Why don't we just get you some new jeans?"

"Nah, these are just for knocking around. That's all."

* * *

28 January

"Oy. Barry, I give up," my father says as I enter his apartment. "That steam room knocks the shit out of me."

"So why do you go?"

"Because it feels wonderful. Where did it all go? I was sixteen two weeks ago. Shit! But it could be worse. I could be in one of those pushcarts like a lot of the guys here. Don't get me a wheeler. I won't use it."

"Okay."

"So why am I in better shape than everyone here? Guys in their eighties, mind you. I'm pushing ninety-three. Hey, you know, a lot of these guys at the place never fought in the war."

"You sure?"

"They don't talk about it. I'm the only one."

* * *

29 January

We enter the elevator on the way to the dining room. A woman is already present.

"How goes your life?" my father asks, cheerfully.

Nothing from the woman.

"Behave yourself," my father says. "It's a public place."

Nothing.

"If you can't, take my number," he says.

The woman lifts her finger, points.

"Stop looking at me like that," she says. "I know who you are."

We arrive at dinner. Sherman arrives moments later, just as the woman at the next table does. They both have walkers. Due to the arrangement of the tables and space constraints, they can't keep both walkers close by. Neither is budging. Sherman bangs his walker into one of the other chairs at the woman's table, trying to "park" it.

"What do you think you're doing, buddy?" asks a friend of the woman with the walker.

Sherman keeps maneuvering a chair.

"Hey, hey," the woman says, "you can't keep your walker here." She points to her friend: "She needs hers close by."

"I need mine close by," says Sherman dryly.

"Move your walker somewhere else," says the friend of the woman to Sherman.

Sherman, untroubled, keeps pushing his walker where he wants it.

"He's been warned about this," says the woman with the walker.

Sherman survived Auschwitz. I'm thinking this warning has had less of an impact than she might think.

"How the hell can you eat the soup AND have the meal?" my father asks Sherman. "It's too much."

"The soup is okay tonight," says Sherman. "I'm surprised."

"Nah. But you shouldn't have the soup," my father says.

"You're not going to finish your meal. That's why I don't order the soup. I fill up."

"Every night," Sherman says to me, "your father orders the chicken. That's all he eats?"

"I can't eat the soup," my father responds.

"But chicken, every night? Why don't you be like your son?" Sherman asks, pointing to me. "He always looks so good. He's gracious."

"Who, him?" my father asks, pointing in my direction. "What does he know? He's been in Oklahoma his whole life."

Sherman orders the chicken.

Later . . .

We're at the "River Silk" casino where, evidently, my father got nauseous and threw up in the restroom. I'm telling you this because he told me he threw up, count 'em, seven times.

"*Vhoosh*," he says over and over, indicating to me the route the vomit traveled from his stomach through his chest and out of his mouth. "It must have been that goddamn chicken."

Which was not the funniest line of the night. That came, while we waited for the car at valet, when we saw an attractive couple walk by—I figure the man was mid-seventies, the woman late fifties—and my father, still queasy, unsteady, stopped in his tracks and said, "Look at this, would ya? The guy's a hundred years old. So how does he get something like that?"

* * *

31 January

"Say, Ba, did you know Cynthia died?"

"Yes."

"So what was her problem, anyway?"

FEBRUARY

2 February

At the "River Silk" buffet tonight, my father gets a plate of peel-and-eat shrimp.

"Look at this," he says about the shrimp. "Did you ever?"

"What's the matter?"

"They make you peel the shrimp yourself. They can't do it for you?"

"I'm not sure they have the manpower, Dad."

"This is impossible. Until you get the skin off. Ach! I give up."

"Can I get you a piece of meat, then?"

"Nah, I'm full from the goddamn shrimp."

* * *

10 February

"What does he want from my life?" my father asks as we head to the "River Silk" buffet, even though they take that "goddamn buck" (the fifty-cent vig before hands of blackjack).

"He? Oh . . . HIM? What do you mean?"

"How much longer I got, Ba, how much longer?"

"Five years."

"Five years? Why five years?"

"One, because ninety-seven is a good age to go, and two, it's when you run out of money and I'm trying to time this just right."

"You know, I had a dream last night about your mother, and she was screaming, 'Jack, where the hell are you? When you coming?'"

"Mom said that?"

"Well, it was a dream, of course."

"Of course."

"Everything hurts. Shit! You know, I'm not used to being old."

* * *

12 February

His doctor (he was my doctor, too), sadly, killed himself a few years back. Dr. Block was born Jewish but flirted with Christianity. At the memorial service, Block's son-in-law mentioned how Block had found Jesus, accepted Jesus, wanted everyone else to find Jesus, at which point my father, irony notwithstanding, said, "Jesus Christ, enough already. Talk about the guy a little." Anyway, tonight at my father's apartment, his Rolodex was on the dining room table (yes, he still has a Rolodex), and I noticed it was flipped to the section that included Dr. Block's name and number. On the card, my father had written in pencil, "Committed Suicide" and underlined it twice.

"Why did he take her and not me?" he asks as we drive back from Mondo's, our Italian restaurant in town. "She didn't drink."

"Dad, there's no answer for that."

"Yeah, I know, I know, but she was too young, and she so loved Las Vegas [which she didn't], so loved working on the shows [which she never did], and so loved the house I had [which he didn't have until years after she died]. Would it have killed him to give her a few more years? She was still a pretty girl."

"Yes, she was."

"Boy, don't make plans."

"Why's that?"

"Because if you make plans and God makes plans and your plans conflict with his, you lose, baby."

"Got it."

"You know she died of breast cancer."

"I know."

"I mean, did you know?"

"I knew."

"How did you know?"

"How did I know? I knew."

"Something with the breast. I don't know. It was warped."

"Lovely."

"You know what I mean."

"Absolutely."

He is silent for a minute. We drive by a Braum's, which is known mostly for its ice cream but also carries groceries, on our route.

"Look at that," he says.

"What?"

"They got butter for sale."

"What?"

"Look." He points.

Sure enough, on the marquee, "Four four-ounce quarters. Two for five dollars."

"Two for five, is that good?" he asks.

"Yeah. Not bad."

"Two for five, really?"

"Do you need butter, Dad?"

"No. But they have butter for sale. Who knew they had butter for sale?"

* * *

19 February

I call. The TV is loud enough to disturb people at the Methodist Home across town.

"Dad, let's put off dinner for tonight."

"What?"

"Let's put off—"

"—What? Speak up."

"Turn down the TV."

"What?"

"I said, 'Turn down the TV!'"

"What the hell is the matter with this phone? Why does it only ring when I'm in the bathroom?"

"What?"

"Why do you only call when I'm in the bathroom? Were you trying to reach me? I was in the bathroom."

"We're speaking now."

"Speak up. What's the matter with this goddamn phone?"

"Dad, you'll have to turn down—"

"—What?"

"The TV. Turn it down."

"Yeah. I'm in town. Where the hell else would I be? I have no wheels. Where are you?"

"Dad. The TV. Turn it down!"

I hear him turn the TV off.

"Good. Thanks. The TV was killing me."

"The TV isn't even on," he says.

"I know. That's because you just turned it off."

"What do you mean?"

"You just now turned it off."

"No, I didn't. It was on earlier, but I'm not watching it now. It's not on. I was watching something earlier, that's all. What's up, sweetheart?"

* * *

25 February

"So," I ask my father, "how was your exercise class this morning?"

"You know, I go on Mondays and Wednesdays. I take the bus to Walmart on Friday. I don't buy much. Paper products, usually."

"I know. That's why I asked about today. How was the class?"

"Well, it's not really an exercise class. It's stretching. You sit, you get up, you put your hands over your head. Don't misunderstand me. It's good. But it's more of a limbering class. It's good because you get limber. The girl is good. But don't forget. I used to play tennis every day in Vegas—four-game sets. Played with an Army colonel. A Jewish guy. Did you ever? No joke. He was a colonel. I don't know how religious he was, but then the legs went."

I see "the girl," Malyn, who leads the "limbering class," and ask how my father is doing.

"He moans a lot," she says, "but he's fine. He told me that when he goes to the doctor, all the doctor wants to talk about is his knee injury from the war, the one he got the Purple Heart in when the bomb went off."

"Great story, huh?"

"Is any of that true?"

"Well, he does have a doctor."

* * *

26 February

I have bought my father three electric razors in the past six months.

"When you come over, you've got to fix this goddamn razor."

"I just bought it Friday."

"I took it apart to clean it and it won't go back together. I mean, it goes back together, but it just keeps falling apart again. You know what I'm talking about? The piece that won't stay on?"

"I have no idea until I see it."

"Maybe I'll just buy another one."

"You don't need another one!"

"What the hell am I going to do? What does it want from my life?"

"I'll come fix it. Don't worry."

"You know how?"

"Yeah. I'm good with razors."

"What? I don't know. That one's totally gone. There's a piece missing now. I don't know. Ach! I give up."

* * *

27 February

My father just found an old toupee in a bedroom drawer. He put it on, looked at himself in the mirror a long time, and said, "Ba, I gotta tell you, it looks good."

MARCH

1 March

We're headed to Owl Head.

"Think I'm going to start running," my father says.

"Running? Really?"

"I want to try it. You know what I mean?"

"When was the last time you ran?"

"What are you talking about? When? I used to play tennis in Las Vegas . . . every day. But I think I want to run. I'll try it. What the hell? I can barely walk. My legs. I feel great, except for my legs."

"Your legs? How are you going to run?"

"When did Mom die?"

"1999."

"Why did he take her and not me?"

"There's no 'he' who did this."

"Yeah, you're right. So when did my father die?"

"Your father? 1961."

"Oh, that's right. So how old would Mom be now?"

"Eighty-nine."

"Yeah, she would be old by now, almost my age. She'd be a wreck like me."

"Very nice."
"You know what I mean."
"I do."
"Promise me when I die—"
"—I know. I'll get you up there—"
"—next to your mother at the grave."
"I will."
"I know it will be expensive shipping the body, so if you have to burn me here in Tulsa and take me up that way, that's fine."
"Burn you here. Got it!"
"Wait till I'm dead, of course."
"Of course."
"Ah, Ba, how much longer I got?"
"Five years."
"Why five?"
"Again, because that's when you run out of money. I'm trying to time this just right."
"Nah, it's not that. I just hate being a burden to my children."
"You're not a burden."
"Yeah, I am. I have no wheels. I can't go anywhere. Ach!"
"You're not a burden."
"I am. I know. To Wayne, to Susan . . . even to you."

* * *

3 March

"Call Melissa," he tells me, "and I'll take the whole mob to dinner at Mondo's. We'll split the check."

* * *

5 March

"I've been fighting the hemorrhoids," Sherman says to us at dinner at the Hebrew Home. "You should be happy you don't fight with the hemorrhoids."

"What?"

"Hemorrhoids."

Next to Sherman is a piece of brisket, which he has pre-requested before ordering to see if it meets his approval. He has pronounced it good, so he asks for it as his entree. It arrives with a piece of squash.

"What is that?" my father asks, poking it with his fork.

"Vinta squash," says Sherman, his Russian accent very pronounced.

"What?"

"Vinta squash!" he repeats.

"It's called 'sport'?" my father asks.

"Vinta squash," Sherman says again.

"What kind of sport?"

"Vinta squash!"

I am thinking the "Vinta" might be the problem here.

"Dad," I say, "squash. It's squash!"

"What's squash?"

"That's squash," I say, pointing to Sherman's plate.

"It's good," Sherman says to my father. "You should try."

"Is it legal?"

"All you eat is chicken," Sherman says.

"I don't have much of an appetite anymore," my father says. "I get the small portion."

The meal continues.

Sherman, a ninety-eight-year-old tailor who spent years in a concentration camp mending uniforms for Nazis, gives me a list of suits to buy.

"Don't buy Joseph Bank or Men's Wearhouse. It's crap. You buy good."

"Okay, got it," says I. "What about Hugo Boss?"

"No," he says. "For a young man. Not you."

"But if I buy something, you'll tailor it?"

Sherman laughs. "Why shouldn't I tailor it? What? Your money's no good?"

* * *

8 March

We're talking about an upcoming trip to see Susan, his daughter, my sister.

"So, Tuesday, I pick you up and we fly to Susan."

"Susan?"

"Susan."

"Susan? You mean Susan?"

"Yes. Your daughter."

"Susan! What about her?"

"We're going to see her."

"Yes, that's right. Good. She's always very friendly and every once in a while she makes a nice meal."

* * *

10 March

A woman, a resident, comes over to the table at the Hebrew Home and says, "I hear you two are going away soon."

"Yes," says my father. "Who told you?"

"You did."

"Oh, that's right. Yeah. To Florida to see my daughter."

"New York," I say.

"Not New York," he says. "Long Island."

"That's in New York."

"Then who's in Florida?"

"Leo."

"My brother, Leo?"

"Yeah."

"I know that. Susan's not in Florida."

"Right."

"So why are you confusing me? Susan doesn't live in Florida. She's in New York. Wayne is in California."

"I need a shot of heroin."

"What?"

"Nothing."

"Well, you two boys have a nice time," the woman says.

"But you can still use my apartment," says my father.

"What are you saying?" she asks.

"You know," he says.

"What?"

"I'm just joking, but I expect you to clean it."

The woman looks at the waitress, who happens to walk up to the table at that moment. "He doesn't have an 'off' switch, does he?" the woman asks.

"No," says the waitress. "He doesn't."

Later, the waitress, whom I know, returns and sits down in the booth next to me. I say something, I can't remember what, and it makes her laugh.

"What are you laughing at?" my father asks.

"Nothing," she says. "Your son is funny."

"Did he tickle you?"

"No, he didn't tickle me."

"Where did he tickle you? Because there's a lot of that going around."

"Jack, he didn't tickle me."

"I was just wondering, that's all. You were laughing. I thought he tickled you."

* * *

12 March

In a conversation with the gate agent at Tulsa International Airport, my father tries to move the venue of the parrot joke from a bar to an airport. It does not go well. He also made the parrot a chicken, which may have had something to do with why the joke went badly. He then asks the gate agent where he should put the bomb he brought.

Rosemary, a Southwest Airlines employee at Dallas Love Field, is wheeling him to Gate 3.

"Do we have time?" my father asks.

"For what?" she responds.

"Sex."

"No," she says, being a good sport.

"Then just go home."

"You're funny," she says as she continues wheeling him through the terminal.

"Hey," he says, "try to miss a bump, would you?"

On the plane, doing the *Wall Street Journal* crossword puzzle, my father says, "These *fakakta* clues. These people are miserable bastards."

* * *

24 March

From the Bahamas, I make a call.

"Sue, I've decided to let you have Dad. I'm not coming back. He's all yours."

"I will hunt you down."

APRIL

3 April

Jesse and Chris, my sister's oldest sons, drove my father back to Tulsa from Long Island. Jesse (he's the pastor, and where did that come from?) and Chris (he who makes the big bucks) like to drive. Weird kids, these two.

"Hey, Ba, have you heard from Bernie?"

"I don't know Bernie."

"He was my cousin. He died. How do you not know him?"

"I don't know him. He was YOUR cousin. You hadn't talked to him in forty years."

"Ida is still kicking, though. She don't give up, that one. Leo died in his sleep. Did she tell you?"

"Why would she tell me? I've seen her three times. She's also your cousin."

"She married Leo Meltzer."

"If you say so."

"You don't know anything about me, do you? How do you know I'm even your father?"

Later, on the way to Panera with his grandson Jesse in the car: "And did you know that after the explosion and the Purple Heart, they gave me more money? Yeah. Fifty dollars more per pay period."

* * *

4 April

My father, sitting next to a large woman at dinner, just said, "I may move over and sit on your lap."

* * *

5 April

"Ah, Ba, listen, we may have a problem," he says over the phone. "They're amassing downstairs and they're saying this and that and we're not going to do what they say, okay?"

"Okay. But what the hell are you talking about?"

"Oh! What AM I talking about? I'm really engrossed in this movie and they're getting ready to attack. Anyway, what's new, sweetheart?"

* * *

7 April

"So," my father says to a woman he doesn't know in the lobby outside the Hebrew Home dining room, "what is the dietary attributes that make chicken Kiev chicken Kiev? You know, because they have chicken in France. I was wondering if it was the same one. Is it the same? It can't be. I mean, I don't know."

"I don't know. I used to make it at home," says the woman. "Was a lot of work. Now you can just buy it all ready-made."

"Yeah, I was just wondering what made it Russian. It's chicken, I know. You know, Kiev is a city in Russia. Did it start there? It must have. And how did it get here?"

"I don't know. My son came by today. I can't find anything on my iPad. He found it like that," she says, snapping her fingers. "It makes me so mad he finds it like that."

"I'm from Austria."

"Now?"

"Now?"

"Are you from Austria now?"

"I'm from Vegas."

"What are you doing here?"

"I live here. This is my son."

"Hi," I say.

"Hi. How old are you?"

"Sixty-one."

"I got a son sixty and seventy."

"Nice."

"So what's in the chicken Kiev?" my father asks again.

"I don't know," she says.

"I was just wondering, that's all. I mean, chicken, I know, but what's the Kiev?"

"I don't know," she says again.

And, hand to God, when we get to our table, my father orders the chicken Kiev, even while asking the waitress, "What makes it Kiev? What's inside the chicken, is that it?"

"I don't know," she says.

"All right," he says, apparently deciding that he doesn't have to unravel all the mysteries of the universe. "Whatever it is, it is."

* * *

16 April

At the Hot Rod for the first time in months, he says to LeAnna, "You look good. You sure you're not pregnant?"

* * *

20 April

"Ba, I appreciate you coming over with the food. The juice, the milk. You know, I bought paper products yesterday and the pre-shave. But listen, I buy the double quart because I have the cereal every day. What did you buy?"

"A half gallon."

"No, it's very nice. I can always buy more milk."

* * *

21 April

Tonight, at the elevator on the way to dinner at the Hebrew Home, my father and I run into Sherman.

"There's trouble!" my father screams.

Nothing.

"There's trouble!" he screams again. "He can't hear nothing. He's deaf."

"Yeah, he's deaf?" I say.

Sherman notices us.

"Where you been?" he asks me. "Every day your father eats chicken. Every day. Fish, meat? No. Chicken he eats."

"I don't know, Sherman. What can I tell you? And where have you been? Haven't seen you in a while."

"Ach! With the hemorrhoids and the teeth, I don't always make it down."

We get to the dining room.

"Old age is not for sissies," Sherman says. "Many people this age commit suicide. They can't take it."

My father orders the chicken.

"See, what did I tell you?" Sherman asks.

One of the managers comes by because, apparently, the previous night, Solomon, who always gets a to-go bag consisting of oranges and small cans of Coke, did not, for reasons not entirely clear, get the bag.

"I'm so sorry," says the manager.

"Usually I get it," Solomon says. "I don't know what happened."

"Well, I don't know what happened either," she says. "I apologize again."

"I always get it," he says. "And I didn't."

"I know. And If there's ever anything I can do, you let me know and I'll take care of it."

And this is my favorite part of the story. Solomon thinks for a moment and says, "All right. Put an extra orange in the bag tonight."

* * *

23 April

Jim (a.k.a. the Big Guy) comes by dinner tonight to talk about the benefit I'll be hosting for him at the Hebrew Home.

"So what kind of meeting was it?" my father asks.

"Talking about doing a show."

"What kind of show?"

"Song-and-dance. What do you mean 'what kind of show'? Comedy."

"You?"

"Yeah."

"Are they paying you?"

"No."

"Why not?"

"It's a benefit. There's no money. Besides, I'm thanking them for you being here."

"Me? What do you mean?"

"You living here. They did a lot to get you in here."

"Oh, that's very nice. But you're not getting paid?"

"I don't want to get paid."

"Why not?"

"Dad, just . . . really. It's something I want to do. It's nothing."

"Well, what do I get, then?"

"What do you mean 'what do I get'?"

"Do I get extra meals for you doing this?"

"No, you don't get extra meals."

"I don't want any. That's not the point. I just thought I got something. That's all." Moments later, he adds, "Tell me something. When I was last at the cemetery, I saw Normie didn't have a stone. You know he went blind? What happened?"

"I don't know. Why would I know that? I saw him twice in my life."

"Well, why don't you find out?"

* * *

28 April

"I still don't understand what the hell you're doing there," he says, as I deposit a check of his into his account using my phone.

"I take a picture of the check. The bank sees the routing number, the account number, and the amount. That's all they need."

"What do you mean 'that's all they need'?"

"That's all they need."

"They don't need the check? You know . . . the check?"

"Nope. Just the information. I email it to them. It's complicated. Don't worry about it."

"I'm not worried, but they told you this? So what if I deposited the check by hand after you took the picture?"

"It's called check kiting, and eventually they'd discover it."

"But what if I did it anyway? I wonder if they really would find out."

"Pretty sure of it."

"Let me have the check, just in case I want to try it. If they ask, I'll just say I didn't know. That's all."

"What could go wrong with that plan?"

"What?"

"Nothing."

"So you're going to leave me the check, or what?"

"No."

"Why not?"

"Aside from everything else, how are you going to get to the bank?"

"Right. I need wheels. You took my wheels."

MAY

12 May

At Mondo's Italian restaurant, old movies are played.

My father sees Stan Laurel.

"He just died. I read it in the paper the other day." [*Died in 1965]

Later . . .

"Iceland?" he asks about a trip I just took. "They got a lot of ice?"

"It was actually pretty mild when we were there."

"But I mean generally."

"I don't know how much ice."

"I mean, it's north of France, right?"
"Yes."
"*Je vais me promener un* Champs Élysée."
"You're going for a walk on the Champs Élysée?"
"*Un gros oiseau noir.*"
"And something about a blackbird."
"Tell me, though. They got Jews in Iceland?"
"I'm sure of it."
"How many?"
"I don't know how many."
"I mean, generally."
"I have no idea, but I'm certain there are Jews."
"Really?"
"Yes."
"You sure?"
"Almost positive."
"Maybe they don't let them in."

* * *

14 May

Around six people came over to the table at Mondo's to say hello tonight, including five women, all of whom are attractive. (That's important to the story.) Each time, my father, being the gentleman he is, stands up to greet them, and, for reasons that defy understanding, to speak French to them. It gets to a point, though, where it's too much. So, after Somer, a woman I know, comes by, I say to my father, "Look, you're ninety-two. You don't have to stand up. You can sit. Nobody will blame you."

"No," he says. "It's respectful. You have to stand."

"Again, very sweet. But you don't have to stand. Everyone will understand."

"No. I want to stand. That way they'll know I'm strong enough for sex."

* * *

18 May
"How are things?"
"Barry?"
"Yeah."
"Oh, I thought it was Wayne."
"Why would it be Wayne?"
"Because we spoke the other day. What's up, sweetheart?"
"Just calling to see how you're doing."
"Fine, fine. I took a shower, did some work."
"What kind of work did you do?"
"Well, I didn't do any work. But, you know, I was thinking about what I had to do."
"You don't have to do anything."
"Yeah, but I was thinking of making some copies of stuff for what's-his-name, who's on extension."
"It's taken care of. Don't worry about it."
"You mean what's-his-name?"
"Yeah."
"All right. So let me ask you something."
"Okay."
"Why am I still here?"
"Because you're here."
"I took a shower and everything feels fine."
"So that's good."
"Yeah. But I'm wondering when it's not going to feel good."
"Don't put a *kinahora* on it. It feels good. You feel good. Enjoy yourself."
"So why did he take your mother and not me?"
"There's no answer to that. I don't know that HE did anything, took anything."
"I'm very serious. He took her at sixty-nine, and here I am pushing ninety-four."
"You're ninety-two."

"You know what I mean."

"I don't know what to tell you."

"I'm sitting here for, what, more than twenty years? Ach! I give up. I mean, she had a life, she wasn't cut short, but I gladly would have given back five years."

"Five? You would've given back five of your years to Mom?"

"Yeah."

"Not the whole twenty?"

"You know what I mean."

* * *

19 May

Rabbi Emeritus Charles P. Sherman of Temple Israel is exiting the Hebrew Home when he sees me about to get into my car. My father is already in the passenger seat. I had to go back to his apartment to get his glasses.

"They let you out?" the rabbi asks.

"Just because I'm with my father. They said, 'Don't bring him back.' Anyway, come to the car. Say hello."

He does.

"Dad," I say, "this is Rabbi Sherman."

"Rabbi, really? There's a lot of that going around."

"Nice to meet you again," says the rabbi. "We met a long time ago."

"I'm Jewish, you know," my father says.

"I know."

"I was bar-mitzvahed."

"That had to be at least twenty years ago."

"You kidding? I'm pushing ninety-four."

"Good for you."

"I've done a lot of bad things."

"Really?"

"Adultery. But not armed robbery. But I've been forgiven."

"This is not Yom Kippur," the rabbi says, calmly. "Save it."

"I was just saying to this girl I was attacking in an alley—"

"—Okay," I interrupt, "that's probably good for now. Rabbi, always good seeing you."

"You too. Be well."

* * *

23 May

"The hell am I doing here, Ba? I should get ready to go."

"Go where?"

"You know. Up . . . up there," he says, sweeping his arm upward, "to see everybody."

"What if they're not there? What if nothing is there?"

"Then I'll come back. Or I'll be reincarnated into a little baby. That's what happens. You come back as a baby. But you don't know from nothing. You're a baby. Then one day, you have a memory and think, 'What the hell is this?' It's no good, Ba. It's no good. Ach, I give up."

* * *

26 May

Residents of the Hebrew Home, twenty or thirty of them, are in the Bernstein Auditorium singing "Blowin' in the Wind."

* * *

27 May

I head from the pool to the Hebrew Home to see my father and to remind him of the activities for tomorrow.

"Now, remember," I say, "you're going to hear the mayor speak tomorrow at four and then we go to the buffet at six."

"What?"

"You're going to hear the mayor speak tomorrow at four and then we go to the buffet at six."

"The mayor?"
"The mayor."
"What kind of mayor?"
"Of Tulsa."
"Why is he coming here?"
"To talk to the residents."
"Here?"
"Here."
"At what time?"
"Four. Go up and say hello to him afterward. He'll probably know who you are."
"Who will?"
"The mayor."
"The mayor?"
"The mayor. I write about you, I've interviewed him. I know him, he knows me."
"You want me to do what?"
"I want you to say hello to the mayor tomorrow."
"How do you know the mayor?"
"I know him."
"You know him?"
"I know him."
"You want me to say hello? At what time?"
"Four, after he speaks. And then you and I will go to the casino afterward at the buffet."
"Which one? Uh, Fiesta?"
"Fiesta? You mean Hot Rod?"
"Yes, yes, Hot Rod."
"C'mon, if you're going to get it wrong, get it right."
"When?"
"Tomorrow. After you see the mayor."
"What about tonight?"
"Tonight's tonight. This is tomorrow."
"When do I eat?"
"At the buffet with me, after the mayor."

"What, tonight? It's three o'clock. I'm not even hungry. I just had the chicken and cheese."

"Tomorrow, not tonight. Tonight you eat here."

"Here? You mean at the hotel?"

"Yeah, whatever."

"What, were you swimming?"

"Yeah."

"How's the water?"

"Cold."

"That's why I don't want to go. My legs, Ba, my legs. Why did the legs go first? Anyway, what the hell's going on with that thermostat?"

"I fixed it."

"Yeah, yeah. The guy told me how to fix it."

"I'm the guy who told you."

"You?"

"Me."

"Oh, yeah, it was you. I thought it was someone else."

"So you got it about tomorrow? The mayor at four, and then I pick you up at six."

"So I don't eat here tomorrow?"

"No, we eat at the buffet."

"I don't have much of an appetite."

"I know. But tomorrow—"

"—I got it. You want me to meet the mayor and then wait for you?"

"Yes."

"What time, again?"

"Four, and then I'll come get you at six."

"You know, I'm cold. Could you turn the thing up to seventy-nine?"

"It's seventy-eight now."

"Yeah, but I'm chilled. That's all."

[The thermostat is adjusted.]

"Okay. I'm leaving. You got it for tomorrow?"

"Yeah, yeah, I meet what's-his-name—the mayor, really? Why would he come here? At what time, again?"

"Four."

"Four, got it. But tonight I eat here. But call to remind me."

"Okay."

Downstairs, on the way back to the pool, I walk by the room where the mayor is to speak. Hand to God, written over his picture and "Tuesday at 4" is the word "Canceled."

Son of a bitch!

* * *

30 May

"You know, Ba," he asks after a discussion about not being a fan of fried chicken because of the crumbs, "how long was I married to your mother?"

"Forty-six years."

"Yeah?"

"Why did we split up?"

"You were a pain in the ass."

"Me? What did I do?"

"What did you do?"

"What I did? What did I do?"

"You were tough to live with, apparently."

"Yeah. But then your mother came back."

"I know."

"It was the best time of the marriage."

"That's what I heard."

"Did you know we had sex every day?"

"Not until this moment."

JUNE

1 June

    I call. "Dad, I'm coming over. I'm bringing you chicken."
"Chicken? Chicken? I got plenty of cheese."
"I know. That's why I'm bringing you chicken."
"I don't eat chicken."
"You eat chicken every day."
"No. I eat the chicken and cheese."
"Right. I'm bringing you the chicken part of that."
"I thought you meant you were bringing the other thing."
"What other thing?"
"The turkey."
"Would you prefer I brought you turkey slices?"
"There's just me, you know."
"I know."
"No, no. Bring the chicken. Or the turkey. What's the difference?"
"One's turkey, one's chicken."
"Bring whatever. I trust you."
"That's wonderful."
"But, Ba, remember, don't bring the cheese. I got plenty of cheese. You brought the whatchamacallit cheese last time. Was better than the last time. I got plenty of cheese. Don't bring any cheese!"

* * *

4 June

    "Ba, when it came to the bed scene," my father says of his wife on the way to Hard Rock, "your mother was fantastic."

* * *

7 June

"Hey, Ba," he says, getting into the car for our drive to his wellness check, "I saw something on TV this morning. It's a hat that grows hair. It's got a red light on it. You think I should get it?"

"Absolutely."

"God knows what that costs."

"Yeah."

"Ach! Where am I going, anyway? I don't need it. Let me ask you something. Why did he take Mom at sixty-nine, and I'm still sitting here at ninety-four?"

"Ninety-two."

"Well, I'm going to be ninety-three. My point is, why did he take your mother and not me, when I was probably more corrupt than her?"

* * *

15 June

When my son, Paul, was eight months old, I came home from work and saw my father on the floor talking to Paul, who was in his playpen.

"Show your father what I taught you," he said, at which point Paul stood up by himself and held on to the mesh, smiling and cackling.

It was the first time I had ever thought of myself as a father and a son.

Not bad. Not bad at all.

It's Father's Day tomorrow.

* * *

16 June

"Hey, Dad, Happy Father's Day!"
"Who is this?"
"Your son."
"Which one?"
"Your favorite."
"Wayne?"
"Very nice. It's Barry."
"Barry? Oh, yeah, I know."
"You doing all right?"
"Yeah, yeah, fine."
"Again, Happy Father's Day."
"Hey, listen, did you file my taxes this year?"
"Yeah."
"What year?"
"This year."
"Okay, just wondering. Thank you for the call. Have a good day."

* * *

25 June

It being Tuesday, we head to the Hot Rod, but the line is so long ("Ba, I don't even think our girlfriend can get us in"), we instead go to the snack bar, where my father orders a burger and fries. I get the chicken club. An hour later, he finds me in the casino and tells me he's nauseous.

"I don't know what the hell happened. I'm up eighteen dollars but I don't feel well. Ach! This old age is shit."

He tells me he met a woman who admired how he played. He bets five dollars a hand.

"You want something to drink?" I ask.

"Nah, I had a, you know, a drink. But I should never have had that goddamn burger. I should never eat meat."

"Chicken can make you sick too."

"Yeah, but the meat, God knows what they put in it, but the chicken has to be fowl."

"'Has to be fowl'?"

"You know what I mean. Not the verb, the noun."

"Dad, plenty of people get sick on chicken."

"What did you have?"

"Chicken."

"Did you get sick?"

"No."

"Well, I had the meat, and I got sick. What does he want from my life?"

"You're blaming God for this?"

"Who else?"

"Good point."

"Did I tell you I'm up eighteen bucks? What the hell! At least we made back dinner."

* * *

28 June

I'm talking to Sam at the Hebrew Home—he's a short, bald

Jewish man, which I know doesn't narrow it down much—after dinner when my father says, "You should thank me."

"Why's that?" asks Sam.

"Because I saved this country from Hitler in World War II."

"Dad," I interrupt, "you were in the Philippines."

"Shut up," he says, then goes back to Sam. "Let me show you a picture," he continues, pulling out his wallet and finding a heavily taped photo of himself at twenty, bare-chested, on a cliff.

"Good thing," says Sam, "you're now wearing a shirt."

JULY

1 July

At a store called Ida Red in Tulsa, did my father tell Brooke, one of the clerks, three milliseconds after meeting her, about the bomb that went off in the Philippines and how "I won the war!" and then ask if she wanted to be his girlfriend.

You have to ask?

* * *

4 July

"Ba, don't buy the regular flakes from now on," he says in a call early this morning. "Buy the sugar ones. You know, the ones with the sugar."

"I didn't buy the regular ones. You did."

"What do you mean I did?"

"I mean, you bought them when you went on Friday."

"Yeah, I go on Fridays on the bus. What's your point? I buy paper products and the pre-shave."

"Well, you bought the regular corn flakes instead of the frosted flakes."

"I did?"

"You did."

"Well, I wanted the others. That's why I say, 'Don't buy the regular ones.'"

"Got it."

"I have them for breakfast every morning. With the coffee, so don't get the regular flakes. I don't like them."

"All right! You shouldn't buy the regular flakes either."

"I like the sugar ones, what can I tell you?"

"You know there's plenty of sugar in the regular flakes."

"What?"

"Never mind."

"Why am I getting this gut, by the way? I eat one meal a day —just the dinner. It's because I don't play tennis anymore. I used to play tennis every day. Four-game sets. Played with an Army colonel. Jewish guy. No joke. He was a colonel."

* * *

5 July

My father's driver's license has expired—it's time for renewal. He's not driving, so he doesn't need one but wants it anyway, in case, he says, there's an emergency and he has to drive himself to the hospital.

"Dad, if there's an emergency, you'll be in an ambulance or someone will take you. You won't have to drive yourself to the ER."

"You know what I mean."

At the DMV, I show the clerk his license. "Do I need to bring him in?" I ask.

"I'm sorry, but you do, along with a birth certificate, in case something goes wrong with the picture."

"What could go wrong with the picture?"

"Well, like in this one, he's wearing a hat."

"That's not a hat. That's a toupee."

She looks again.

"Oh, I'm so sorry," she says, unable to control her laughing. "I think I remember him. Oh, my! That isn't a hat. I'm so sorry. You bring him in, I'll take care of him."

"Thank you. You know, you keep being so nice, he'll ask you out."

"I'll only go if he's wearing the toupee."

"Oh, sure. A moment of amusement for you, four years of strife for the rest of us."

Later that day, I return with him to the DMV.

"If I had known they were going to take my picture, I would have taken a shave."

"I told you we were doing that."

"Yeah, but I didn't think you meant today."

"But we were headed there today. That's why we're here."

"But what about my hair? I need a brush."

"Just smooth it back with your hand."

"Am I going to have to take my hat off?"
"Yeah."
"But I have no hair in the front."
"In the front? It's really okay. You're ninety-two, you're not supposed to have hair."
"But what if it grows back?"
"We'll go get another license, I promise."
"Yeah, we'll just tell them we lost this one."
"Great idea."
He did ask the aforementioned woman to marry him.

* * *

9 July

Because the Sweet'N Low was milliseconds late getting to the table here at the Hot Rod, and because the only things my father had to sweeten his decaf were his orange Creamsicle and flakes of black-forest cake, and because the coffee was "too goddamn hot," which necessitated him adding, count 'em, three ice cubes from his root beer, my thoughts turned to a conversation we had earlier in the day. One of the Hebrew Home dining room managers told me that my father was walking around the lobby today and she invited him in for a cup of coffee.

"I know how your father likes his coffee now," she said. "Wow! He told me I wasn't leaving enough room for the cream and to pour some of it out. Anyway, tell him he can come down anytime he likes."

"Dad," I say to him later, "I heard you went downstairs today and had a cup of coffee."

"What do you mean?"
"You went downstairs today for a cup of coffee."
"No, I didn't."
"You didn't?"
"Well, I went down and then had a cup of coffee, but I didn't go down to have a cup of coffee."
"The manager said you can come down anytime you want."
"What do you mean?"
"She said anytime you want a cup of coffee, she wants you to come down. It's not a problem."
"Where?"
"The dining room."
"At the hotel?"
"Whatever, yes."
"You know I can go down whenever I want."
"That's what I heard."

* * *

12 July

The call this morning:

"Ba, no joke. I don't need the plugs. I hear fine without them."

This is a direct result of yesterday's trip to the audiologist, where ninety years of wax was removed from his ears.

"But you really do need the hearing aids."
"You know, I'm going shopping at ten on the bus."
"Dad, listen to me. You need to wear the hearing aids."
"Yeah, I take the bus on Fridays."
"Dad, please put the hearing aids in."
"I don't need them. I hear fine."
"You'll be around a lot of people today. Please wear them. It will be easier on everyone."
"All right, I'll wear them, but I don't need them since the guy

took out the wax. I'm telling you. Ach! All right. But I'm going to wear them without the batteries."

* * *

13 July

"You know how much it costs these days to get a plot?" my father asks me. "Ten thousand dollars. It's not cheap, baby. No joke. It's twenty to thirty thousand dollars," now raising the price.

"She must have killed him," he says of Lylah. What's odd here is that Lylah was married to a guy named Bernie, Bernie Metz, not Bernie Newman, my dad's cousin, who died. Bernie Metz is also dead, but my father isn't baffled about what killed him—only about how Bernie Newman died. "She's a tough cookie," he says about Lylah, and then quickly changes the subject back to Bernie Newman. "And did you know Pitsy is Bernie's sister? And Leo died in his sleep. How do you die in your sleep? What, you cough, but you don't wake up? You don't wake up the person next to you? I don't get that. Listen, if you have any questions, call Ida. She has all the answers."

* * *

16 July

Tonight at the "Hot Top" (a.k.a. Hot Rod), LeAnna is not working.

"Say, Ba, what's-her-name, DeAnna, is not working tonight."

"LeAnna."

"Yeah, she's not working. I wonder where she is."

"Maybe she's sick."

"No. I wonder if she's pregnant."

"Pregnant? She's at least fifty, Dad. She's probably not pregnant. And we just saw her last week."

"No. She just got married."

"It doesn't mean she's pregnant."
"You know I used to run with her?"
"I know."
"She got married, nu? Did you know? I guess she knew the guy."
"Good bet."
"What?"
"Nothing."
"I wonder where she is, though."
"Probably just took the night off."
"But it's Tuesday. I mean, they knew who I was, so it was no problem getting in. No, but she's very nice, though."

* * *

20 July

"Where the hell is Bernie buried? All right, he died, I know. But where is he buried? He's not in the Family Circle plot. You know what those things cost? And what about the Bernie in Albany?"

There's a Bernie in Albany?

* * *

23 July

Dinner at the Hebrew Home tonight.

A resident, Carol, approaches the table.

"Jack, how did you get such a handsome son?"

"Ah, Miss America. Who, him?" he asks, pointing in my direction.

"Yes. He's so good-looking."

"I'm the father, you know. Him? No. I got two others."

"I know."

"This is my oldest."

"Second-oldest," I say.

"Second-oldest. I have two other sons."

"One other son. And a daughter."

"You know what I mean. So how do you know him?" he asks her.

"I've seen him perform, and I read him."

"You mean in the . . . in the . . . what's the name of that, again?" he asks me.

"Not important."

"I can't think of the name."

"Don't worry about it."

"What is it again?"

"*Tulsa Voice.*"

"What?"

"*Tulsa Voice.*"

"Tulsa what?"

"*The New York Times.*"

"What?" he asks, excitedly.

"Nothing."

* * *

27 July

"Dad," I ask him this morning after seeing his bank statement, "why do you keep charging when you have cash on you?"

"I don't have cash on me."

"You have a hundred and fifty dollars cash on you."

"Oh, that."

"Yeah. That. Use that cash."

"I don't use that cash. I save that for emergencies."

"What emergencies do you have?"

"You know. Emergencies."

"What emergencies?"

"What if I'm walking around and meet a hooker and she needs cash?"

* * *

30 July

The call comes: "Ba, I'm not going swimming in the ocean anymore. All the sharks want to do is bite. I'll swim in a pool but not the ocean. They just keep biting. And they don't just bite and take a little bit. They have to get the whole leg."

At "Casino Night" at the Hebrew Home, he informs me they're not actually gambling. Each resident is given a certain amount of fake money and can simulate betting on craps, blackjack, or roulette. My father is wise to such an obvious ruse. "Who needs this shit?" he asks.

AUGUST

3 August

Jack Friedman, upon seeing Hope, his daughter-in-law—she and Wayne and their daughter, Francesca, are in town for a visit—for the first time in years: "You didn't know Leo Meltzer. He died in his sleep. Ida said he coughed and then he died. And Bernie and his wife both died together. I don't know how they died together. And Jerry married Pitsy. You didn't know Mel Karp, did you?"

* * *

9 August

Yesterday in his refrigerator, I saw a half gallon of milk (double quart, if you side with my father on this), half-filled, about to expire. I go to the store, buy a half gallon of milk, Kellogg's Frosted Flakes, and orange juice. I return.

He sees me pouring the old milk down the drain.

"What are you doing?"

"The milk was expired."

"Expired. What do you mean expired?"

"Expired. Either bad or going to go bad."

"I use it every day on the corn flakes. How could it be expired?"

"How?"

"I mean, I use it. Expired?"

"Expired."

"I use it every day. It tastes fine."

"Better to throw it out."

"I have it every morning."

"I got you new milk."

He looks. "Ach, I buy the gallon."

"But the gallon will go bad before you use it up. And it was the half gallon that went bad."

"That's because I use it every day."

"But you didn't finish this size, and it went bad."

"But the big one I use, the double quart."

"This is a double quart."

"You know what I mean."

"The gallon?"

"No, the double quart."

"You mean the bigger one, the gallon?"

"Yes."

"That would be the double-double quart. You don't need that much milk sitting in the refrigerator."

"That's because I use it on the cereal. That's why I need the big one."

"Dad, you didn't finish the half gallon before the expiration date. Imagine how much will be left in the gallon jug."

"Well, I use it every day on the cereal. That's all."

"I know that. I'm saying. I'll buy you the half gallon from now on. The milk will be fresher."

"You know I use the milk every day for the cereal?"

"I think you've mentioned it."

"But I—"

"If you run out, though, I'll buy you another half gallon."

"What? You're going to schlep out here every few days to buy milk?"

"I schlepp out here every other day anyway."

"Look, in the morning, I have the coffee and the cream and the cereal with the milk. It's very satisfying. Oh, and I need juice. Oh, I see you got juice. What kind of juice?"

He checks.

"Good, I have juice in the morning and I was out. Well, I wasn't out, I had some, but I was going to need some. All right, you bought milk, I see. Why didn't you buy the big one?"

"Again. The half gallon will be fine. It will be easier to lift, too. Trust me on this."

"Yeah, OK. The other one is heavy. You're right, I can't lift it. Well, I can lift it, it's just heavy. Anyway, all right, but I use it on the cereal every day."

"I know!"

"All right, don't get so shook up. I'm just telling you that I have cereal every morning. The flakes. That's why I want the big one. Oh, I see you bought the better frosted flakes. I got the other ones."

"Don't scrimp. You're pushing 100. You deserve Kellogg."

"It's better, you're right. That's why I always buy that kind."

"But you had the other kind up there."

"Well, I didn't last time. That's all."

* * *

17 August

"You know, Ba," he says of Melissa, "she's a good-looking

woman. Very good. No joke. Even when she's not dressed properly."

* * *

21 August

I explain to my father about my recent upper endoscopy, and he says, "Look, you better live. Because if you die, I'm in trouble."

* * *

22 August

My father tells me his favorite joke tonight at the Hebrew Home.

There's a fence that separates heaven and hell, and St. Peter and Lucifer have a deal in which they alternate repairing the fence whenever there is a need. Such a repair is needed, so they meet at the fence.

Peter: "It's your turn to fix the fence."
Lucifer: "Well, I'm not going to."
Peter: "What do you mean?"
Lucifer: "I'm just not doing it."
Peter: "We have an agreement. We alternate. I did it last time. Now it's your turn."
Lucifer: "I don't care. I'm not doing it."
Peter: "See, Devil, this is why nobody likes you. Now, fix that goddamn fence or I'm calling a lawyer."
Lucifer: "Really? Where are YOU going to find one?"

Best thing about the joke, to me, is that in my father's version, St. Peter has no problem saying "goddamn" fence.

* * *

27 August

Moments before we leave for the casino, one of my father's remaining tax clients sends him a copy of a letter from the New York City Department of Finance pertaining to the client's 2018 corporate tax return. Apparently the department didn't get the client's 2018 corporate tax return, and it is being taken personally.

"What the hell do they want from my life?" asks my father, handing me the letter.

"The guy's return, apparently."

"What do they want? His return?"

"Yeah. His return."

"His return? What year?"

"2018. Specifically, according to the letter, they're interested in the money he made from real estate."

"Real estate?"

"Real estate."

"How much did he make?"

"Why and how would I know that?"

"Well, call him and find out, and then put it down in a letter and send it to them. That's all."

"I think they want it itemized—not just one figure. On an actual form. Expenses, occupancy, you know."

"Then just send them a letter and tell them he's on extension."

"I don't know if that's going to work, Dad."

"It'll work. And if it doesn't work, they'll send him another letter."

* * *

28 August

He calls to tell me, "You know, Ba, here I am in my nineties, and I was just thinking about my life and you and Wayne and

Susan . . . you know, my family, so to speak. Nothing special. So, what's up, sweetheart?"

SEPTEMBER

3 September

Say hello to Precious, who has come to clean my father's apartment at the Hebrew Home.

"Tell me something," he asks her. "Is that your real hair or is it just something on your head?"

He tells her the Purple Heart story.

* * *

6 September

"Hey, Ba, I'm going to Walmart, but not to buy hardware for the kitchen, just some paper products, so if you come over, I won't be there until I get back."

* * *

7 September

At the Hebrew Home, tipping is an optional matter. The residence requests, however, that if one decides to give a gratuity, the resident should give one lump sum to the management, who will then divvy up the money accordingly between housekeeping, the restaurant staff, security, etc.

I mention this to my father (for the 112th time, but let's not get bogged down in detail), to which he says, "That's a great idea. How much should I give?"

"I don't know. Give a hundred a couple times a year."

"Great idea," he says. "I'll split it with you."

* * *

14 September

On the way to Owl Head, he taps my stomach. "So, how are you, baby? I was just thinking what I would do if you weren't here."

"You wouldn't be in Oklahoma."

"Oh, that's right. I was wondering what the hell I was doing here. Anyway, you know Panera has a nice soup."

"Nah. Let's go see the guys at the bagel place."

"Yeah, Panera, they only fill the soup halfway. Fill up the bowl, for crying out loud!"

"Bastards!"

We arrive at Owl Head and the talk gets around to his retirement from accounting, once and for all.

"Now, remember, Dad, when you're done, you're done. We throw everything out."

"No," he says, "you must keep a copy. The preparer must keep a copy."

"The client has a copy. You don't need to keep one."

"No, you do. You must keep a copy. The preparer must keep a copy."

"What if the preparer dies?"

"Well, that's something different. But if you don't die, you must keep a copy."

***

16 September

We visit Diane and Amy, mother-daughter owners at 61 Nails.

"They're very good, Ba, very good," he says. "The girl did the nail that was hit by the bomb beautifully. I wonder if they think we're brothers. By the way, I need milk. Don't buy the double quart, though. Buy the half gallon. I eat the cereal every morning. EVERY morning. I have it with the coffee. It's a good combination."

***

18 September

I call my father to tell him I can't make it out to the Hebrew Home today.

"Ba, do what you have to do," he responds. "I got dinner today, tomorrow I take the trip to Walmart. I got plenty going on. And I know you need to make a living. You come out here enough. Believe me, I know you're a concerned person."

***

22 September

"So how the hell do you die in your sleep?" he asks on the phone.

"You just do."

"What? You don't thrash around? It doesn't wake you up?"

"I don't know."

"And Jerry Parker married Pitsy after his friendship with Mel ended?"

"I guess so."

"And Bernie died, Red Meltzer died. They were my cousins. And Leo, my brother, does he get around?"

"Yeah."

"I don't mean dancing. But does he walk? And how old was my mother's second husband, Sam?"

"Abe."

"That's what I meant. Now, which one is your daughter?"

"Nina."

"She's the one with the ring in her nose?"

"Yes."

"You know I'm putting on weight."

"I know."

"It's because I don't exercise. In Vegas, I played tennis. Listen, if I go first, take the quarters off the wall. Do that first. There must be, like, sixteen dollars in there."

"Okay."

"Get that first. Very important. Ach, Ba, I give up!"

"You want some potato salad?"

"Oh, yeah. Great idea. Put some on a plate."

* * *

24 September

A woman whom I have known for years and whom my father knows I have known for years, comes by the table at the Hebrew Home to say hello. We hug.

"How do you know him?" my father asks, seeing the hug. "Now hug me. This is my son, by the way. You know each other?"

"Jack," she answers, "we've known each other for years."

"But how do you know him? I'm the father. I made him. And do you know"—he points to me—"what it took to make this thing? I needed two women."

*　*　*

28 September

After a discussion about a gig I will have next year in the Bahamas, probably in April, I tell my father how we'll both fly to New York, see Susan, his daughter, and then I'll leave him there, fly to the Bahamas, do two weeks of comedy, fly back to New York, get him, and then we'll fly back to Tulsa.

"Wait a minute!" he says. "Then what happens to the meals at the hotel?"

"You don't live—ah, never mind. What do you mean 'meals'?"

"The meals. Since I'm not going to use them when we go, what happens to them?"

"Happens?"

"Can you use them?"

"I'll be in the Bahamas."

"Will they roll over until the next month?"

"No."

"What do you mean 'no'?"

"Why are you worried about this? It's next April. No, they're not going to roll over."

"I'm not worried. I'm just concerned about the meals, that's all. Can Melissa use them?"

"What do you mean?"

"Can Melissa come and eat the meals that I normally would eat?"

[Note to self: Check with Melissa to see if she wants to eat at the Hebrew Home, by herself, around retired Jews who can't hear, complain about the portions, and stockpile desserts.]

"I'll ask, Dad."

"Yeah. Tell her she can use the meals, what the hell? But it seems strange they don't roll over. They're mine, right?"

"Right."

* * *

29 September

Rosh Hashanah at the Hebrew Home.

"Dad, I think you're supposed to wait until after the prayers before you start eating."

"I know, I know. I'm just having a carrot and some lettuce."

OCTOBER

5 October

"What are you doing tonight, Ba? Am I going to see you, or what?"

"Actually, I got a gig."

"Where?"

"It's at an arena in town. I'm opening for Rachel Maddow."

"Who?"

"She's got her own show on MSNBC. She's an author. It's kind of a big deal."

"Oh, yeah, yeah, I know her."

"You know who she is?"

"Yeah, I mean, uh . . . is it just the two of you?"

"Yeah."

"Anyone else performing?"

"No."

"Just the two of you? How long can the show be?"

"I don't know. However long she decides to do. How many do you think there should be?"

"Do you know her?"

"No."

"Will the comedy club be mad you're not performing there?"

"I don't think so."

"Who is she, again?"

"She's on television, hosts her own show, and she's here in Tulsa giving a lecture, promoting her new book, followed by a question-and-answer period. I'm, in a sense, her opening act."

"Okay. Hey, how old is my brother Leo?"

* * *

7 October

My mother, Florence Friedman, would have been ninety today.

Many years ago, before she got sick and before the metastatic breast cancer returned, she told me that she and my father, at about the midpoint of their marriage, agreed that if either of them ever came down with a terminal disease, the other would take out a gun and shoot the one who was suffering, to alleviate any more pain.

But they never followed through.

"Hey, Ma," I asked her one day, "on some level, mostly criminal, that's actually a beautiful thing you and Dad decided. How come you never got the guns?"

"With your father, c'mon, he'd be like, 'Ah, she was complaining, she was sick, so I shot her. Go know it wasn't serious.' So, Ba, I called it off."

After my mother and father's separation, which lasted eighteen months, she returned to Greenlawn, New York, where they were living—he had kept the house. My father told me that the first night together, they were sitting in the living room talking, looking at each other.

"Then," my father said, "your mother said to me, 'Jack, we have to talk more, but I'm so tired. I have to go to sleep.'"

"So I said, 'Of course, of course.' Then your mother said, 'I don't know where I'm supposed to sleep.'"

"What did you tell her, Dad?"

"I told her she's sleeping with the owner."

* * *

10 October

We pass a woman (I figure she's in her late thirties, early forties) who's in a chair outside the new Hebrew Home cafe.

"All alone?" my father asks her. "Are you desperate?"

She looks up, too astonished, it seems to me, to form a response, a response he doesn't wait for anyway.

"Yeah," he says. "There's a lot of that going around. All right, have a good day."

* * *

14 October

Jack Friedman—who wanted to know if anyone in his family reached 100, who wanted to know how old Bernie was when he died, who wanted to know what I did with his hair when he moved into the Hebrew Home and whether I know non-Jews are also there—is having a birthday today.

"Ninety-three! Ninety-three? What the hell happened? I was sixteen two weeks ago. I feel good, though, I really do. No joke. But the legs. When I walk, they bother me. When I'm sitting, they feel fine. Ach, I give up!"

At Mondo's for his birthday dinner—and thanks, Michael Aloisio, for the spumoni with the candle—my father tells me he was married to someone named Martha after he and my mother split up for a year and a half. When Melissa and I convinced him he was not and that there was never anyone named Martha in his life, nor was he ever married to anyone other than Florence Friedman—who was not, we have to insist, a dancer—he says, "Oh, yeah, that's right. I was thinking of someone else."

He also kisses me on the forehead.

* * *

18 October

"Ah, Ba, what the hell am I still doing here?"

"You're here. Life is good. You just turned ninety-three."

"Ninety-four!"

"Here we go. No, you're ninety-three."

"That's right. So why did he take your mother and not me?"

"Why don't you ask him when you get there?"

"Florence is somewhere, but she doesn't know she's Florence."

"Sounds reasonable."

"Question: There's you, Wayne, and, uh, Susan, right?"

"Yes."

"Are you a regular son?"

"What?"

"A regular son, you know."

"What do you mean?"

"I mean, you're not a, you know, adopted or a grandson. You're a regular son."

"Yes, I'm a regular son."

"And Cynthia and Vivian are dead?"

"Yes."

"Vivian was my sister, you know."

"I do."

"Why the hell did Cynthia die?"

"Why? I don't know."

"Was she sick?"

"Probably."

"You know I can't sit in that chair anymore, the soft one that you're in."

"So sit in the hard one."

"That's what I do. . . . Where's it all going, Ba? Where's it all going?"

"I don't know."

"I know I'm a pain in the ass. And I want you to know I appreciate this so. I know you have a life."

"Who said you're a pain in the ass?"

"Nah, I know. I am. I take time away from you and Miralda—"

"—Melissa."

"What'd I say?"

"Doesn't matter. Close enough."

"She's got Jeffrey—"

"—Gregory."

"You know what I mean."

"Dad, you're not a pain in the ass. There's no place else I want to be right now."

"When did my mother die?"

"1983."

"And my father?"

"1961."

"Was I there?"

"Yeah."

"I don't remember. You know that picture I have? Everyone is dead in it. Listen, tell Mizzilou—"

"—Melissa."

"Eh, yeah. Tell, uh, Missy, tell her I want to take you all out to dinner. I'm buying."

"I will. You want to split it?"

"You got a deal. . . . I want to show you the jar I have with quarters."

"I've seen it. It's mostly pennies."

"You don't know what you're talking about. There's silver in there. All right, whatever, take it when I'm gone."

"Probably four dollars in there."

"And don't forget the quarters on the wall."

"I won't."

"Ach, Ba, am I going to die at this place? I mean, is this the last move? Ach, I give up. Shit!"

"It's a good place, don't you think?"

"Yeah. It is. It's beautiful. The dinners, they call every day, they do the laundry. I tip them a little."

* * *

27 October

My father's Remington electric razor, just a few months old, is not working.

"Ba," he says, "I did nothing. It's not working."

I check. It's not.

"I'll get you another one."

"All right, I didn't like this brand anyway. Get me a Howard."

"A Howard? There's no such thing as a Howard razor."

"You don't know what you're talking about. I've been using them since before you were born. It's called a Howard . . . or a Forward. You'll see."

"A Forward?"

"Yeah. A Howard Forward."

"I'll go to Walmart and look."

I arrive there and see a Remington, which is too complicated, and a Braun, which is perfect for him.

I return.

"Dad, no Howard. No Forward. I got you this one." I hand it to him.

"Yes, yes. This is the one."

"It's a Braun."

"Who makes it?"

"Braun."

"Braun?"

"Braun. It's a German company."

"Braun. What kind of name is Braun?"

"German."

"German?"

"German."

"No, this is the one I wanted."

"Really? Not Howard or Forward?"

"Braun. That's what I meant to say."

"Good."

"But where do they come up with these names? Braun, Howard. Hey," he adds, new razor in hand, "can I shave my legs with this?"

"Not with this one. Maybe with the Howard."

"What?"

"Nothing."

* * *

31 October

Sitting at my father's dining room table at the Hebrew Home, he suddenly grabs my hand, cups it in his, and says, "Don't think for a moment I don't appreciate what you do for me. I would be lost with you. Now, go, I don't want to keep you. I know you have things to do. Work, whatever. What kind of work do you do, again? You in maintenance?"

NOVEMBER

1 November

At dinner at the Hebrew Home, my father is eating brisket.

"Dad, you like the brisket?"

"I can't finish it."

"Why not?"

"It's that goddamn soup. I always fill up on the soup. That's why I don't order it with the matzo balls. Just the broth."

"But you just had it with the broth."

"You know what I mean. I can't eat the . . . the . . . you know."

"Matzo balls."

"Right, that's what I said. I should know not to order the soup," he says again, banging the table. "It was good, don't misunderstand me. That's why I don't eat the salad, either."

"But you ate the salad."

"I had a little, that's all. And they put it out. What? I'm not going to eat it?"

"Don't eat it if you don't want it."

"But I'm very serious. I shouldn't have the soup. I always get filled up. That's why I don't ever get it."

"It's not a big deal. Really. Eat what you want."

"You know a lot of people here are retired. How do THEY eat so much?"

"I have no idea."

"You know they're not all Jewish, either. One woman has a cross. She's very nice."

* * *

3 November

We head to Owl Head this morning after a rough night. He tells me he had a dream where he went out with the guys—I don't know what guys he's talking about—and woke up in his apartment and didn't know how he got back there. Called at 1 a.m., called at 8 a.m. He also, more important, is calling to tell me he's out of potato salad.

"Ach, Barry, I give up," he says. "It was such a dream. And then I woke up in my apartment and thought, 'What the hell is going on? Did the guys drop me off, or what? Anyway, I appreciate you coming. I just feel bad that I take you away from Melissa."

"She understands."

"Tell her I appreciate it."

"I will."

"That's why I give her twenty bucks every time I see her: to thank her."

* * *

7 November

Yesterday, we saw Dr. John Schumann. My father's blood pressure was 138/69.

"Is it elevated," my father asked, "because of the war? I have a Purple Heart, you know? I was running the wrong way."

* * *

9 November

On the way back from Owl Head . . . "So Bernie is dead, his wife is dead, Bucky is dead, Marvin is dead. George Topperoff is dead. That was a good-looking guy. And his brother, too. He was older. Also good-looking. Did you know him? He's probably dead, too. Leo Meltzer is dead, died in his sleep. I still don't know what that's about. So, what the hell am I still doing here?

"You're lucky, you got good genes, you live without stress, you played tennis, you have a good son."

"You? What do you have to do with it?"

"Nothing. Just the driver."

"I should start running again. I stopped a few years ago."

Just then we pass the site of the old Furr's Cafeteria.

"What happened to that place?" he asks, pointing to the gym that's now in the location. "I miss going there."

"You do?"

"Don't you?"

"No. The food was terrible and expensive."

"Yeah, I know. But I loved it so."

* * *

11 November

"Hey, Dad, thanks for saving the country."

"It was nothing."

"Hilarious."

"Hey, Ba, let me ask you something. I'm reading the paper about a guy in the war."

"Yeah?"

"And I'm thinking, 'I did more than him. I got a Purple Heart. Why are they writing about him? He's only ninety.' Anyway, what's up, sweetheart?"

* * *

16 November

This is just never not funny.

Jack Friedman walks into the house tonight for dinner with his daughter, my sister, Susan, who has been here all week, and says, "Did you hear that Bernie Newman just died? What the hell happened? He died? His wife, too. Both of them. Did you ever hear such a thing? How did he die? And Leo Meltzer died in his sleep. That one I don't get."

* * *

17 November

At dinner at Mondo's with Susan and Emily, her daughter, my niece, and Susan and I were laughing at how everyone knows about Bernie.

"Bernie?" my father asks. "Who's that?"

* * *

18 November

Susan and Emily headed back to New York today. On the way to the airport, they stopped by the Hebrew Home.

"Dad, I love you," Susan said, kissing her father. "Bye for now."

"Next time you see me," he replied, "I'll probably be dead."

"Really, Dad, that's what you're leaving me with? Right after I kiss you goodbye—that's what you went with?"

"Well, you know what I mean."

"Unbelievable," Susan whispered to herself. She looked toward the ceiling and the heavens, adding, "He's yours whenever you want him, Mom."

Susan then called to tell me about the exchange.

"I mean this, Barry. If you ever need me, to vent to me or just to call and breathe in the phone to me because of Dad, please do it. You need an outlet. Drinking and smoking weed couldn't hurt, either."

* * *

23 November

All night, my father, for reasons that defy understanding—he's never done it before—has been addressing Gregory, Melissa's son, as "Paul," my son, who died 12 years ago.

Gregory, who's fourteen, has been running around all night, laughing, playing, coming to the table, leaving it. My father, staring at Gregory's half-eaten dinner on the table, asks, "Hey, Ba, is Paul coming back?"

It's a nice thought.

Later . . .

At the bar mitzvah celebration of my young cousin Oliver, a waitress offers my father a meatball.

"It's spicy," she says.

"Oh, really?" Jack Friedman replies. "Will it make me horny?"

* * *

28 November

Today at the Hebrew Home, the staff, the exhausted staff, beautifully set up the dining room for Thanksgiving.

Mayra, the manager, comes over to say hello.

"Hi, Jack. Are you OK?" she asks.

"You don't look like you slept at all," he says. "Are you OK? You don't look good. Does your husband know where you are? Hey, when I die, if I have children, can they use my apartment?"

DECEMBER

3 December

My father's phone bill came today—there were eleven calls to directory assistance, at $2.49 per call.

"Dad, in the future, call me if you need a number. They're gouging you. Don't call Information."

"I'm telling you, I never do that. Never!"

"You are. Maybe you don't remember, but you are."

"I don't remember."

"Looks like Information to New York and New Jersey and Nevada. You would call looking for those numbers."

"I didn't do that, I don't remember doing that. OK, I won't do that anymore, but I'm telling you I never did that."

"All right, just promise me, no more."

"I won't do it, but I'm telling you, it's someone else. Someone's coming in here and using the phone."

"Someone is breaking into your apartment to call Information?"

"What do you want me to tell you?"

* * *

8 December

"Every morning I have my corn flakes," he says, "and I put a banana in it."

"Good."

"What does a banana do?"

"What does it 'do'? It's a good source of potassium."

"Potassium?"

"Potassium."

"But what's its function inside the cereal? I'm very serious. What function does it serve?"

Later . . .

"Dad, you ever hear from the guy in Florida we went to see ... Marvin?"

"Marvin? You mean Kraftchen?"

"How many Marvins were there?"

"There was Marvin Kraftchen and Marvin Feldman."

"Really?"

"Yeah! These are the guys I ran with. There were two Marvins, Miltie, Morris, who drove a cab, and Mel."

"And that's just the M's."

"What?"

"Nothing."

"Anyway, they're all gone, except Mel, who's in California. He takes naps."

* * *

10 December

Tonight at Mondo's, before the meal, Jack Friedman gave me the greatest piece of advice—his greatest piece of advice—ever offered from father to son.

"Don't fill up on bread."

He said it while eating bread.

* * *

24 December

Tonight, along with America's Comedy Dad, Jack Friedman (and thanks to Dahlia Lithwick for bestowing the title on him), dear friend Aaron—"Q" to those of you scoring at home, co-owner of Owl Head Bagels—comes over for a special Christmas dinner of pizza, tomato and buffalo mozzarella, and chocolate cheesecake (the last two provided by him).

At one point, Aaron asks my father, "Hey, Jack, what was your favorite memory of Barry when he was growing up?"

"Uh, let me think. Well, one time . . . oh, yeah, Barry did

something and his brother, Wayne, didn't like it—or maybe it was the other way around. I can't remember what it was about, but it was about something."

* * *

27 December

My phone rings. (His TV is blasting in the background because he doesn't need the stupid "ear plugs.")

"Barry, it's Dad. Did you see it?"

"See what?"

"You're in the magazine."

"What magazine?"

"*The Messenger.* From the . . . temple."

"Synagogue."

"What?"

"Nothing. Not important."

"Anyway, you're in it."

"I am?"

"Yeah. It says you did something. What did you do?"

"I don't know. It's probably the book."

"The what? No, let me read it to you. It's on page two. 'Mazel tov to Barry Friedman for writing *Four Days and a* . . . something. He had a . . . at Magic City Book . . . on December 17 . . . about the loss . . .' Well, it goes on. Yeah, yeah, it's in *The Messenger.* It's got that famous guy—oh, what the hell's his name?—on the cover. You know who it is. Anyway, you're on page two. Do you have a copy?"

"Of the book?"

"No, the magazine. You gotta get a copy. You're on page two. It says 'Mazel Tov' and then 'Barry Friedman.' Really. I'll save this copy, but you have to get the magazine. You know, *The Messenger.* Do you know what I'm talking about?"

* * *

28 December

After my father and Sherman had an argument about how much chicken my dad eats, and after Mort, the other guy at the table, died, my father eats alone.

"Hey, Dad, do you want me to get you at a table where you can eat with people, so you won't have to eat alone?"

"No. Don't push it."

"There's no pushing it. It won't be a problem."

"Let it be. It's better this way."

"How's it better?"

"Well, people walk by, they see me sitting alone, they probably think, 'Who's that guy? He must be special. He's got his own table.'"

I had heard from "the Big Guy" that Mort had a stroke. It was on a Thursday. His daughter wanted him to have physical therapy and Mort told her, "I want to be in the ground by Sunday." Later, Jim, the Big Guy, said Mort said he was worried how his daughter was going to take the news of his death.

"Jim," I asked, "my father ever say he's worried about me?"

"Nah."

Best part of the story: When Mort's daughter asked her father whether he was excited about his new great-granddaughter, Mort replied, "I'm very excited. Cut her a check. I'm done."

three
2020

JANUARY

2 JANUARY

"Ba, I want to take you to dinner. I'm buying. You do so much for me. We'll go to Moodo's."

"Mondo's."

"Yeah, yeah. What'd I say?"

"Close enough."

"I'm going to give you thirty bucks."

"Hold it. You just said you were buying. It's going to be more than that."

"How much more?"

"Depends what we order."

"All right, all right, whatever it is, I'll split it with you."

"You're killing me. Now you're splitting it with me?"

"What time are you coming?"

"Five thirty."

"Five thirty? Tonight?"

"Yeah, we just talked about it."

"So you're coming here?"

"Yeah."

"We eating here?"

"No, we're going out."

"Right, right, I forget. We're going to your guy with the shrimp."

"My guy . . . Mondo's."

"Yeah, yeah, I like that place."

Later . . .

"What are you doing here?"

"We're going to dinner, remember?"

"Yeah, yeah, we're going to, uh, what is it—the Paladium, right?"

"Mondo's."

"Yeah, yeah, they make a great chicken dish with the shrimp."

He reaches into his pocket. "Oh, before we go, I want to give you this," he says, and pulls out a . . . twenty-dollar bill. "You know, for dinner tonight."

* * *

4 January

"Big problem, Ba," my father says to me at Owl Head, as I bring him his decaf with four packs of Sweet'N Low and five different-flavor creamers. "What happens if you go first? You know, if you die before me. Who's going to take care of things?"

"Well—"

"—You know, they make great coffee here."

* * *

6 January

"So, Ba, how old are you?"

"Sixty-two."

"Is that good?"

"Is it good? That's a great question. All right, now that you ask, yeah, it's good."

"Okay. You know I have dinner at five tonight at the home."

* * *

13 January

"Ba, I got two phone calls from the front desk," my father says, "raving about your thing in the paper. What did you do?"

"Wrote a book."

"Yeah . . . what? I know, I know. But how did they find out?"

"Who?"

"The front desk."

"I guess the person at the front desk reads the paper."

"How did they know you had a father?"

"They know I have a father."

"But how do they know me?"

"You live there."

"But how do they know I'm your father?"

"How do they know? Dad, they know you're my father. I got you into the place."

"You did?"

"I did."

* * *

25 January

"Ba, I forgot to shave," he tells me at Owl Head, "but I decided I'm not going to shave because this is not a date. If it was a date, I would shave."

* * *

28 January

Today, Malyn, exercise guru and pool life coach extraordinaire, told me that yesterday my father came to the exercise and stretching class (no small achievement for a ninety-three-year-old man) and was huffing and puffing throughout the class. Afterward, he approached Malyn and apologized for being out of breath and unable to perform all the stretches. Malyn said, "Don't worry, you did great," to which my father responded, "It's because of my chest wound from the war."

FEBRUARY

8 February

"Hey, Ba, it's Dad. Where the hell are you? I know you're away. What is this, your answering machine? Question: Did you file my tax return last year? Call me back tonight after eight. You know I eat dinner at five."

* * *

11 February

"Jack, how are you?" Myra, one of the buffet managers, asks him tonight at dinner.

"Want to do some heavy breathing?" he asks. "I learned anatomy from the Braille system."

* * *

20 February

"Dad, how are you? I'm in Poland."

"Poland? Anyplace special?"

"Warsaw."

"Warsaw? Oh, yeah! That's a very famous place because of the war."

MARCH

2 March

At the Hebrew Home, there is an exercise class every Monday, Wednesday, and Friday morning. Often I call my father to remind him because he likes to go. He just forgets he likes to go.

"Just reminding you about the exercise class this morning at ten."

"It's not really an exercise class. It's more stretching. It's light, nothing special. You know, for the old-timers."

"Which is you."

"There are people in there over 100."

"No, there's not."

"Well, you know what I mean."

"Frighteningly, I do."

"What?"

"Nothing. So, are you going?"

"I only go when I don't feel achy."

"And?"

"I don't know yet. I may feel achy."

* * *

5 March

This morning, Petar, my father's eighty-seven-year-old client, a Serbian doctor with a thick, indecipherable accent, called my father, a ninety-three-year-old accountant who can't hear, doesn't listen, has no short-term memory, and shouldn't be even doing taxes, to tell him about a New York City tax bill that he, the Serbian doctor, got for $23,000.

I hear my father say, "Forget about it!"

It's amazing they both don't wind up in jail.

* * *

8 March

On the way to Owl Head today, as I am starting to do lately, I quiz my father on the moments and people in his life.

"Now let me get this straight," he says. "I had three children: Susan, Wayne, and Barry."

"That's right."

"But Barry died."

"No, Barry didn't die. I'm right here."

"Not you—the other Barry."

"What other Barry?"

"The first Barry."

"There's only one Barry. You had only one Barry."

"What do you mean 'there's only one Barry'? The other Barry—the first one."

"There's no 'first Barry.' There's only one Barry, me."

"You?"

"Yes, me."

"Are you sure?"

"Am I sure I'm Barry? That's actually a great question."

"Hey, I heard Bernie Newman died. Somebody told me that. How did he die? Do you know? And Red Meltzer died in his sleep. How the hell does that happen?"

* * *

11 March

"Hey, Dad, who's your favorite son in Oklahoma?"

"Irving Schlamowitz."

"Correct."

"Okay. Say, Ba, why don't you get my Social Security increased?"

* * *

15 March

"What is it with this cookie you brought yesterday?"

"What do you mean?"

"I take a bite and I either get the vanilla or the chocolate. I can't take a bite and get both—unless I bite it in the middle and then the cookie breaks."

He then proceeds to do just that and the cookie, as predicted, breaks.

"See," he says. "Why do they make it like this? Ach, I give up!"

* * *

17 March

While the Hebrew Home/Hotel is on a bit of lockdown—COVID has hit—I call my father from the street below his apartment.

"Hello," he says, his voice booming, almost as loud as the TV.

"Dad, it's me."

"Barry?"

"Yes, Barry. Listen, I'm outside your window. I'm going to throw two tubes of toothpaste up to you."

"You mean here?"

"Yeah, come outside."

"You mean outside?"

"To your balcony."

"The balcony?"

"The balcony."

"Oh, you mean the outside balcony?"

"Yeah."

He appears.

"What are you doing down there?"

"I'm going to throw this up to you, OK?"

"Okay."

I do. And he catches them.

"Oh, thank you," he says, "I really needed these."

"So you were out of toothpaste?"

"No, no. I got one tube. And I think I have another. But this is good. I need these."

My father has only four of his own teeth remaining in his mouth.

He now has a tube of toothpaste for each.

Life, while not good, is hilarious.

* * *

19 March

"What is with the *fakakta* South?" my father asks during this morning's phone call.

"This should be good. What are you talking about?"

"The guy with the one arm?"

"Guy with the . . ."

"Yeah, he puts on the uniform and he loves the girl and he wants to fight and then they kill him."

"You're watching television."

"Yeah, all right, maybe so, but, c'mon, what? He wanted to see the girl. You had to kill him? Why did we let them back in, anyway?"

"Who?"

"The South."

* * *

21 March

"Hey, Dad," I say on the phone, "how was dinner last night? They brought it up to you, right?" The Hebrew Home, because of COVID, is bringing the residents' food to their apartments.

"Oh, yeah, very good. I had what I usually have but they wrapped it up nice. Excellent."

***

23 March

"Ba, I understand, keeping people away and I can't go out so I don't get sick—and, OK, I'm getting my dinners. They're very nice, by the way. I have no complaints, but how long are they going to keep me interred here?"

***

25 March

"Dad, listen, I'm coming by tomorrow with some food for you. Going to leave it at the front desk. They'll call you. When they do, just come down and get it. Listen, I need you to bring down your empty pill trays."

"Barry?"

"Yeah, it's me."

"What did you say?"

"I'm bringing you food tomorrow, leaving it at the front desk, like last week, but I need you to bring down your empty pill trays."

"Food? Yeah, OK. What are you bringing?"

"The usual: chicken, cheese, cookies, soda, milk, cereal, and Half and Half."

"I'll need some Half and Half. I'm out. Well, I'm not out. I got. But I can always use."

"I got some for you, don't worry. But the trays. You'll bring the trays down?"

"Back up."

"To what point?"

"What trays?"

"That the pills come in. That I fill up for you."

"You mean the bottles?"

"There are no bottles. I fill up the plastic trays."

"I don't know what the hell it is you're talking about. I don't have trays. The bottles, you mean?"

"Forget the bottles. There are no bottles. You have trays. Your pills come in trays, right, that you take every morning? They're marked: Monday, Tuesday, Wednesday—"

"—Yeah. What's your point?"

"That's my point. I need the empty trays, those trays, so I can fill them with more pills."

"I don't have trays. Trays? What kind of trays? Trays?"

"Trays."

"Trays?"

"Dad, in the morning, how do you take your pills?"

"I take the pills. I take down the thing—"

"—The thing! Yes, that thing—that's the tray!"

"What thing?"

"That the pills are in."

"Barry, I don't know what you want. I take the pills every morning. I take them out of the . . . you know . . . the . . . what do you call it? The tray?"

"YES! The tray! It's called the tray."

"What about it?"

"I need them. I need the trays."

"You want me to bring down the trays?"

"Please."

"But they're empty. Anyway, what's going on with this goddamn disease?"

* * *

26 March

"Hey, Dad, I'm here," I tell him in a call from my cell. "Come to the balcony."

"The balcony?"

"I'm downstairs. You'll be on the balcony."

"Outside?"

"Yeah, I'll be outside."

"But I can't come out. And you can't come in."

"No, you're staying on the balcony. You come out there, and I'll be outside, below, so we can talk."

"Talk?"

"To each other."

"All right, hold on."

He appears. "We're not going to make it, sweetheart," he says. "Did you see the news? We're not going to make it. I don't just mean me and you. This whole country is going down the tubes."

* * *

28 March

"Where the hell's my TV in the bedroom?" my father asks in a call. "What did you do with it?"

"You told me to take it, remember? You didn't need it."

"I know, I know, I'm just wondering. I don't like watching TV in bed. My head hits the pillow and I fall away."

"All right, so you're good, then?"

"I wash my hands twenty times a day . . . with soap! I scrub my fingers. I tell you: I can't stand to look at my hands anymore."

"It's an odd sentiment, I gotta tell you."

"What is?"

"Nothing. Anyway, tomorrow, yes? I'll be there with the croissant and the egg. I'll toss it up it to you and I'll hang around and we'll talk."

"Make sure you double-bag it so it doesn't fall out."

* * *

29 March

We begin at the Owl Head Drive-Thru, where dear friend Aaron Quinton is manning the operation. I order, then get to the window.

"You're really going to toss this to him?" he asks, handing me a package consisting of a fried egg on a toasted croissant and two salt bagels.

"I sure am."

"Love you, brother."

I arrive at the Hebrew Home and call.

"Dad?"

"Barry?"

"Yes, it's me. Come to the balcony."

"I don't think the phone will reach. Tell you what: I'll put the phone down and then come to the balcony."

"Good idea."

He appears.

"All right," I yell, "I'm going to throw this up to you."

"Throw what?"

"Breakfast."

"Breakfast?"

"Breakfast."

"Oh, you mean . . . what?"

"The egg sandwich."

"I already had coffee."

"I didn't bring coffee. You ready?"

"Aim toward the door so it doesn't fall short."

"Thanks, coach. You ready?"

"Go 'head."

The trajectory is a little off, the catch muffed, but the sandwich is saved.

"Ach," he says, "they should have wrapped it better."

* * *

30 March

"How are you?" I ask. "Were you sleeping? Did I wake you up?"

"No, I wasn't sleeping, I was dozing."

* * *

31 March

"Barry, it's Dad. I'm watching TV. What the hell's going on with this thing? I can't go outside?"

"No, you can go outside. It's the groups. The more people you're around, the better chance someone has COVID, which means there's a better chance of you getting it, so they want you to stay in. Conversely, if you have it—"

"—No, I feel fine. Really. Nothing aches."

"Always good."

"So who the hell came up with this?"

"Nobody came up with it. It's a virus, a new virus. And since nobody is immune to it, it keeps spreading."

"So what's with the hands?"

"You mean the washing?"

"Yeah."

"If someone has the virus and they sneeze or cough into their hands and then shake hands with you, and you then touch your mouth or nose, well, that's how you get it."

"I know, I know. That's why I don't touch people."

"What?"

"I don't touch people."

"That's good, Dad."

"No, no joke. I don't touch anybody. So what else is new? How's Carole?"

"She's fine." I have no idea who he's talking about.

"Let me ask: Can you get this thing?"

"Yeah, I can get it. I'm also avoiding groups, but I can come see you. Tell you what. Tomorrow, I'll come visit. I'll come to your balcony and throw you another egg sandwich, just like the other day. Sound good?"

"Oh, yeah, very good. But wrap it good so the egg doesn't come apart in the wind."

APRIL

1 April

Let me start by saying that you may be cool but you're not "Jack Friedman on a balcony snagging an egg sandwich in midair" cool.

"Dad, I'm here." I'm standing below his apartment at the Hebrew Home.

"You mean downstairs?"

"No, the balcony."

"That's what I meant. Let me turn the TV off."

He doesn't.

"Dad, get your hearing aids."

"My what?"

"Hearing aids."

"I'm going, I'm going."

He opens the sliding door, then reappears and is putting in his hearing aids. I toss the egg sandwich up.

The catch is made.

"Hey, how's the family?" he wants to know.

"Good, good."

"Sylvia okay?"

"Susan."

"Who?"

"Never mind. She's good."

* * *

2 April

"Dad, how are you?"

"I see people in the paper: eighty-six . . . seventy-eight . . . eighty-three . . . eighty-four. They're all dead. What am I still doing here? Hey, you think when I die, I'll make the paper?"

"I'm sure of it. I know people."

"Who do you know?"

"I know. Don't worry. I know."

"So what's going on with this shit? Can I go out on my balcony?"

"Yeah. That's a great idea."

"If someone has it, they can't reach me up there?"

"No."

"How's Wayne?"

"He's good."

"Yeah, I know. He called me yesterday. Let's see. Who else do we have in the family?"

"Nice. Susan, your daughter."

"Oh, yeah, yeah, she called too. She calls every day. And her kids."

"I hear they make big bucks."

"Yeah, but Jesse [Susan's second-oldest] wants to be a pastor. That I don't get. A pastor? Nu? Where did that come from? And you're all right?"

"Yes."

"How's Melissa?"

"Good."

"No, no joke. I love you, Ba, I really do. You're fronting me all this stuff."

"I'm not fronting you the chicken and cheese. God, that's hilarious. Anyway, I love you, too."

"But call me once in a while. Or come by."

"Great idea. I'll do that."

* * *

3 April

"Hello."

"Dad, how are you? Good God, turn down the TV."

"So is this the end of the world? Is this World War III?"

"I don't think so."

"I'm going to stay inside. And hide."

"Great idea."

* * *

5 April

"Dad, how are you?"

"Hello, sweetheart!"

"Wow. You sound good today."

"Barry, I'm ninety-four."

"You're ninety-three."

"Whatever. I'm going to be ninety-four. The point is, I feel good, but I'm bored. I'm watching TV, I'm washing my hands four, five times a day."

"Wait, wait, wait. You were washing your hands twenty-five times a day yesterday. Why the change?"

"Where the hell did this thing come from, anyway?"

"First known case was in China."

"Ah. So if I see a Chinese person, I should worry."

"Only if they're Republican."

"What?"

"Nothing."

"Question: Would I be better if I were not in Oklahoma?"

"Wouldn't we all?"

* * *

6 April

I call to tell him, "Dad, come to the balcony."

"I'm coming, hold on."

He appears. TV is not off, hearing aids are not in, jacket is not on. He clearly has no plans for a long visit.

"All right, I'm ready," he says, holding out his hands for the egg and croissant sandwich wrapped in tin foil in a paper bag.

I throw it. He doesn't make the catch.

"I got it, I got it, don't worry," he says, retrieving it from the chair upon which it fell. "Okay, thank you," and he starts to head back into the apartment.

"Whoa, whoa," I say. "What happened? We break up? We're not going to talk?"

"I'm freezing out here."

"Dad, how are you?"

"This sandwich is magnificent. What a combination! What is it?"

"It's an egg on a toasted croissant."

"It's perfect. Did you make it?"

And suddenly the world seems right again.

* * *

8 April

I make the call.

"Listen, you know what today is?" I ask.

"What?"

"Mom died twenty-one years ago today."

"How long ago?"

"Twenty-one years ago."

"How old was she?"

"Sixty-nine."

"And Leo?"

"All right, let's move on. Leo was ninety-eight."

"And what about my father?"

"Your father? I think he was sixty-five."

"And where were you?"

"I was three. This was 1960."

"Where was I?"

"I don't know. Probably in the vicinity."

"So what the hell am I doing at ninety-three? Ach, I give up."

I throw him his egg-on-croissant. The bag containing the sandwich clears the railing by three feet, but as he goes for the catch, he misjudges and the bag hits him in the chest and falls to the ground.

"Why do you throw it and it always hits the railing?"

"It didn't hit the railing."

"So why don't you throw it so I can catch it?"

* * *

10 April

"Dad, how are you?"

He turns off the TV. "Ach, I give up! I give up! I give up!"

"What's the matter?"

"Nothing, really. It's my age, I think."

"What's your age?"

"Everything hurts. I feel lousy. But then I feel good, then I feel lousy, then I feel good, then I feel lousy. I mean, I feel good, just physically. Ach, I give up!"

"Hold on. How do you feel now?"

"I feel good."

"So that's good."

"Nah. Because I keep waiting for it to turn. I keep waiting for a catastrophe."

* * *

11 April

Scene: Ext. balcony. Jack Friedman, dressed in sweats and a FUBU shirt, appears. The toss is made, beautifully, I might add —nice arc, perfect end-over-end rotation, contents double-bagged and wrapped in tinfoil. Jack Friedman gets under it and, again, blows the catch.

"What kind of football player are you?" he screams as he bends down to pick up the bag.

"You're blaming me on that one? It was right to you."

"Right to me? Right to me? I had to reach up."

* * *

12 April

8:03 a.m. My phone rings.

"Barry, it's Dad."

The "it's Dad" makes it art, as, no doubt, he doesn't want me to think it's that other kvetchy ninety-three-year-old I talk to every morning.

"What's up?"

"Barry, I need the world."

"What do you mean 'need the world'?"

"I need coffee, orange juice, and roll paper."

"And?"

"That's all."

"All our worlds should be so small."

* * *

15 April

"I can't believe, with this thing going around, how well I'm feeling," he says in a call to me. "Except the legs. Everything but the legs. Why do the legs go?"

"Because you're going to be ninety-four."

"That's no answer."

* * *

16 April

The egg-on-croissant exchange gets lost in the sun again, though he was wearing sunglasses.

"EMSA?" he asks, seeing an ambulance. "What's that?"

"It's an ambulance, Dad."

"They picking somebody up or dropping them off?"

"EMSA doesn't usually drop off new residents."

"Barry, I'm ninety-four."

***

19 April

"Dad, it's Barry. Coat, hearing aids on, TV off. I'm outside."

"All right, all right, I'm coming."

The door opens and he steps out. He feels the chill.

"Is this considered spring, or what?"

"It's April, Dad."

"Yeah, but is it spring?"

"It's spring."

"What is this, winter? It's cold."

"It's spring."

"It's chilly, you know. What kind of *fakakta* weather is this?"

"I don't know. Weather's funny like that. Anyway, you all right?"

"Yeah, except I don't sleep. You know why? Because I'm so inactive. But when I walk or run, I get out of breath."

"When do you run?"

"I don't run-run—well, you know what I mean."

"All right, I should know better, but I've gotta ask: Do you need pills?"

"Pills? I take pills every day."

"I know. But do you need your trays filled up?"

"My what?"

"Your trays."

"My trays? What trays?"

"That the pills come in."

"I take the pills every day. Nine pills I take. What the hell am I taking, anyway?"

"I'll explain it next time, I swear. For now, I need the empty trays."

"What are you talking about?"

"We're doing this again—astonishing. That the pills come in. The trays, the plastic containers, the box, the . . . the pill pillows."

"You mean the pills?"

"I don't even know what I mean anymore. The things the pills come in . . . that I hand to you."

"What about them?"

"Are any of them empty?"

"Yeah. I need pills."

"Okay. Would you toss the empty . . . I have no idea what to call them . . . down to me?"

He then tosses five plastic trays from his balcony, one by one.

"Watch out for the wind!" he screams. "They're moving!"

"Thanks, Coach."

* * *

21 April

My father went to the emergency room today. As it turns out, there is some kind of intestinal blockage. It doesn't appear serious, but he will be kept in the hospital for a few days for more tests, at which point we'll know if surgery is required. When the doctor called to give me the latest, he said, "Your dad was pleasant to talk with. I really enjoyed him, and he's in really good shape for a man his age." Apparently, the blockage is a result of scar tissue from surgery my father had forty years ago and isn't from his war wounds from seventy years ago, though I'm sure he'd prefer it if they were battle-related."

* * *

22 April

"Mr. Friedman," the doctor says to me, "I have to tell you: Your dad is a hoot. I told him I was going to examine his chest and he said, 'I have to charge you for that.' And when I told him, 'That's okay, because I am already charging you,' he said, 'What? I am going to talk to my lawyer about this . . . as soon as he gets out of jail.' Is your father always like this? It's wonderful talking with him. He's really all there and then . . . you think, 'Whoa! How did we all of a sudden get into this rabbit hole?'"

"Yeah, you have to hold on, because when talking to my father, it's like a dance. And he leads."

"He's in good shape. He really is. He remembers the war and keeps asking for women."

"Perfect."

"I'll tell you, if I'm ninety-three and I'm like that, I'm good."

* * *

23 April

"Is this Barry Friedman?"

"Speaking."

"Hi. I'm Rachel, your dad's nurse. Excuse me a second, but is this Barry Friedman the columnist?"

"Yes, it is, Rachel, best nurse in all the land. YES, it is!"

"I love your writing."

"And I love you."

"And my father adores you. He loves your politics. He reads everything you write."

"Well, tell the best father in all the land I adore him too."

"Wow, he's going to be so jealous I got to talk to you."

My father could be in surgery at the moment having his lung reinflated, and I'm letting Rachel go on about me as long as she wants.

"That's very nice."

"Can I tell him I talked to you?"

"Absolutely."

"Okay . . . about your father."

"Oh, yeah . . . him. It's always about him, isn't it?"

"He was okay today. There's still the obstruction, he's a little uncomfortable, but he did poop."

"Will a day ever go by that I won't hear that word?"

***

24 April

"Mr. Friedman, how are you?"

"Fine, Doctor. How are you?"

"Good, good."

"And how's my father?"

"He's fine. Had a good day. Seems like his old self. Ate solid foods, he pooped."

"Bingo."

"And he was so charming. He's a riot. Just so you know, I'm taking him home with me."

"Great. I'll pack his things."

"You're the son who dragged him to Tulsa and just left him at the hospital."

"Yes, that's me. We have some issues left to work out in our relationship, so I figured this was the best course of action. Just dump him at the first hospital I came to. What else did he tell you?"

"He showed me pictures of his wife, your mother, I guess, and I said, 'Jack, how did you get such a good-looking woman?'"

"And he said?"

"He told me he was very charming."

***

25 April

At 3:15 p.m., a masked Jack Friedman is wheeled through the exit door of the hospital after being discharged.

"Oh, Ba, so good to see you. I didn't know where the hell I was. What the hell was I doing in there?"

"You were sick."

"Well . . . sick. I don't know that I was sick. I was just . . . what the hell was it, again?"

"You had a blockage."

"Yeah?"

"Yeah."

"What kind of blockage?"

"A blockage-blockage. It was in your lower bowel."

"Yeah, I couldn't go, but then, wow-wee-wow, did I go! No, it's good, Ba, I feel good. Thank you so much for coming."

We arrive at the Hebrew Home/Hotel. I walk him inside to the front desk, and first thing he asks Jackie at the desk, "You have my paper?"

He's back, baby!

* * *

26 April

The phone rings. It's 7:30 a.m.

"Barry, it's Dad. I'm at the hotel. Yesterday, they gave my paper away."

"Those rat bastards!"

* * *

27 April

He calls to tell me, "Ach, I give up. Am I going to die here? Am I going to die soon?"

"Yeah, here, but not anytime soon."

"All right, I'm ninety-three, ninety-four. Where am I going? Just don't die. Barry, don't die. I'd be lost without you."

"I won't die, promise."

"I'm just joking. Live your life the way you want."

"Thanks. I think."

"Barry, whatever money I have is yours. Take it all."

"Very nice. But you don't have any money."

"Well, whatever I have, take half—you know, if it's an emergency."

***

28 April

Today, after I tossed my father an egg on a toasted croissant, the woman who lives in the apartment on the first floor right below him told us to stop screaming.

"Sorry, ma'am, he's hard of hearing," I say.

"It's all right," she says. "I understand. Would you bring me breakfast tomorrow?"

"Bagel be okay?"

***

29 April

I do.

***

30 April

"Ba, I was feeling lousy earlier. They put some cockamamie sauce on the chicken last night. I should know not to eat the chicken."

"But you love chicken."

"Well, you know what I mean. What kind of sauce was that?"

"How would I know that?"

"It was some kind of sauce. Anyway, I feel better. It's ebbing now."

MAY

1 May

"Dad, how are you?"

"Ach! I don't know. I feel a hundred and one."

"A hundred and one?"

"Well, you know what I mean. I need orange juice. The big one."

"I'll bring you some."

"You know . . . with the handle."

"With the handle. Hey, it's your daughter's birthday."

"Yeah?"

"Yeah."

"Which one?"

"How many do you have?"

"One."

"That's whose birthday it is."

"Cynthia?"

"Susan."

"Susan. I knew that. How old is she?"

"Fifty-five or fifty-six, not sure."

"You know I'm going to be ninety-four."

* * *

2 May

"Dad, whoa, the TV!" I say after he picks up. "Make it lower."

"What do they want from my life? I got too many buttons here. All right, it's off."

It's not.

"Ach, Barry, sometimes I feel ninety-five."

"You're ninety-three. You feel two years older? Hey, did you call your daughter on her birthday?"

"What?"

"Susan."

"What about her?"

"Did you call her on her birthday?"

"Yeah, yeah, she calls."

"You know your other children have birthdays this week

too."

"I was just thinking that."

"No, you weren't."

"I was!"

"You were not!"

"You miserable bastard. I was too. I'm telling you. I swear to God."

"Fine. When's our birthdays?"

"Okay, I thought about it for a moment, but it was fleeting."

* * *

3 May

"Ah, Barry, where did it all go?" he asks in a call. "Where did it all go? Ach!"

"Hey, hold it. Wish me a happy birthday."

"Oh, that's right. I forgot. It's your birthday. How old are you?"

"Sixty-three."

"No, but I feel all right, but I take it slow. I go down and I get the paper. It's the best exercise. But how long is this going to go on?"

"Probably a month more. Let's get back to my birthday. Wish me a happy birthday."

"I did already, sixteen times! You know, Susan called me yesterday. Was very nice. She calls regularly. Once or twice a week."

"Nice."

"And I know you do, too. Hey, do I have any money left?"

"Yeah."

"You want to buy something?"

"No. What do I need? Clothes I got. Tell you what: Take a thousand."

"I'm not taking a thousand, but very nice. Did I mention it's my birthday?"

"How old are you?"
"Sixty-three."
"Is that gross or net?"

* * *

5 May

I call from the car. "Dad, turn the TV off, put your hearing aids in, put a jacket on, and meet me at the balcony."

"What a set of instructions! Just so you know, the hearing aids are already in, the TV is off, and I'll get a jacket."

He opens the sliding door. I can hear the TV, and it becomes apparent pretty quickly that he's not wearing his hearing aids.

"You just told me you had the hearing aids in."

"I didn't think you meant today."

"Yes, I was reviewing your hearing-aid usage for the week."

"What?"

"Nothing."

"I put them in yesterday. And I can't hear you anyway."

"All right, you ready?" I ask, showing him the package.

Toss and catch made.

"Attaboy," he says. "I got it. So, let me ask you. If I walked out of this place, could I get back in?"

"Probably not without a test. You planning on walking out?"

"That's not my point. But could I walk out?"

"How much time are you spending planning your getaway?"

"No, I'm just curious, that's all."

"You could leave. Where do you want to go?"

"Nowhere. Where am I going? Hey, there's a short word for this thing and a long word, right?"

"Yes. COVID-19 and Coronavirus."

"But it's only one thing?"

"Yes."

Due to a temporary glitch in the Owl Head operations, I got, count 'em, two egg-on-toasted-croissant sandwiches. I ate one, and let me just say, "Holy f*ck!" He's right. What a combination!"

* * *

6 May

I call. (I can hear his TV before he even picks up.)

"Hold it a second, hold it a second. Let me make this lower . . . okay."

"Dad, how are you?"

"Fine. Watching TV."

"Hey, did you check your mail recently?"

"Every day I check. When I get the newspaper."

"Did you get a check from the government?"

"Where?"

"In your mailbox."

"Why?"

"Stimulus money because of the virus."

"I didn't check."

"I thought you said you checked."

"Not every day."

"Didn't you . . . never mind. Go down today and check your mailbox and see if there's a check. If there is, leave it at the front desk so I can deposit it into your account."

"What front desk?"

"Where you pick up the newspaper."

"You mean where I pick up the newspaper?"

"Where you pick up the newspaper."

"They'll have the check."

"No, your mailbox. There, there might be a check."

"All right. I'll find it."

"You don't have to go now. Sometime today. Even tomorrow."

"I'll check. If I have the check, I'll call you, but I checked already."

"You checked?"

"Well, not today."

* * *

8 May

"Barry, it's Dad. I got a check. Twelve hundred dollars. What's that for?"

"Stimulus money because of the virus."

"Why me?"

"Dad, everyone gets one."

"Everyone?"

"Everyone in America."

"That's thoughtful."

"Donald Trump is nothing if not thoughtful."

"What?"

"Nothing. Tell you what, Dad, leave the check at the side desk and I'll put it into your account."

"So what do you want me to do with it?"

"Leave the check at the side desk and I'll put it into your account."

"You want me to leave the check at the side desk and then you'll put it into my account?"

"Yes."

"You want me to endorse it?"

"No."

"No?"

"No."

"Why not?"

"Okay, sign it, if you want."

"I'll sign it."

"Okay."

"All right, front desk—uh, side desk. I won't endorse it."

"Perfect."

"Twelve hundred dollars? I wonder how they came up with that figure."

Later...

"Barry, it's Dad. I just want you to know I left the check at the side desk in an envelope that says 'For Barry Friedman' in big red letters."

"I'll pick it up today."

"It's at the desk."

"Yes."

"In an envelope that says 'For Barry Friedman.'"

"Good. I'll come by today."

"So you're going to come by today?"

"Yes."

Later...

"I forgot to tell you the check is at the side desk, not the front desk."

"You told me."

"I didn't know if I told you."

"You told me."

A few minutes later...

"Barry, it's Dad."

"What a surprise!"

"Did you pick up the check yet?"

"No."

"What do you mean?"

"I didn't."

"What do you mean?"

"You just called me."

"When did I call you?"

"Ten minutes ago."

"Yeah, because I want to know if you picked up the check."

"Dad. I'm still at the house."

"That's why I called. To see if you picked up the check."

Later...

"Barry, it's Dad."

"Yes."

"Did you want me to endorse the check?"

"No."
"Because I didn't endorse the check."
"You didn't have to."
"So I don't have to endorse it?"
"No."
"Okay, I left it at the side desk—well, really it's the front desk now because the other desk, there's nobody there."

Later . . .

"Dad, it's Barry. I picked up the check and I left you an egg sandwich."
"Did you pick up the check?"
"Yes, I have the check."
"You found it?"
"They gave it to me."
"Did they know who you were?"
"Yes."
"Listen, take half."
"I'm not taking half. It's your money."
"Put it in checking, then."

Later . . .

"Barry, it's Dad."
"How are you?"
"I called to tell you the sandwich is delicious."

11 May

I call. "Dad, I'm coming by this morning. You need anything?"

"Barry? Yeah. I need some soda."

"What kind of soda?"

"What kind do you think?"

"How about cream?"

"Cream?"

"Cream."

"Yeah, cream. Cream is good."

"You want root beer, too? You like root beer."

"No. Okay. Root beer is good."

"Anything else?"

"No, that's it."

I bring the cream soda and root beer, as well as some potato salad, which he loves because it's a great nosh. And then, having already stopped at Owl Head, I toss him an egg on a toasted croissant.

Moments later, he calls.

"Ba, I forgot. I need cereal. You know the flakes."

"Okay."

"You know what I mean? The flakes."

"I got it. The chocolate-frosted flakes."

"No. I need the chocolate."

"That's what I said."

"I have the regular."

"So you don't need the regular—just the chocolate?"

"I don't need the regular. But I am completely out of the chocolate. I have it every morning."

"I know."

"How the hell did I get this old? That was a great sandwich, by the way."

"Glad you like it. Anyway, cereal. No regular, just the chocolate. I'll tell you what. I'll bring both."

"You know what, bring the regular, too, but I don't really

need. I've got plenty, but what the hell, bring a box, even though I have."

"You need milk?"

"I got milk."

"You sure?"

"Positive. I finished the half gallon and just opened the double quart."

* * *

12 May

"Dad, how are you?"

"You know, I'm cold. They turned down the heat."

"Well, actually, you turned down the heat."

"That's what I mean, so I turned it up to eighty, and put on a sweater."

"That'll take care of it."

"They still pushing this disease around?"

"Yeah. It's all over."

"How come I never heard of it before? And they're sending out checks. Can you believe it? I'm ninety-three. How the hell did that happen?"

"If there were an answer, I would tell you. I really would."

"My question's academic. But, I mean, what the hell happened? Who sped up the years?"

* * *

13 May

"Barry, how much money was that government check?"

"Twelve hundred dollars."

"Listen, I'm going to need about a hundred."

"Okay."

"You know, for miscellaneous things when I go out."

"But you don't go out."

"Oh, right. But I thought I should have some cash for the miscellaneous items anyway."

"What miscellaneous items?"

"You know, the miscellaneous this and that. Like . . . I can't think of anything, but the miscellaneous shit. I mean, I don't need anything. But I thought I should have money around in case I need something, so you don't have to run out and buy—it's just the miscellaneous stuff. That's all."

"Okay."

"But I don't really need anything. I really don't. I have everything."

*　*　*

15 May

He calls. "Barry, I gotta get out of here."

"Why? What's up?"

"My nails on my toes. They're way out of whack and they're killing me. Didn't you have a girl who did this? We went a few times."

"Yeah, sort of. I have a girl. But you can't leave, and I don't think the place is open now."

"What do you mean 'I can't leave'?"

"For the same reason as ever: the virus."

"You mean I can't leave for the nails? Ach! C'mon."

"Dad, you can't leave."

"You know, one of the nails, since the war, it doesn't grow, and your girl did such a good job."

"Again with my girl. Dad, you're going to have to be patient. I'll call the Big Guy, but I don't think he'll let you out."

"So I tried cutting them myself. Just three of them."

"Don't, don't . . . DO NOT do that! Put the scissors away, put the clippers away."

"Why?"

"Because you're ninety-three, you can't bend down, you're

going to cut yourself, it's going to get infected, and then I don't know what happens."

"All right, all right, I didn't do anything. I just cut two."

"No more cutting, okay? I'll call the Big Guy and he'll send someone up. But no more cutting. Promise me."

"I didn't. I didn't do anything. I thought about it."

* * *

19 May

I call. The TV sounds like a jackhammer is being used to pulverize your bathtub, while you're in the bathroom . . . taking a bath.

"Dad, for the love of—"

"—Speak up, I can barely hear you."

"Turn off—"

"—What?"

"—the TV. You have to turn it off."

"Barry?"

"Dad, TURN OFF THE TV!"

He does.

"I did, I did. It's off, it's off. It's been off."

"No, it hasn't. You just turned it off."

"Because of the TV, that's all."

* * *

20 May

"Barry, it's Dad. I need a haircut."

"Okay. As soon as I can get in to see you."

"Yeah, because I need a haircut. Just the back, though. I have to plaster it down now because it's too long. You know what I mean? Just a trim . . . in the back."

* * *

22 May

"Dad."

"Who is this?"

"Here we go. Barry."

"Speak up, I can hardly hear you."

"The Big Guy is allowing visitors, so I get twenty minutes in a special room he had designed and built for such things. We can get together."

"Where?"

"In a room Jim has set up."

"A room? What kind of room?"

"It's a room, Dad. I don't know. A room."

"A room?"

"A room."

"Okay."

"So I'll meet you downstairs."

"Where downstairs?"

"Downstairs by the side entrance, where you get the paper."

"There are two entrances. The side entrance where I get the paper and the front entrance that's closed."

"By the side entrance, then."

"What time?"

"At ten forty-five."

"So you want me downstairs?"

"Yes."

"What time? Eleven?"

"Tell you what. Let me call you when I get there."

"But I won't be upstairs to answer the phone because I'll be downstairs."

"Wait upstairs until I call you."

"So don't come downstairs?"

"Right, not until I call you."

"So what time will you be here?"

"Around ten forty-five."

"You know, Ba, I'm wondering: With this corona thing, I

mean, are we ever going to have, what do you call it, community again? Because I worry about that."

"That's a fabulous question. Yeah, we will. Slowly. But, yeah, we will."

* * *

23 May

"Dad, it's Barry. Okay, I'm downstairs. But we're meeting in the front."

"The front? Not the side?"

"Not the side. The front entrance."

"You mean in the front?"

"Yes. Come off the elevator and walk straight."

"Come now? Where?"

"In the front. Main entrance. Come now, yes. And don't forget your hearing aids."

"Hearing aids? What about them?"

"Put them in."

"I don't wear them during the day."

"Wear them today."

"I'll put them in, but I don't need them."

As he makes his way down, I tell the woman at the front desk, "I'll bet you a buck he doesn't have the hearing aids in."

"I'm not taking that bet," she says.

Smart woman. He's not.

He appears. She gives him a mask.

"Dad," I say, seeing him, "you look good. But with these masks . . . you can't hear anyway . . . it will be tough to hear me. Hearing aids next time."

"What?"

"Hearing aids!"

"No, I feel good. I really do. You know, not bad. Nothing hurts. You know, it's very good what they do here."

"They're keeping you safe. You should wear a mask every day."

"I do, I do. Well, I didn't this morning when I got the paper. But I should. You know, one thing: They should have a doctor come in and check all the people here. Go door to door. They'll know who's sick. So what do we hear from the other side of the family?"

"The other side?"

"You know."

"Oh, yeah. They're all good."

* * *

24 May

"Dad, how are you?"

"Slow and sluggish," he says, turning off the TV. "When is this thing going to be over, already? It's getting ridiculous."

"I agree. But things are loosening up. Probably by the end of June, we can go out again."

"Good. I can't wait to get out of here."

"Say, you have everything you need?"

"You mean here?"

"Yeah."

"No, I got everything. I mean, yeah, the milk is about half gone, juice is about half gone, Half & Half is about half gone. So, I need, but I don't need. You know?"

"I do."

* * *

25 May

"Barry, it's Dad."

"Hey, how are you?"

"I need toilet paper."

"Okay."

"But I'm feeling good. Everything is reasonable."

* * *

26 May

We meet at the Hebrew Home entrance.

"Oh, Ba, thanks for bringing this. I see you have the toilet paper, the coffee, the potato salad. . . . Very good."

"My pleasure. And the sandwich."

"I see, I see. Yeah, it's in the special bag. But I'm going to need milk next time you come. I need a double quart. You know, the gallon. I have about a quarter left of the half gallon."

"Okay. By the way, you look good."

"It's a rented body."

"Never gets old."

"What?"

"Nothing."

* * *

28 May

The call is made from Walmart.

"Dad, Barry."

"Huh?"

"Barry."

"Yeah, yeah, I know."

"Meet me downstairs. In the front. Downstairs. In the front."

"What do you mean?"

"The front."

"You mean in the front?"

"Yes. You need to wear your mask, your hearing aids, and bring your empty pill trays."

"My what? My milk trays?"

"Pill trays."

"What trays? I don't understand you."

"PILL trays."

"Spell it."

"P—"

"—What?"

"P—"

"—What?"

"Fucking P!"

"B?"

"P . . . P . . . the pills you take every morning. The trays they come in."

"What trays do I have?"

"For your pills."

"My what? Oh, oh, the pills. Yeah, what about them?"

"Bring the empty trays down."

I arrive. Since the milk, juice, Half & Half, and soda are heavy, the woman at the front desk offers to bring them upstairs to his apartment and then escort him downstairs. She and the Hebrew Home/Hotel are great like that.

She returns. "Barry, he has his trays, his hearing aids, and his mask."

"He does not."

"He does."

"What are the odds?"

"I know."

My father appears and we take our place on opposite sides of the blue lobby table.

"How are you today, Dad?"

"Good. Sleeping well. Everything is fine. I'm just bored. So when am I moving again?"

"You're not moving again."

"But if I do. What about all my stuff, and where does it go? And how did it get here?"

"I moved it for you."

"You? It was here when I got here."

"No, we moved it here."

"And if I move, what happens then?"

"You're not moving again."

"What do you mean I'm 'not moving again'?"

"You'll be dead for your next move, so don't worry about it."

"What do you mean I'll 'be dead'?"

"You'll be dead. This is your last place. You're not moving anymore, so you don't have to worry about the hassle of the furniture."

"I'll be dead. I don't like that."

"I don't either. I'm just saying you don't have to worry about moving again."

"Will the place still make my bed?"

"Probably one more time after you die, and we get your body out of there."

"All right. Whatever it will be."

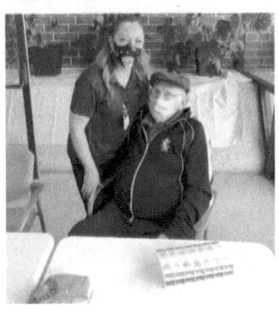

***

29 May

"Barry, did you try calling earlier? I need toothpaste."

"How can that be? I brought over four tubes last month and you only have, like, three of your own teeth left."

"Well, I use it to brush the dentures."

"No, no, no. Don't do that. It's not good for the dentures."

"Why not?"

"It breaks down the . . . whatever, of the plate. It scratches them and then food can lodge inside them. Very bad. Just soak them."

"I don't. That's why I don't brush them. I just soak them."

"You just said you brush them."

"Well, you know, I don't all the time, just sometimes."

"Dad, really, don't use it on the false teeth."

"I don't. Just the teeth I have."

***

30 May

"Hey, I gotta ask you," he says in the lobby of the Hebrew Home. "There's Wayne in California, there's Susan in Long Island in New York—"

"Right."

"And there's you here?"

"Right."

"That's the immediate family, so to speak."

"Yeah, so to speak. Your children."

"But what happened to you?"

"What do you mean 'what happened' to me? Nothing happened to me."

"Didn't you—I don't know, I thought something happened to you."

"Nothing happened."

"You sure?"

"Far as I know."

"All right. I thought something happened."

"Nothing happened."

"Question: When did my mother die?"

"1983."

"Where was I?"

"You were in New York. You were there."

"And my father?"

"1960."

"Where was I?"

"I assume you were there, but I don't know. I was three."

"Oh, that's right."

* * *

31 May

"Dad, how are you?"

"You know I'm going to be ninety-four?"

"I heard, yeah."

"Okay, twenty years ago, that was something—seventy-four. But ninety-four? What the hell happened? But then I think what some people my age got and I think, 'Don't knock it, baby.' But, no, I feel good. I don't sleep well because I sit around all day. I wake up and think, 'What am I going to do today?' and then I watch TV all day. I got plenty of food. What a load you brought. The chicken and the other stuff. All right, but I walk downstairs every day and get the paper. It keeps the blood flowing. So, you? Everything cool?"

"I'm working."

"I'm ninety-four. What the hell happened?"

"I don't have an answer for you."

"My question's academic. Maybe when I'm 104, I'll be impressed with myself."

JUNE

2 June

We sit for our 2 p.m. meeting at the Hebrew Home/Hotel entrance.

"Dad, your hearing aids."

"I had them in earlier. I took them out."

"Why would you do that?"

"I take them out sometimes."

"You did not have them in before."

"Not before, but I had them in."

"You had them in sometime in the past, is what you're telling me?"

"What?"

"You need to wear them."

"I feel fine."

"And you really should wear the mask."

"I can't breathe."

"You can breathe."

"No, I wear it, I wear it. But it bothers me. But I wear it."

"But you're not wearing it."

"You know what I mean."

"Why are you in such a bad mood today?"

"Because they got me strapped in here."

"They don't have you strapped in. Sit on your balcony. Come downstairs. You can walk outside. Just stay close to the building."

"I tried that. They locked me out."

"They didn't lock you out. They should have, but they didn't."

"What do you mean? Why should they have locked me out?"

"Because you're a pain in the ass."

"Ach!"

"Ach!"

"No, no joke. I went out and the door was locked."
"This door is never locked during the day."
"Not this door. The back door."
"There is no back door."
"It was the side door, then."
"That door is open during the day, too."
"No, some woman had to let me in."
"So she let you in. It's closed. It's not locked."
"What if she wasn't there?"
"Someone else would have let you in."
"Who?"
"Some other woman. How should I know?"
"Ach! I'm leaving here."
"Where you going?"
"I don't know. But I'm leaving New York."
"You're not in New York."
"You know what I mean."
"Would you stop complaining?"
"Who's complaining?"
"Who's complaining? You are. Now, c'mon, let's take a walk."
"Nah, I don't want to take a walk. A walk?"
"A walk."
"A walk? Nah. Listen, I need something, but I can't remember what. What would I have been thinking about? I know it wasn't potato salad. I got plenty."

*　*　*

5 May

I arrive at the Hebrew Home/Hotel entrance to find my father in a sweater, tweed hat, and sweatpants. He is wearing a mask. His hearing aids are not in.

"Dad, why are you wearing a sweater?"

"I didn't know what temperature it was. Is it hot, is it cold? What?"

"Why don't you open your sliding door to the balcony and find out?"

"I do that."

"Did you do it today?"

"No, not today. What kind of weather do you get around here?"

"You've been here for five years."

"I haven't been here for five years."

"You have been in Oklahoma for five years."

"No."

"Yes."

"No."

"Dad, I'm telling you."

"Really?"

"Yeah."

"I forgot. When did I leave Vegas?"

"Five years ago. Anyway, the point is you don't need a sweater and tweed hat and sweatpants in June in Oklahoma. In fact, you can put those away until probably October."

"So, Ba, what's new with you? Feeling all right?"

"Yeah. I've been trying to lose some weight."

"Yeah?"

"Yeah."

"You know, you look a little withdrawn."

"That's actually hilarious."

"No. Your face. It looks, what do I say, gaunt. Not gaunt. But you know what I mean."

"I do."

"You know I hate these masks."

"Would you stop with that?"

"What? I can't breathe."

"You can breathe fine. You just can't hear."

"I can hear fine. It's these masks. The sound comes in muffled."

"But the sound goes to your ears, not your mouth or nose."

"Why am I wearing it, again?"
"Because it's safer for you and everyone you're around."
"I know that!"
"Then THAT'S the answer."

* * *

7 June

The call comes in.

"Barry, it's Dad. I need hand soap. You know, the bars of soap. I'm out of the hand soap. The bars."

"I got it."

"You know what I mean? The soap you use for your hands and face. The bar soap."

"I know, I know. I'll bring it to you."

"Is there any place I can get it inside the walls here?"

"The walls? You're not in prison."

"What?"

"Nothing. I'll bring it to you. I'll drop it off at the—oh, God, here we go—side entrance."

"The front entrance?"

"The side entrance."

"You mean . . . where? In the front or the back?"

"No, the side."

* * *

9 June

    He calls.

    "Ba, it's Dad. Just want to confirm we're meeting at ten."

    "Eleven."

    "Yes, yes, eleven. In the back."

    "In the front."

    "In the front?"

    "The front."

    "What do you mean 'the front'?"

    "In front of the building."

    "Oh, that one, yeah. I know. I thought you meant the back."

    "No, the front, at the table."

    "Okay, in the front . . . at ten."

    "Eleven."

    "Got it."

* * *

10 June

    He calls. "Did you call?"

    "I did. Listen, I'll see you Friday. I'll bring you breakfast then."

    "What time?"

    "Ten thirty."

    "In the back entrance?"

    "You know, Dad, this isn't a big deal, and I should have my head examined for bringing this up, but there really is no back entrance."

    "What do you mean there's 'no back entrance'?"

    "There's no back entrance."

    "What are you talking about?"

    "There's no entrance in the back."

"Of course there's a back entrance. What do you mean 'there's no back entrance'?"

"There's no back entrance."

"What about the one in the back?"

"Which one in the back?"

"The one over there. The other one."

"The other entrance? By the cafe?"

"Yeah."

"That's not in the back. That's also in the front, but you call it the 'side' entrance."

"Well, for our purposes, we can call it the 'back.'"

* * *

12 June

I arrive at the entrance to the Hebrew Home. He's waiting for me.

"Jack, you like this soda?" Julie asks him.

"It's better than sex."

"Let me take your temperature," she says. She does.

"You know, I do a lot of heavy breathing," he says while she's applying the thermometer to his forehead.

"99.7," Julie says, smiling.

"Well, I'm very warm."

* * *

13 June

I'm preparing my father for a visit with my friend Ken from Boston.

"Why does he want to see me?" my father asks.

"He doesn't. He's here to see me."

"Oh, I thought he was here to see me, that's all."

We arrive.

"Dad . . . Ken."

"You and I met twenty years ago," says Ken. "We gambled together in Las Vegas."

"Was I alive back then?"

"Yes."

"Nice to meet you. What's your name?"

"Ken."

"Dad, let's take a picture."

"You want me naked?"

* * *

17 June

I call. "Dad, how are you? What are you doing?"

The TV is blaring.

"Just waiting for the guy to come and talk about his load."

"What?"

"The guy is coming up to talk about his load and my load."

"You're watching television. There's no guy coming up. Load?"

"No, I'm not saying there's a guy coming up, but he wants to talk about his cattle."

"He wants to talk to you about his cattle?"

"I don't mean me, but he said he was coming."

"Dad, you're watching TV, and the guy is not coming to talk to you about his cattle or his load."

"Not his load—MY load!"

"You don't have a load."

"I'm not suggesting I do."

"Is the TV off?"

"Yeah, yeah, it's off."

"Don't turn it back on for a while."

* * *

18 June

"Dad, how are you?" I ask, entering the lobby. "Hey, why don't you just wear shorts and a T-shirt? It's summer."

"I do."

"But you don't."

"I wear them upstairs and when I come down."

"But you came down and you're not wearing them. You'll be more comfortable."

"That's why I wear them."

"But you don't have them on."

"Well, I didn't know I was coming down."

"Yeah, you did."

"Well, you were coming today. I knew that."

"So you could have put the shorts on."

"I did. I had them on."

"You changed?"

"No, I put these on today." He points to his sweatpants.

"But . . . why don't you just put the shorts on in the morning when you wake up and leave them on?"

"I do."

"You've never worn them down here once."

"I wear them all the time. Upstairs."

"But you always wear long pants."

"No, no, I wear the shorts. I always wear the shorts."

"But you're not wearing the shorts."

"Because I didn't put them on. But I wear them. Every day."

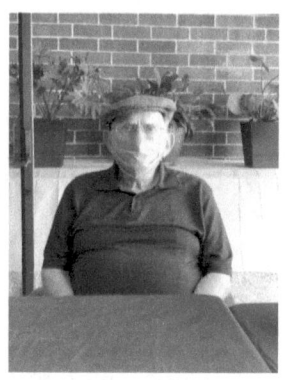

* * *

21 June

"Happy Father's Day, Dad," I say. He's sitting on the bench in front of the Hebrew Home.

"What?"

"Father's Day."

"Oh, yeah, I heard something about that. What's in the bag?"

"Potato salad and orange juice and an egg sandwich."

"Good, good, I needed that."

* * *

23 June

I arrive at the Hebrew Home front/back/side entrance with the customary egg sandwich in the bag. Carol shows me in.

"How goes your life?" my father asks her.

"Pretty good, Jack."

"That bad, huh? Well, don't worry. It'll get worse."

"What a ray of sunshine you are today," I say.

"What?"

"Nothing. Anyway, how are you doing?"

"Good, good."

"You look good. Short-sleeve shirt. Excellent."

"I like these. The material."

"You want me to get you some more?"

"Okay, but not too big. I'm a medium."

I laugh. I hear Carol laugh inside at the front desk.

"Who's that laughing?" my dad asks.

"That's Carol. I don't think she believes you're a medium."

"I am!"

"Carol," I yell inside, "what do you think?"

"I so wish I had a tape measure right now," she replies.

"Dad, I'm going to get you a large."

"Don't get me a large. They're too big."

"You need a large."

"No, no, no. I have a thirty-six-inch waist."

Once again I hear Carol laugh.

"Dad, you're not a thirty-six-inch waist. Look at your stomach."

"That's because I don't exercise."

"Different issue at the moment. Trust me, you're not a thirty-six. You're a forty."

"I haven't been a forty my whole life. I'm not a forty. Forty?"

"You're a forty."

"I have a pair upstairs, I just had them on, that's a thirty-six-inch waste and they fit perfectly."

"You sure it's a thirty-six-inch waist?"

"I don't know. I think so. I didn't look."

JULY

2 July

"When you die, Ba," my father said today, in the Hebrew Home lobby, "you are immediately reborn as a baby somewhere and you don't know from nothing until one day you're walking, you see someone and think, 'Where do I know them from?' It's from your previous life. Why does God do it like that? Ach, I give up!"

* * *

8 July

Today, my father and I went to the office of Dr. John Schumann.

(That's "Dr. Schumann" to you; "the Young Guy" to my father.)

"Say, Ba, is this guy part of the association?"

"What association?"

"You know, the association."

"There is no association."

"What do you mean 'there's no association'?"

"There's no association."

"Oh, I thought there was an association. Why did I think there was an association?"

"I don't know."

"Oh, I thought he was part of the association."

"He's not."

"So, have I ever seen this guy?"

"About six times."

"So who's this guy, again?"

"The young guy."

"He's a doctor?"

"He's a doctor."

"I've seen him before?"

"Yes. About six times."

We enter the clinic. Mai, the nurse, takes my father's vitals.

"You want me to undress?" my father asks.

"No."

"Why not?"

"Dad . . . please."

Dr. Schumann enters.

"Jack, how are you?"

"Good. I'm pushing ninety-four, you know."

"I know."

"I feel good, though, I do—no joke. I stopped smoking."

"Dad, you stopped smoking about forty-five years ago."

"I know. I'm just saying. Was it that long ago? I've got a Purple Heart, you know." He returns to his chair.

"It wasn't in battle," he says, surprising Dr. Schumann and me, for we have the original and revised versions of the story memorized. "A lot of service people think I was, but I was talking to the sergeant and I stepped on something and then *booooom!* I lost the nail on the big toe, but I wasn't really in battle. We won that war."

* * *

12 July

The TV is "Stasi interrogating a perceived West German spy in the mid-'70s" loud.

"Turn down the television."

"Wait a minute. Let me turn down the television."

"Good idea."

"What?"

"Nothing. What do you need? I'm coming over."

"I need . . . oh, you know."

"Potato salad?"

"What?"

"Potato salad?"

"No . . . potato salad? Yeah, you know. Get the big one. I eat it at every meal."

"What else?"

"Roll paper for the kitchen."

"You have, like, eight rolls from the last time."

"I do? What did I do with them?"

"I don't know."

"I have eight rolls? Where?"
"I don't know where. You put them away."
"I put them away? When did I put them away?"
"Last time I gave them to you."
"Let me look. I have eight rolls? I'll call you back."
He hangs up. He calls.
"Barry, it's Dad. I have no roll paper."
"Yes, you do."
"Anyway, I need it for the kitchen. You know which one I'm talking about? For the counter, not for the rear end."

* * *

13 July
"Hey, Ba," he asks on the phone, "where's my hair?"
"What?"
"My hair. Why did he take my hair?"
"Who took your hair?"
"I had hair."
"You didn't have hair."
"What do you mean I 'didn't have hair'?"
"You didn't have hair."
"Of course I had hair."
"No, you didn't."
"I had hair. What are you talking about? I had hair. And now I don't have any. What the hell happened?"
"You haven't had hair for forty-five years, and even then you didn't have much of it."
"So why did he take it?"
"Who?"
"Who? You know who."
"God didn't take your hair."
"Then who took it?"
"Who took it? I don't know who took it. You didn't have any

to take. Some men go bald, some die. You won. Look at the bright side."

"I had hair. And now it's gone. Where did it all go? Ach! I give up."

"You really didn't have hair, Dad."

"I had hair. I had hair in the front and now it's gone."

"You wore a toupee for years, but that wasn't really YOUR hair."

"Ach! Maybe you're right."

* * *

14 July

"Dad, how are you?"

"Did you just call?"

"Yes, we're talking."

"I mean before."

"Yes, I just called, but you couldn't hear the phone ring."

"I needed something, so I made a notation in my mind what it was. But I forgot."

* * *

18 July

The call is made.

"Hey, I've got good news for you," I tell him.

"What's that?"

"You tested negative for COVID-19."

"The what?"

"The thing. Coronavirus."

"Oh, yeah."

"Yeah."

"Yeah?"

"Yeah. From earlier in the week when they tested you."

"You know I'm going to be ninety-four, in October? It's a bad scene if old-timers get this. And you, are you good?"

"Yeah. I'm good."

"I mean, are you working, making money?"

* * *

21 July

"Ba, did you know," my father asks in the Hebrew Home lobby, "I'm going to be ninety-four?"

"Yes."

"No, no. I mean my age."

"I know."

"I'm ninety-three, and I'm going to be ninety-four."

"That is how it works, yes."

"I see people dying at eighty, eighty-four, eighty-two, seventy-six, and here I am ninety-four! And then the TV talks about people who are eighty-five. I'm older. How the hell did I get to be ninety-four? You think it's the pills I take?"

"Yes, that, and that you have a wonderful son."

"You?"

"Wayne."

"You know he called the other day?"

"He's a good son."

"And I heard from Cynthia."

"Susan."

"What?"

"Nothing."

"And the Big Guy waved to me today. He said, 'Hi, Jack.' How does he know me?"

"He knows you. Anyway, what do you need? What are you out of?"

"I need everything. I have nothing."

"What do you mean you 'have nothing'?"

"Well, I have the cheeses, but I don't have the chicken."

"You need chicken? You sure?"

"I mean, I have chicken, but I ate the last piece today, so I don't have."

"So you need chicken?"

"That's what I said."

"Okay, chicken. What else?"

"Nothing else. I got the cheeses. You know, the cheeses—the Swiss and Muenster. I got the milk. I got a full half gallon and you just bought me the double quart, so I'm fine with the milk. The juice. No, I got everything."

"Hey, you want some ice cream?"

"No."

"No?"

"No. Yeah, good idea."

"What kind?"

"The kind you scoop out of the container," he says, miming the scooping motion.

"I know that, but what kind?"

"What do you mean 'what kind'?"

"What kind? Dad, you want chocolate, strawberry, vanilla?"

"Yes. The chocolate, strawberry, and vanilla. It comes in one container. You know what I'm talking about? They're all together. They're in a row. Chocolate, strawberry, and vanilla"—he mimes the rows. "Bring me that, but I have to put it in the freezer."

* * *

22 July

Dr. Schumann and I decided that of all the medication my father takes, the antidepressants, which had been prescribed to him in Las Vegas before I dragged him to Tulsa, do not need to be one of them. So, the slow weaning of the Escitalopram has begun, which necessitated retrieving all my father's medications and the pill trays that held them, and then reducing and eventually removing the antidepressant from the oft-referred-to "pill pillows," which was coined by my friend Dahlia Lithwick.

Today, I returned the trays, along with the Neapolitan ice cream, which can be scooped (for those scoring at home); the turkey slices (he has plenty of cheese, let's remember); and the egg sandwich, which he loves as both lunch and sometimes as a nosh when he eats only half and saves the rest. Julie, our lovely and talented Hebrew Home docent, generously brought the food up to his apartment.

We begin at the tables in the lobby front, not the ones in the back or on the side.

"Dad, here are the new pills," I say, sliding them across the table.

"I thought you said I was down to one pill."

"No, I removed one pill. And start the new regimen today."

"What?"

"Sorry. Just start taking them today."

"What about tomorrow?"

"Take tomorrow's pills. They'll be under Thursday."

"And Friday?"

"Just follow the tray."

"The what?"

"The tray. It's in your hand."

"I know that."

"The days are listed Monday through Sunday."

"So what happens after Sunday?"

"Start the new tray."

"When?"

"Monday. With the new tray."

"What new tray?"

"That's in your other hand."

"Oh, this?" he asks, lifting it.

"Yes."

"Back up."

"Okay, you got a tray of pills that starts today, Wednesday, that's in that hand," I say, pointing to the hand that holds it. "That goes to Sunday. The other tray starts on Monday"—I point to his other hand—"so start that on Monday."

"Today."

"Today is Wednesday."

"And Monday?"

"Monday is Monday."

"Did the girl put the ice cream in the freezer?"

"Julie," I call out, "did you—"

"—Yes," she says from nearby in the Hebrew Home lobby.

"Yes, she did. So, are we good on the pills?"

"Yeah, yeah. Pills. I know."

"Dad—"

"I'll call if I have questions. So, let me ask," he adds, pointing to my phone on the table. "If you're in California and I call you, will it go straight to your cell phone?"

"Yes."

"What if I was in California and you were in California?"

"You could still call me on the cell."

"So the signal would have to come back to Oklahoma before going back out there?"

"That's not really how it works, but you'd be able to call me."

"That's not my point. I know I'd be able to call you."

"I thought that was your point."

"What?"

"Nothing."

* * *

25 July

"When am I going to get out of this place?" he asks when I arrive at the Hebrew Home lobby. "They got me trapped. Why can't I get out?"

"Because you're ninety-three."

"I'm going to be ninety-four!"

"I know. And ninety-three-year-olds about to be ninety-four-year-olds get sick very easily from this disease."

"Don't misunderstand me. I'm not knocking you. You do a nice job bringing me things, but I'm trapped. What if I decide to leave?"

"Where you going to go?"

"That's not my point."

"If you're going to plan a breakout and be on the lam, you should have some idea where you're headed."

"Ach, I give up!"

"All right, when I come back, what do you need?"

"Cookies."

"Okay, I'll bring you cookies."

"No, that's it. I'll tell you, Barry, I'd give you a hug right now if I could. But I can't get over there. Hey, what if I give you the hug [he points to Julie] and then you give him [he points to me] the hug?"

"Jack," she says, "I don't trust either one of you."

* * *

28 July

He comes downstairs to the front (not the side or the back) of the Hebrew Home. He sits.

"Aw, Barry, how much longer I got?"

"Five years."

"You know I'm ninety-three. I'm going to be ninety-four."

"I know. You're going to live to ninety-nine."

"You can't give me to one hundred?"

"No."

"You miserable bastard. Don't misunderstand me. Nothing hurts. But I'm trapped here. Hey, what about my tax clients?"

"You don't have tax clients."

"What do you mean I 'don't have tax clients'?"

"You retired."

"What do you mean I 'retired'?"
"You don't have tax clients. You retired. You're done."
"What are you talking about? I used to do, like, 104 returns."
"A hundred and four?"
"You know what I mean. And who's doing my taxes?"
"I am."
"You have no forms."
"I have forms."
"I'm going to be ninety-four!"
"I know. And you're retired. No more accounting work."
"You're right. What am I knocking my brains out for?"
"Exactly."
"What about my taxes?"
"Again, I'm doing them."
"You're doing them?"
"Yeah, I'm doing them."
"All right, good. That way, if they don't come out good, I can blame you."

* * *

29 July

Yesterday, I veered from the usual Oreo, and its many varieties—mint, double stuffed—and instead brought him the Keebler Chips Deluxe Rainbow Cookies and Keebler Chips Deluxe Original Chocolate Chip.

I call.

"Dad, how are you?"

"I don't know yet. I haven't taken my pulse. How'd I get to be ninety-four?"

"You have a good son."

"Is that it? I should leave you all my assets."

"You have no assets."

"What do you mean I 'have no assets'?"

"You have no assets. The plan is for you to live until you're broke and then drop dead. Hey, how do you like the new cookies I brought over yesterday?"

"Passable. Not bad."

"Passable?"

"Yeah. You know what the problem is: I bite down on them and they're good, but I forget sometimes there's a piece of hard chocolate or candy on top and if I don't remember to chew it, you know, the top, it blocks the airways. But they're not bad. Not the best I've had. But they satisfy me."

* * *

30 July

"I'm bringing you pills," I tell him in a call.

"And get some juice. I'm almost out. Well, I'm not out, but I have about a half left of the double quart."

"So you have . . . never mind. You remembering to take your pills?"

"What pills do I take?"

"The pills you take every morning."

"Oh, those pills. I thought you meant something else."

* * *

31 July

"So where is Normie buried?" he asks in the lobby about his cousin Cynthia's husband.

"Normie? In New York. Long Island. At the family cemetery."

"You know there's a place for you."

"I do know."

"He was blind, you know, Normie."

"I do know that."

"Imagine that. How do you get around? Ach!"

"I don't know."

"What about Vivien, my sister?"
"Same place. Along with Cynthia."
"Cynthia died?"
"Yes."
"When?"
"I don't know when."
"I don't mean when. I mean, you know—"
"—She died years ago."
"She was married to Normie."
"Yes."
"What was her problem?"
"What was her problem?"
"What about Hy, my brother?"
"He died. He's there too."
"And Leo?"
"He died. He's in Florida."
"Why isn't he buried up there?"
"I don't know."
"So I'm the only one left, right?"
"From that generation, pretty much."
"What the hell happened?"

AUGUST

1 August

"I'm glad," he says when he calls, "the home is doing what it's doing in terms of the meals and the masks. They say men over sixty-five are at higher risk, so this is no joke, baby. You know I'm pushing ninety-four."

* * *

3 August

"Barry, I need milk," he tells me. "I need the big one, the double quart, you know, the gallon. I mean, I don't need it right away. I still have about a quart."

"So you're good until Wednesday?"

"Yeah, yeah, I have about a half of the big one left."

* * *

5 August

"Barry, I got a needle stuck in my ass."

"What are you talking about?"

"You know, a needle."

"Needle. I got that part. Why?"

"I give myself an injection every day."

"No, you don't."

"What are you talking about? Of course I do. Every morning I stick myself, well, a few days ago, I got the needle stuck in my ass and I can't get it out. I keep pulling and pulling but I can't see back there and I don't know what the hell is going on."

"There's no needle in your ass."

"Don't misunderstand me. It doesn't bother me, but I can't get it out."

"Dad, you don't have a needle in your ass. You don't use a syringe every day. And if you did, which you don't, you'd be in pain."

"Well, not a syringe, but, you know. Anyway, it's all right, but I can't get it out. I keep pulling and pulling and I can't get it out."

"Again, it's not a needle."

"Then what the hell is it? All right, forget it. It doesn't bother me."

* * *

7 August

Two days later, he calls.

"Barry, you have to take me to an emergency room. I got this needle stuck in my ass and I can feel the thread. I sat on a sewing needle."

"You have no sewing needle in your apartment on which to sit."

"But I can feel the string."

"You didn't sit on a needle with a string."

"Then what did I sit on?"

"I don't know, but tell you what. Leave your apartment, head right, two doors down on the left is the nurse's station. Have her check it out."

"Who?"

"The nurse—she'll know what to do."

"She won't know."

"She'll know. She's a nurse."

"She'll know? She's going to know about this?"

"She'll know."

"She's not going to know."

"She'll know.

"All right, I'm going, I'm going. But she's not going to know."

I call the nurse and tell her my father is probably wandering around the building looking for her office. She says she'll go find him. A few minutes later, she calls.

"Barry, your father does not have a needle or syringe in his rear end. He has a skin tag back there, a big one, and it's bleeding because he kept picking at it. He'll be fine. I put a bandage on it, but he should have it removed."

"Can't you remove it?"

"Afraid not. We don't do that here."

My dad goes back to his apartment. I call him and tell him that if he can wait until Wednesday—I've already called his doctor—the tag will be removed at the office. Otherwise, we have to go to an emergency room, which is crazy. Crazier still (I called), three minor emergency clinics in town don't remove skin tags.

"All right, all right, I'll wait. But how did I get this injury?"

"It's not an injury. It's a skin tag, like a mole, and it's bleeding. But it's not serious."

"Ach, I need this like a hole in the head. Ach, I give up!"

* * *

9 August

My father gets in the car, which is outside the front (not the side or back) entrance of the Hebrew Home.

"Why are we going to the doctor, anyway?"

"To remove the skin tag."

"The what?"

"The mole on your ass."

"Does he know why we're coming?"

"Yeah, I told him."

"Why me? Why me?"

"It's a skin tag. It's nothing."

"All right, don't get so shook up. He's going to know what to do?"

"Yes."

"The doctor, I mean. We're going to the Young Guy?"

"Yeah."

"You know, I can feel the string?"

"There's no string."

"Then what do I feel?"

"Probably the contours of the tag."

"The what?"

"The ridges on the mole."

"How did I get this injury?"

"It's not an injury!"

"You know I'm going to be ninety-four? I need this now?"

At the office, in an examination room, after my father makes his way to the table and undresses—before removing the tag, which was done in about five minutes—the doctor asks him where the mole is specifically, and my father, hand to God, says, "It's on the cheek and not on the asshole, so to speak."

* * *

6 August

"Dad," I say on the phone.

"Wayne?"

"Barry."

"Oh, it's you."

"Yeah, I thought I'd visit my father."

"Oh, really. You have a father who lives here? I'm just kidding, so what's new, sweetheart?"

"I'm coming to see you."

I arrive. Julie meets me at the front (not the side or back) entrance of the Hebrew Home. She takes my temperature.

"Your dad is a mess."

"Yeah, I know. What did he do now?"

"Well, let me ask you. What's with the Purple Heart story? Does he have one?"

"Nobody really knows. It may be his. He may have lifted it from someone else's bed."

"He told me the other day he hasn't had sex in twelve years."

"Twelve years?"

"Twelve years."

"What did you say?"

"I said, 'I can't help you there, Jack.'"

* * *

8 August

I visit at the front (not the side or back) entrance of the Hebrew Home.

"Ba, I have to tell you, the cookies you brought, the last batch, the Oreos . . . delicious. Much better than the others. Don't misunderstand me, the others are good, but these are the best cookies I've ever had. But let me ask: What do you do all day?"

"I write, Dad."

"What?"

"I'm a writer."

"Yeah, I know. But what do you do?"

* * *

11 August

I visit at the Hebrew Home front (not side or back) entrance because my father was out of . . . well, here's the conversation:

"Dad, I brought you sugar. You don't need it, but here it is. Tell me again why you need sugar?"

"No, I don't need it. I use it for the coffee. That's all."

"You don't put it in your coffee."

"Yeah, I know. I use the Sweet'N Low."

"Right. But you wanted this, the loose sugar, you called it."

"Right, because I'm out."

"You don't use it, though."

"It's good to have around. Sometimes I put it on the corn flakes."

"You eat chocolate frosted flakes—are they not sweet enough?"

"No, but you're right, I don't use it. I use the Sweet'N Low, usually, in the coffee. I have the corn flakes every day with the milk. And I have plenty of juice. Ba, I just realized I'm going to be ninety-four."

"'Just realized'?"

"Well, I'm ninety-three, and in two months I'm going to be ninety-four. October 14th, 1926. What the hell happened? I was sixteen two weeks ago."

"Why do I never get tired of this?"

"What?"

"Nothing. Listen, next time I come back, what do you need?"

"You know, just the food. But that's an ongoing thing."

* * *

13 August

Today's installment comes post-front (not side or back) entrance visit to the Hebrew Home. From our dear friend Julie:

"I don't know what I missed, but you missed Jack asking me if he can schedule an appointment to have sex with a woman in that room. I refuse to supervise that. He said it would be good for his health."

* * *

21 August

"What's in the bag?" he asks at the Hebrew Home front (not side or back) entrance.

"Pineapple soda and mint Oreos."

"Oh, good. You know, the Oreos are just for a nosh. And the roll paper you brought the other day . . . perfect. I cut it up into little squares."

"Why do you do that?"

"Well, you know, sometimes I don't need the big sheet, so I just use the smaller sheet. I prefer the smaller sheet, that's all. That's why I like the rolls with the smaller, you know, the . . ."

"Perforations."

"What?"

"Where you can separate the paper."

"I use it in the kitchen but not in the bathroom. This is not for my ass. I have other paper for that. There are lot of old-timers here, you know. A lot of Jews."

* * *

24 August

"Dad," I say in a call, and I hear as I'm saying "Dad" that he has, in fact, turned off the television.

"Hi, Ba, how are you?"

"Fine. You?"

"Good, good. The pills are working very good, by the way."

"I'll tell the doctor."

"No, you lay them out very well."

"That really is the key to modern medicine: how you put the pills in the tray."

He laughs.

I made a joke. He laughed. What a great day.

* * *

25 August

I enter the Hebrew Home front (not side or back) entrance, and my father is already trying to get out the door.

"Whoa, whoa, Dad, where you going?"

"Let's go for coffee."

"We can't go for coffee."

"What do you mean 'we can't go for coffee'?"

"We can't go for coffee. You can't leave the building."

"What do you mean I 'can't leave the building'?"

"They want you to stay inside. It's safer."

"What do you mean they want me 'to stay inside'?"

"This is going to be a long day."

"What?"

"Nothing."

"What's with all these cars?" he asks. "Are they for the workers or the inmates?"

"Residents."

"You know what I mean."

"I do. Your shirt is dirty."

"What do you mean my 'shirt is dirty'?"

"Your shirt. Dirty."

"Where?"

I point it out to him.

"Oh, that. That's a little dirt. Nothing special."

* * *

28 August

I meet my father at the Hebrew Home front entrance, where the indefatigable Julie graciously offers to take the Neapolitan gallon of ice cream.

"Did you buy the every day ice cream or the single day?" he asks me.

"What do you mean?"

"Well, is it the kind of thing where you have, like, a sandwich and that's it, or is it the, you know, scooping kind?" he asks, once again, as he has been known to do, miming the scooping motion.

"No, it's the scoop."

"Oh, good, I like the ice cream once in a while."

He sees Julie inside: "So, you want to get pregnant?"

SEPTEMBER

3 September

I arrive at the Hebrew Home front (not side or back) entrance with my father's chicken and cheese, egg sandwich, and milk, which the incredibly wonderful Julie takes up to his apartment. He arrives in the lobby. As does she.

"Ba, where did I park my car?"

"Park it? You don't have a car."

"That's what I thought."

"So you didn't park it anywhere."

"I know, I know. But I didn't know why I worried about where I parked it."

"Right, because you don't have one."

"I know. So why did I want to know where I parked it?"

"I don't know. Maybe you forgot you don't drive."

"No, I know I don't. I know I don't drive. But why don't I drive?"

"Because you kept getting into accidents."

"I don't remember. *Fakakta* drivers here."

"Here we go."

"So I don't have a car?"

"Again. No."

"I didn't think so. Isn't it funny that I thought I forgot where I parked it?"

"Not hilariously funny, but not bad."

"I don't have a car?"

"Nope."

"I know, I know. I'm actually relieved. Where the hell am I going, anyway? What's in the bag you brought?"

"Chicken, cheese, an egg sandwich, and milk."

"I know, I know. The recurring items."

* * *

6 September

"Barry, I need the world and get me three tubes of toothpaste."

"You have four teeth."

"Don't forget the flakes. And the toothpaste."

"Got it."

"Three tubes."

"Okay. Here we go: Now, listen, you have to meet me by the side entrance, not the entrance where we usually meet because that one is closed. The other one."

"Side entrance? You mean . . . which one?"

"The other one. Where the receptionist is."

"In the back?"

"Yes, in the back. The big table. Near the coffee shop."

"Coffee shop?"

"Yeah, you know. The coffee shop in the front of the building."

"Yeah, yeah. You mean the one on the side?"

"Right. That one."

"The one by the other front. On the side, near the coffee shop, where the girl sits."

"Yes, that one."

"I know, I know. I've been there lots of times."

* * *

8 September

I arrive at the Hebrew Home front (not side or back) entrance with his egg sandwich and bananas in a bag.

"Bananas? Why did you bring me bananas?"

"You said you wanted bananas."

"I said that?"

"You said that."

"I don't remember saying that."

"I didn't make it up."

"No, no, it's good, but they don't look ready to eat. I mean, one does."

"Did that on purpose. Eat that one today and then in the ensuing days, the bananas will be ready for consumption."

"But they're green."

"They won't always be green. I know bananas."

"All right, very good."

"And there's an egg sandwich in there."

"I know, I know. There always is."

"What else do you need?"

"I need dessert items."

"Dessert items?"

"Yeah. What am I supposed to do, Barry?"

"Dad, all you have to do is don't die."

"Don't die?"

"That's it. Don't die."

"You know I'm going to be ninety-four?"

"I heard something about that. Still . . . don't die."

"Why not?"

"There are too many forms to fill out."

"Okay, I won't die. But what if I get shot?"

* * *

9 September

"Ba," he says on the phone. "I need fluids—the milk, the juice, the Half and Half, the sodas, you know . . ."

"The fluids. Got it."

* * *

12 September

"Ba, it's Dad. I just want to call to thank you for all the attention you give me. I want you to know I appreciate it, and I know I'm a pain in the neck."

"Not at all, Dad."

"No, I want to thank you. And as soon as they release me from this place, we're going to dinner and I'm buying."

"You got a deal."

"Remember, I'm buying!"

"Okay. Got it."

"God bless you, sweetheart."

* * *

13 September

I call. "Dad, how are you?"

"Ach, I give up! Why am I still here? Bernie's gone, Leo Meltzer's gone. And I'm still here. Nu?"

"Dad, you have a good life."

"I know, I know. I'm very comfortable. I get the meals here. Just promise me you're not going to move anywhere, like to Cincinnati."

"Promise."

"You sure you don't have plans to move to Cincinnati?"

"No plans. None. I'll tell you if that changes."

* * *

15 September

I enter the Hebrew Home front (not side or back) entrance with two bags: one with cookies and chicken, one with potato salad, a newspaper, and his pills.

"Dad, how are you?"

"What's in the bags?"

"What you needed—"

"—Oh, cookies," he says, looking inside. "Yes, I needed these." And then, spying the potato salad, "I live on this stuff. And a newspaper. Hey, is it hot out or what?"

"Perfect day to sit on your balcony."

"I did that last week."
"You know, you can do it again."
"I know, I know. I do it at night sometimes when I'm bored."
"At night?"
"Well, I did it once. So, what's new, sweetheart?"

* * *

18 September

We meet outside the Hebrew Home front (not side or back) entrance. I slide his egg sandwich across the table. We see a chair.

"Hey, Ba, why is the chair outside?"
"I don't know."
"Look at that. There's a chair outside. Nu?"
"Yeah, it is."
"I wonder why."
"I don't know."
"Usually the chair is inside."
"Maybe it's another chair."
"Yeah?"
"Yeah."
"I guess people are going to use it."
"Well, it's a nice day. People might use it, yeah."
"Isn't that funny?"
"It's a chair."
"Yeah, but usually the chair is inside—and now they moved it out. Ach, I give up!"
"Over a chair?"
"No, you know what I mean."
"I do. Hey, you want to walk around to the other entrance?"
"You mean the back?"
"Yeah."
"Or the side?"

"Both . . . either . . . neither. The one over there, around the building."

"Yeah, I've done this walk, like, twenty times."

"Really?"

"Yeah."

We attempt to. He gets tired. We head back.

"I get tired, Ba."

"I know. It's all right. You're ninety-three!"

"Ninety-four! Where did it all go? I was sixteen two weeks ago."

We sit on the green bench.

"The chair is still here."

"Yeah, it is, Dad."

"Look at that."

* * *

22 September

I call the Veterans Administration and talk to LaShon.

"Hi, calling for Jack Friedman, about his appointment tomorrow to get some blood work done."

"Who am I speaking with?"

"Barry Friedman, his son."

"I thought so, because if not, I thought, 'I have GOT to get some of whatever he's on.' You do not sound ninety-three."

"Thank you for that."

"Well, he's all set. Just need to ask a couple of questions for screening for COVID. Has your dad experienced fever or chills, cough, shortness of breath or difficulty breathing, fatigue, muscle or body aches, headache, recent loss of taste or smell, sore throat, congestion, nausea or vomiting, or diarrhea?"

"Nope. He's just a pain in the ass."

"Don't talk about your dad like that, boy!"

"You're right. I'll just bring him to you then."

"Bring him to me," she says, laughing. "I'll take him."

* * *

23 September

"Where are we going, again?"

"The VA clinic."

"Does this have anything to do with the Veterans Administration?"

"It is the Veterans Administration."

"I know, I know. You know, I'm a veteran."

"I am aware. That's why we're going."

"How do they know I'm a veteran? What . . . will they take my word for it?"

"I sent them the paperwork."

"YOU did? Where did you get it?"

"I have all the paperwork."

"Did you take it from me?"

"Yes."

"I'll need it back."

"You're not getting it back."

"Do they know I have a Purple Heart?"

"Yes. Even though it's probably not yours."

"What do you mean 'not mine'?"

"You probably stole it off the guy in the next hospital bed, remember?"

"What do you mean?"

"The Purple Heart was not actually on YOUR bed. You thought it was your bed. That's the story you told me."

"It's on my discharge papers."

"No, it's not."

"It's not?"

"No."

"Maybe you're right, then. So what is this going to cost me?"

"Nothing. You're a veteran. The taxpayer is picking up the tab. You're a sponge on society, a taker, a mooch. By the way, did you thank me today, as a taxpayer, for being so generous on your behalf?"

"Did you thank me for saving the country?"

"Yes."

"When?"

"A week ago Tuesday."

"I don't remember."

"Stay here. I have to go to the business office."

When I return, I hear him from down the hallway talking to one of the nurses: "Yeah, I was just walking along the street with the sergeant when the bombs started falling and then KA-*BOOM!* I then woke up in the hospital a week later and got the Purple Heart. What's your name, again, love?"

* * *

26 September

We see "the Big Guy" in the lobby.

"This guy giving you trouble?" Jim wants to know.

"When doesn't he?" I say.

"You got a great place here," my father says. "Don't misunderstand me, it's very comfortable. You got the meals. Very nice. But I'm very serious. I sit and watch TV all day. I need sex. You can't provide any girls for sex?"

"Aren't you glad you stopped by, Jim?"

"I'm going to leave you two boys alone now," Jim says, smiling.

OCTOBER

1 October

At the Ernest Childers Tulsa VA Clinic, after my father asks, "Free? This is all free? Why? Because I'm a GI?" we get the following:

"So, Mr. Friedman," the doctor says, "I have to ask you this: When you were in the service, did anyone in the military make any unwanted sexual advances to you?"

"What?" my father asks.

"Let me ask you again," the doctor says.

"Oh," I think, "don't do that."

"When you were in the military, were you forced to have any sexual contact against your will?"

"Sex?"

"Yes, did anyone—"

"—sex?"

"Were you forced—"

"—What do you mean?"

"When you were in the military—"

"—In the Philippines."

"What I want to know—"

"—I have a Purple Heart."

"Let me help here," I say. "No, he didn't."

On the way back to the Hebrew Home, we drive by Furniture Outlet.

"Furniture Outlet? What the hell is that?"

"A place where they sell clearance stuff. At least that's the promise."

"Outlet?"

"Yeah, outlet."

"What about a Furniture Inlet?"

* * *

5 October

The call is made. "Ba, I have no physical ailments."

* * *

6 October

We meet outside at the front (not side or back) Hebrew Home entrance.

"I hate these masks, you know. You can see people, but you can't kiss."

"Someone you want to kiss?"

"I'm just saying."

* * *

9 October

Today as we walk around the Hebrew Home, we stop and admire the landscaping.

"Say, Ba, what's with the rocks?"

"What's with them?"

"I mean, the rocks."

"I know. I don't know what to tell you."

"Whose rocks are they?"

"The Hebrew Home owns them, I would imagine, unless you can rent rocks."

"Where did they get them?"

"I don't know. From a man who sells rocks, probably."

"Yeah?"

"I don't know."

"How much were they?"

"Why would I know something like that?"

"My question's academic."

"Of course it is."

* * *

11 October

The call is made.

"Dad, how are you?"

"I got problems."

"What's the matter?"

"The men were here and then they left."

"What men?"

"The men with the horses."

"The hell are you talking about?"

"The men! The men were here!"

"There are no men with horses at the Hebrew Home."

"No, they said they were going to come back and now they're not coming back."

"You watching TV?"

"Yeah. The men . . . they said—ach, you don't understand. They were coming back and now they're not, and Randolph Scott—"

"—Randolph Scott?"

"Yeah. He's now getting involved. It's a mess."

"You want me to call you back so you can get this all straightened out?"

"Yeah, call me back."

* * *

13 October

Today, I meet my father outside the Hebrew Home front (not side or back) entrance.

"Dad, how are you? Do you know what tomorrow is?"

"I'm going to be ninety-four, I know."

"How do you feel?"

"Hey, how did my furniture get here?"

"We moved it."

"I moved it?"

"Guys in trucks moved it."

"What if I want to move again?"

"You're not moving again."

"What do you mean I'm 'not moving again'?"

"You're here until you die?"

"What do you mean I'm 'here until I die'?"

"Dad, this is the last move. The next one you're not going to know about."

"I'm going to die here?"

"Yeah."

"What do you mean 'I'm going to die here'?"

"Yes, you're going to die here. Not for many years, I hope, but this is it. And it's good, because this is the best place for you."

"I know, I know. They got the meals, they're very nice, but what if I want to get an apartment in New York City?"

"Do you want to get an apartment in New York City?"

"No."

"So why do you ask?"

"I don't know. I'm from there, you know."

"I'm aware."

"Ach, I give up!"

"Dad, tell me, do you need anything? Listen, about your birthday—does the name John McCain ring a bell?"

"Yeah . . . yeah. John . . . who?"

"McCain. He was a senator."

"Yeah, yeah."

"Well, his mother just died. She was 108."

"A hundred and eight—wow-wee-wow! That's fourteen years more than me."

"Right. That should be your goal."

"Fourteen years. But what if I live twenty more by accident?"

* * *

14 October

On this, his birthday, I remember two pieces of advice from my father.

The first:

Never fill up on bread at a restaurant.

The second:

When I was nineteen—my father was fifty—we were driving around Long Island City, New York, one summer night, looking for doughnuts. I was home from college, a truly unimpressive year at the University of Miami, and I was dating a girl named Jill from Coral Gables, who, even more inexplicably, had agreed to move up to New York with me after school ended.

"You know, Ba," my father said, "enjoy yourself with this girl, but don't think you're the only one."

"What do you mean, Dad, 'the only one'?"

"When I was your age . . . don't worry."

"'Don't worry'?"

"I did plenty."

"'Plenty'? Not following. All right. Good."

"I ran. I did."

"I'm happy for you."

"No, no, don't misunderstand me, there was plenty of tumulting. I did plenty of tumulting."

"'Tumul—' . . . I don't know if that's the word you're thinking of. 'Tumulting,' really?"

"You know, running around, the girls, the sex, the whatnot. I did. I ran plenty. Don't worry."

"All right. I'm not worried. Tumulting it is, but I still don't know what you're trying to say."

"Just that you also have to do something with your life, you know. You can't spend it in bed. That's all."

And then we found chocolate and Boston Cream doughnuts and drove home.

* * *

17 October

I call around noon.

"Barry," he says, "I need Cynthia's number. She sent me a birthday gift, a First Cavalry shirt. You know, I was in the First Cavalry, in the war, and I want to thank her. Yeah, the First Cavalry. No joke. We didn't have horses, but that was the name. I need to call Cynthia."

"Susan."

"What did I say?"

"Never mind."

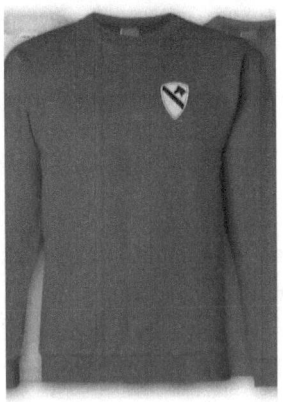

* * *

20 October

Today, at the Hebrew Home front (not side or back) entrance, my father and I meet and talk age, sides, and masks. And a special guest stops by.

"You know I hate these masks."

"Hey, how do you like the new potato salad I got you? That's from Trader Joe's."

"I don't."

"You don't?"

"No, it's too dry. I like the other kind. It's moister."

"'Moister'?"

"Yeah, you know, moist. I like it a little wet. The other kind, not this kind."

"Okay."

"I mean, it's not bad. It's dry, not as moist."

"Got it."

Just then, Mayra, the buffet manager, comes by. My father waves her over.

"Come, sit in my lap," he says.

"Not in front of your son," she says, joining him.

"Ach, him! Don't worry about him. So how are you, love?"

"Good, Jack, good. I'll see you tonight at dinner."
"Give me a kiss."
"Did you tell your son you wanted a private dance for your birthday?"
"A what?" he asks.
"A dance."
"I wanted a dance? When did I want a dance?"
"You wanted a dance."
"I wanted a dance? What kind of dance?"
"You know what kind of dance. Bye, Jack."

* * *

21 October

I call. "Dad, how are you?"
"I'm ninety-four. How the hell did I get to be this old?"
"Here we go."
"No—ninety-four! Ninety-four?"
"Yep."
"Who the hell gets to be ninety-four?"
"I'm bringing you soda."
"Soda?"
"Soda."
"Soda?"
"Yes, soda."
"Soda. You mean . . . "
"Soda. Pineapple soda. You said you needed soda."
"I don't need soda. Soda? I said I needed soda?"

"Soda! Yesterday, you told me you needed soda."

"I don't need soda."

"You don't need soda? You sure?"

"Oh, soda. You mean in the refrigerator? I thought you meant generally. Yes, yes, I'm down to my last bottle."

* * *

22 October

I arrive at the Hebrew Home front (not side or back) entrance. Outside.

"I spoke to Wayne," says my father.

"Me, too," I say.

"He calls every day. EVERY DAY. He's busy. Works and works and works."

"Amazing, huh?"

"And I talked to Cynthia last night."

"Susan."

"She sent me a beautiful shirt. First Cavalry."

"I know."

"How did she know to get me that? I was in the First Cavalry."

"I know."

"But how did she know?"

"You probably told her."

"I told her?"

"You told her."

"She's making big bucks. And the kids. They're all making money. Big bucks, all of them. They all work. There's, like, seven cars in the driveway." [There are four.]

"Wonderful, isn't it? Oh, here's your pineapple soda and potato salad."

"Good, good, because I need. Well, I didn't need. You know. It's good to have around. I eat the dinners downstairs. So, you doing anything? You working?"

"Nah."

* * *

24 October

"The love of fuck? What are you wearing?" I ask.

"What?"

He found a toupee.

"'What?' You know what. Where did you find it?"

"I was looking for something else."

"What were you looking for?"

"I don't remember."

"Oh . . . and?"

"I put it on. I just wear it around the apartment."

"You're wearing it now. You're not in the apartment."

"I know, I know. I just wear it in public."

"That makes no sense."

"What do you mean?"

"You know what I mean."

He sees a mezuzah on the wall.

"Is that a nose?" he asks, pointing at it.

"A what?"

"A nose. Is that a nose?"

"It's not a nose. Don't change the subject."

"Are you sure it's not a nose?"

"Dad, the toupee. You have to take it off. It looks terrible. Everyone here knows you're bald." This toupee (and, again, he had many) was reddish-brown, curled in the front with the consistency of a small doormat.

"You sure it's not a nose?"

"You cannot walk around with that on your head."

"I wear it around the house, so for people who come to the door, they don't know."

"Are you kidding me?"

"What? I just put it on. That's all."

"Dad, you gotta trust me on this. You look awful. Julie," I say, "please tell him. Back me up on this."

Julie gives it the "thumbs down." "Jack," she adds, "take it off."

"She's just jealous," he says to me.

"Why would she be jealous?"

"She doesn't have hair like this."

"Nobody has hair like this. That's the point."

"Ach, what do you know? I wear it because it makes me look twenty years younger. I look sixty-two."

* * *

25 October

Jack Friedman, with his own hair, and Florence Ulrich, October 25th, 1953—sixty-seven years ago today. Their honeymoon suite at the New Yorker Hotel was $11.50, because he sprung for the breakfast package too.

On his wife: "What did she ever see in me? She was a beautiful woman, your mother."

* * *

26 October

I call. "Dad, how are you?"

"The girl brought up the food."

"What girl?"

"The girl comes up and gives me money for food."

"She doesn't give you money."

"What are you talking about? She gives me money and then she goes shopping and brings up the food."

"No, no, I do the shopping, and Julie, that's the girl, is not bringing you money."

"She gave me fifteen dollars."

"No, she didn't."

"I have it here."

"Maybe it's your own fifteen dollars."

"I have fifteen dollars?"

"Yes. Dad, look, I buy the food, leave it at the front desk, and Julie is sometimes nice enough to bring it upstairs for you. But I bring it into the building."

"You do the shopping?"

"Yes."

"When do you do the shopping?"

"Whenever you need."

"No, I don't need anything. I got the juice, the milk. You get snow here? Is this a Southern state?"

We hang up. He calls back a few minutes later.

"Barry, I'm sorry. I got confused. I thought the girl brought up the food. She did it once—just once. I know you usually do the shopping."

"That's all right."

"It's just I thought she did it, and you actually did it, so I'm sorry."

"Don't be sorry. Not a big deal. She brings up the food, so I can see you'd think she bought the food."

"No, it's not that. It's just I thought she brought the food and you mostly bring me the food. And then the guy—"

"What guy?"

"The guy who brings the food."

"There's a guy who brings the food?"

"Once there was a guy."

"What guy?"

"Some guy. Anyway, I thought she brought the food, but actually you brought the food. Well, she brought the food but you bought the food, so I'm sorry."

"Don't have to apologize."

"Okay, but call me if you're going shopping. What the hell? Maybe I'll need something."

* * *

31 October

I arrive at the lobby.

"Oh, listen," I say to him, "remember yesterday, Halloween?"

"What's that?"

"Halloween."

"Halloween? Yeah, Halloween. What's your point?"

"Remember? Mayra—"

"—Who?"

"Mayra. You know . . . Mayra."

"Mayra? Mayra. Oh, yeah, yeah. Mayra. What about her? I don't remember."

"She helped you with the tie."

"Yeah? I don't remember."

I show him a picture of the two of them.

"That's a great shot," he says, admiring it. "You know, I'm ninety-four."

"I didn't know."

"Yeah. You think I'll make one hundred?"

"Ninety-nine."

'Look how he won't give me till one hundred," he says to nobody in particular.

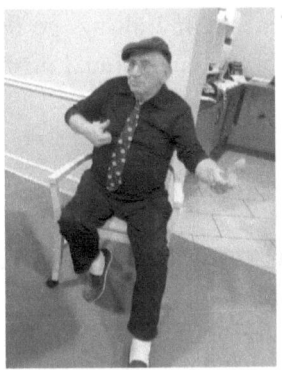

NOVEMBER

1 November

I call. "Dad, how are you?"

"Feeling good."

"Got enough potato salad?"

"Oh, yeah, I live on the stuff. Who can eat all that stuff, though? Hey, am I gaining weight?"

"You're pushing one hundred. Enjoy yourself."

"What if I find myself in a strange bed?"

"Let's take that chance."

* * *

3 November

We meet outside the Hebrew Home front (not side or back) entrance and decide to walk to the Hebrew Home side/back/other front (not front over there) entrance.

"You know, Ba, I just realized that I'm in my nineties. I see a lot of people in their seventies and eighties drop dead."

"Lovely thought. How are the dinners?"

"I go down every day. In the mornings, I have the cereal and juice and coffee, and at night I always go down to the dinners. I don't usually have a formal lunch, but I nosh all day."

* * *

7 November

"Dad, guess what?" I ask in the lobby of the Hebrew Home. "We have a new president."

"Yeah? He beat, uh—"

"Yes, he did."

"What did Truman say?"

"You mean Trump, but I imagine Truman would be pretty happy."

"So he won? Very good."

"And you know I met him?"

"Who?"

"Biden."

"You met Biden? Why did he want to meet you?"

"I'm not sure he wanted to meet me, but he was in town for a fundraiser a number of years ago, and I wrote a story about him and me and, as it turns out, dead sons," I say. I show him the picture of me and Biden.

"Look at this!" he says. "Very nice."

"Yeah, I know the president of the United States."

"So you know him and I know you?"

"Jack, you're one degree of separation away from the president," Julie says from nearby.

"Yeah," says my father. "Will that get me more women?"

* * *

14 November

I arrive at the Hebrew Home front (not side or back) entrance with a power-of-attorney form for my father to sign.

"What is this, again?" he asks.

"It's so I can speak to doctors, credit card company reps, and anyone who needs to talk to you. I can say I'm acting on your behalf."

"My behalf?"

"Your behalf."

"About what?"

"Whatever comes up. This way I don't have to appear to be you on the phone. It's not easy sounding ninety-four."

"You know, I'm ninety-four."

"That's why I used that number, yes. So, anyway, that's what the form is about."

"I trust you."

"That's nice to hear, and as soon as you sign that, I'll control your entire life."

"Yeah?"

"Yeah."

"So I talk to you about getting women?"

"That's exactly right. Oh, listen, we're going to the VA on Tuesday to get your hearing checked."

"My hearing's fine."

"I know. Let's go anyway."

"What is this going to cost me?"

"Nothing. You're a veteran."

"Yeah. You mean a GI?"

"Yes."

"That's right. Does the VA know that?"

"They're aware."

"You told them?"

"I told them."

"I saved the country, you know. I have a Purple Heart."

"I know. You saved the whole goddamn thing. And a grateful nation wants to buy you hearing aids. But promise me you'll wear them."

"What are they going to cost?"

"Nothing. Seriously, they will be free—so, will you wear them?"

"Sure. If they're free."

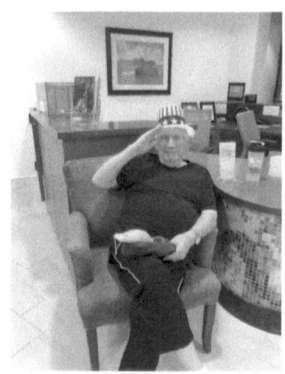

* * *

17 November

As we are leaving the VA clinic, I tell him his hearing aids have been ordered.

"You know, I understand everything you say, but it's true. I don't hear you."

"You understand but you don't hear? That's either brilliant or flat-out daffy."

"I hear! I hear you fine."

"You just said you don't."

"The words, I mean. I don't hear the words. Well, I don't hear all of them."

"Then you don't hear. That's the point."

"Maybe you're right."

"Here's the good news. The guy said you process information well, especially for a guy your age. You just don't hear well. These hearing aids will help with that."

"He knows I'm a veteran? And these plugs won't cost me anything?"

"Nothing."

"So why," he asks, "doesn't the VA also make it so veterans don't have to pay tolls?"

* * *

21 November

I call. "Dad, how are you?"

"Hold it, hold it. Let me turn down this stupid television."

He does.

"What's new, sweetheart?"

"Well—"

"—Do I get Social Security?"

"You do."

"Until I die?"

"Until you die."

"Okay, just wanted to be sure. How much do I get?"

I tell him.

"Some people get more, though, right?"

"Yes."

"I know, I know. Does it depend on how much you pay in?"

"Exactly."

"I know, I know. All right, so tell me when we're headed west."

"We're not headed west."

* * *

23 November

I call. "Dad, how are you?"

"Susan was just here—"

"No, she wasn't."

"I don't mean Susan, I mean my sister, Vivian."

"Nope, she died a long time ago."

"Well, I was talking to someone. I was telling Florence—"

"—Not Mom, either. She died more than twenty years ago."

"Wait a minute. I was talking to my mother."

"Not your mother. She died forty years ago. Maybe you were watching TV and got confused."

"TV?"

"Yeah, TV."

"I got it on. What's your point?"

"Nothing."

* * *

25 November

Susan calls.

"Your father!"

"This should be good. What happened?"

"All right, so I sent him some handkerchiefs, because he always says he needs them. He's always reaching for them."

"Was this before or after the First Cavalry shirt?"

"Hold on, let me finish."

"Okay."

"So I don't hear anything," she says, "which is fine. But I called the other day to ask if he got the handkerchiefs. And he says, 'Handkerchiefs?' and I say, 'Yeah, the handkerchiefs.' and he says, 'Handkerchiefs? Oh, yeah, yeah, some woman sent them to me. It was very nice.'"

"That's hilarious."

"Again with the 'some woman.' I said, 'Dad, I sent them. And I sent the shirt. And the eyeglass holder,' which he told me was great for holding pencils. 'I sent them! Susan.' He then asked me if I knew Susan."

"What did you tell him?"

"I said I was Susan."

"I'm not laughing. Okay, I'm laughing."

"I mean, are you freaking kidding me? Who is this woman? And you'd think he'd wonder who it is who's sending him things."

"Well, he has a lot of admirers, you know."

"I know he's ninety-four, but, c'mon already. I give up."

Like father, like daughter.

* * *

28 November

"Oh, good, you brought the quart size," he says, in front of the half gallon of Half and Half. "So often you get the other size. How did you know to get this size and not the bigger one?"

"I'm good like that."

"No, this is a good size. Because I have the coffee every day. And sometimes you get the wrong size. Who knew it came in this size? But I need cream."

"That is the cream. Half milk, half cream. Hence Half and Half."

"No, not this cream."

"What kind of cream?"

"For my back."

"Cream for your back?"

"Yeah, it itches, so I need cream. You know what I mean? Cream . . . the cream."

"Cream, yeah. Lotion."

"No, I mean the cream. Because my back itches, so I put the cream on and it feels better."

"Okay, I'll get you cream."

"You know what I'm saying?"

"Yeah, cream."

"For the back, you know, because it itches. The cream." He rubs his fingers together to show me where the cream would ooze between them.

"I got it. Cream."

"Yeah, because it feels good on the back. I itch it and then I rub it. That's why I need the cream. I think the cookies are doing it."

"The cookies are not doing it."

"No?"

"No."

"I eat the cookies and then . . . anyway, I need cream for the back that I can rub on it."

DECEMBER

1 December

If this keeps up, Nabisco is going to get a letter.

We meet at the Hebrew Home front (not side, back, or other front) entrance, and talk immediately turns to the evil of snacks.

"Barry, I don't know what the hell's going on with my back."

"Still itching?"

"Yeah, it's those goddamn cookies."

"It's not the cookies."

"What do you mean 'it's not the cookies'?"

"It's not the cookies. Why would you think the cookies have anything to do with the dry skin on your back, anyway?"

"What the hell else could it be?"

"About a million and a half other things. It's cold, your skin gets dry, your clothes rub against your skin—that's probably why."

"Yeah?"

"Yeah. I'll get you some lotion, all right?"

"Lotion?"

"Cream."

"Yeah, yeah, cream for the back. You know, the cream."

"Lotion?"

"Yeah, cream, like I said."

* * *

2 December

At the Hebrew Home front (not side, back, or other front) entrance, I slide his watch, now fixed, across the table.

"There you go."

"Oh, good, the watch. What was it?"

"The battery."

"Was it the battery?"

"It was the battery."

"I thought it was the battery."

"It was the battery."

"Oh, good, just the battery. Thank you so much, Barry. How much did you spend?"

"Fifteen dollars."

"Fifteen?"

"Fifteen."

"For the battery?"

"For the battery."

"Not bad. I had this watch, like, a million years."

* * *

3 December

Mayra asks me about this joke my father tells:

"Jack and Jill went up the hill, both with $1.25, and then Jill came down with $2.50."

Mayra, clearly troubled, wants to know: "Okay, so I need to know if you know the answer to this: Whatever happened to the water?"

* * *

4 December

We meet at the Hebrew Home front (not side, back, or other front) entrance. I slide a Ziploc bag, containing six hardboiled eggs, over to him.

"What's this?" he asks.

"Hard-boiled eggs."

"Why?"

"You told me you like hard-boiled eggs the other day, so I made you some."

"Yes, yes, I eat them every day."

"No, you don't. You don't have eggs in the house. That's why I made them for you."

"That's what I meant."

"I'll bring you some every week if you want."

"Yes, yes. I love them. I always have them."

"When do you have eggs if you don't have eggs? You don't have eggs."

"When? I have eggs."

"You don't have eggs."

"I'm telling you, I have eggs."

"How can you have eggs when you don't have any eggs?"

"That's what I'm saying. I like eggs."

"That's why I brought them to you, so you CAN have them."

"Are they all hard-boiled?" he asks, as he picks up and studies the bag.

"One's not. There's a joker in the deck. Of course they're all hard-boiled."

* * *

5 December

I call. "Dad, how are you?"

"Is this Wayne?"

"No, it's Barry."

"Oh, I thought it was Wayne. He calls a lot."

"I have a question: On your latkes, what's your topping of choice?"

(I participated in a *Washington Post* panel on this, believe it or not.)

"Sour cream," he says without hesitation.

"You're wrong. It's applesauce."

* * *

6 December

I call. "Dad, how are you?"

"Listen, I need a new whatchamacallit."

"Hard to know. Uh, how about a hint?"

"It's the record player, you know. It—"

"—record player. You don't have a record player."

"Not the record player! You know what I mean."

"I don't know. Uh, electric razor?"

"No, not that. Wait, yeah, yeah, I need a new one. I don't know. This stupid one I have broke."

"How did it break?"

"I don't know. I was shaving with it and I lost some of the pieces. Now it's cutting me all over. You can't fix it. I already tried."

* * *

8 December

On the way to my father's ophthalmology appointment, here in Tulsa, Oklahoma, we pass Ascension St. John Medical Center. My father looks up, sees the sign, and says, "Ascension St. John? This is not a Jewish town, is it?"

At the VA, this:

"Mr. Friedman," says the ophthalmologist, "your eyes are in excellent shape, especially at ninety-four."

"I wonder," my father replies, "if that's why they asked me to be a spy when I was in the Army."

* * *

9 December

I decided to pick out my father's eyeglass frames today at the VA. I didn't imagine he'd care. But I called to tell him.

"Do you trust me?" I ask.

"Do I trust you?"

"Yeah, do you trust me?"

"Well, let me think," he says. "If I had a hernia and needed someone to hold it up, then, yes, I would trust you with that."

* * *

12 December

We meet at the side, back, front, but not the usual front entrance, near Doug's, the cafe, which is near the side, back, front, but not the usual front entrance.

"I love these sandwiches so," my father says, eating it the moment I hand him his egg sandwich from Owl Head.

"Good."

"No, I really love them."

"Good."

"Very good."

"Good. So, do you need anything?"

"A hundred thousand dollars."

"What are you going to do with a hundred grand?"

"All right, I'll take fifty. What? I'm not entitled to it?"

"Not saying you're not entitled to it—"

"—You know, I love these sandwiches," he says, taking another bite. "Ach, Barry, what am I doing? Everything hurts. The legs, the legs!"

"Sorry."

"It's a good sandwich, you know."

* * *

13 December

Carol at the Hebrew Home calls to tell me that my father received a package from someone in California. It's from Wayne. A Hanukkah gift. I have not gotten my father a Hanukkah gift.

"Don't give it to him, Carol," I say. "I will not have my brother looking better than I do in his eyes."

* * *

15 December

I arrive at the Hebrew Home front (not side, back, or other front) entrance, as my father slowly makes his way to the long table in the lobby where we meet.

"Ach, Barry, I'm getting old. You know I'm ninety-four?"

"Have heard that, yes."

"I can't breathe."

"You can't breathe?"

"Well, I can breathe, I don't mean I can't breathe."

"Good, because when people say 'I can't breathe,' it tends to worry the people to whom something like that is being said."

"No, no, I can breathe. But I'm out of breath."

"That's because you're ninety-four and you just walked."

"What's that got to do with it? I wasn't out of breath when I was ninety."

"You weren't ninety-four when you were ninety."

"Maybe you're right. Ach, I give up!"

PS: I asked my father what Wayne sent him for Hanukkah. He couldn't remember. I win.

* * *

16 December

I call. "Dad, I'm picking you up at noon and we're getting your hearing aids."

"My what?"

"Like clockwork."

"What?"

"Nothing. Hearing aids. Tomorrow at noon."

"We're getting them? Where?"

"The VA."

"Oh, because I was in the infantry."

"Yes."

"How do they know?"

"I told them."

"You told them?"

"Who else was going to tell them?"

"So you just told them?"

"Dad, I have your discharge papers, your Social Security card, so I didn't just say it. They know it's you."

"Yeah?"

"Yeah."

"I'll be a son of a gun."

* * *

18 December

The phone rings. I pick up.

"Barry, I can't hear you."

"I haven't said anything yet."

"Oh, I thought you said something."

"No, you called me."

"I know."

"Turn down the TV."

"It's not on."

"Dad, it's on."

"I just turned it off."

"But it was on."

"No. It's off."

"Fine. What's up?"

"I'm out of cereal."

"I'll bring you some."

"I'm totally out."

"All right, I'll bring you some tomorrow."

"You know what kind to get?"

"Do I know what kind to get? Is the pope Catholic?"

"Is the pope . . . I've been doing that joke for, like, a thousand years."

* * *

19 December

"So what do you have in the bags?" my father asks in the lobby.

"Cereal and your pills."

"Oh, good, because I need the cereal and the pills."

"How about that coincidence?"

"What else?"

"Soda, some milk, and your newspaper."

"I get a newspaper here."

"That is your newspaper."

He gets up to inspect the bags, already in the cart provided by the Hebrew Home.

"You should have got the double quart," he says, picking up the half gallon of milk.

"You still have half of the old double quart in your refrigerator."

"No, you bought me a big one."

"But you still have half of it left."

I see he is clean-shaven. "So," I say, "you like the new razor?"

"Oh, yeah. The last one you got me was the worst thing I have ever owned."

"Worse thing ever? Really? Never owned ANYTHING worse?"

"Well, it cut my face to shreds. I couldn't use it. But this one. Wow. Where'd you get it?"

"Same place as the first one."

"This one . . . terrific. The last one was terrible. I mean, terrible."

"All right!"

I also notice he is wearing his watch. "And the watch is working too?" I ask.

"Yeah, yeah, perfectly," he says. "Your guy put a new battery in it."

* * *

23 December

Jack Friedman upon meeting the receptionist at the VA Audiology Center:

"Hi, Mr. Friedman," says the receptionist, Diana. "How are you? I remember you from the other location."

"Good to see you, love," he says. "Do you do a lot of heavy breathing?"

To the audiology doctor, my father declares, "I am very active in sports. I play a lot of ball and I was wondering if that's when these earplugs usually fall out."

"No, they shouldn't fall out," says the doctor, incredulously, but not flinching at his endeavor in electronic and miniature aural craftsmanship being characterized as "plugs" by my father.

"You play a lot of ball?" I ask, unable to control myself. "When do you play a lot of ball?"

"You know, tennis, basketball."

"The hell are you talking about? You don't play tennis anymore. Remember, the legs? And basketball? Have you ever played basketball?"

"What do you want? I'm pushing ninety-five."

"My point. You're not playing tennis anymore, so you don't have to worry about the plugs falling out."

"Yeah, I guess you're right, but I'm just saying, if I did pick up the game, would they fall out?"

On the way back to the Hebrew Home, I tell my father his hearing aids come with a five-year warranty.

"You mean I can get a new pair when I'm one hundred?"

"Just gotta stay alive."

"That's not so long from now. You know, I'm ninety-four now."

"I know."

"And they won't cost me anything?"

"Not a dime."

"Wow-wee-wow!"

* * *

24 December

As my father's appointment was scheduled for yesterday afternoon at 4:30, he was going to miss dinner, usually brought to his apartment at the Hebrew Home at 5 p.m., if not by, then certainly under the auspices of, our good friend and restaurant manager extraordinaire Mayra Hudson. I wrote Mayra earlier in the day to see what other plans we could put in place, and she, very kindly, said she would either have dinner waiting for him in a takeout bag when we got back to the Hebrew Home or, if I preferred, have dinner brought up to him at 6:30 (upon which I decided). And, oh, by the way, she wanted to let me know: She was on vacation, in Mexico, with her family, but, no problem, she would take care of it, which she did . . . perfectly.

As it turned out, dinner was brought up to my father, who had removed his hearing aids to eat (don't ask, if you're just joining us) at precisely six thirty.

This morning, I called him. "Dad, just so you know, yesterday, Mayra—"

"Who?"

"Mayra. You know, Mayra. From the dining room."

"You mean here?"

"What other dining room . . . yes, there!"

"Oh, yeah, yeah, I know. Yeah, yeah. The girl. What's her name?"

"Mayra."

"Yeah, yeah, I know her."

"Of course you do."

"What?"

"Nothing. Anyway, not only did Mayra make sure that you would have dinner at 6:30, but she was in Mexico, on vacation with her family, and made all the arrangements from there. How about that, huh? Isn't she terrific?"

"Mexico? What was she doing there?"

* * *

25 December

I call. "Dad, how are you?"

"Good, good."

"Got your hearing aids in?"

"No. I had them in yesterday, as a matter of fact."

"Perfect. You know it's Christmas?"

"No mail today."

"Right, because it's Christmas."

"I mean no meals. I'm looking at the calendar. It says 'Christmas Day. No meals.'"

"Ach! We can't have that. You want me to bring you something?"

"I mean, I don't know if that means no meals at all or just no meals."

I call. "Dad—"

"Barry?"

"Yeah. Just wondering if you had lunch."

"No."

"You didn't? You didn't eat?"

"No, I ate. They brought up lunch."

"So you did eat? You got lunch?"

"Yeah, I get lunch every day. They deliver it."

"Actually you get dinner—never mind. So they brought up the meal?"

"Yeah, yeah. I thought when the thing said no meal, it meant no meal, not that they weren't going to not bring up the meal. But they did. I get the meals delivered every day because of the thing . . . the whatchamacallit. I get the soup, the salad, but I don't always eat the soup because it fills me up, but, yeah, they brought the meal up."

"So you ate? That's what I'm checking on."

"Yeah. I had the lunch."

"Good. And the hearing aids—the TV sounds loud. You wearing them?"

"No, no, but I had them in earlier."

"Wear them all the time, Dad, so you can get used to them."

"Yeah, you're probably right, but I wear them when I mix it up with people."

I call. "Dad, it's Barry. Just checking. You got the plugs in?"

"Well, I'm watching TV, so I don't really need them, but I'm wearing them. What the hell? But I don't really need them."

"Of course you don't. The neighborhood can hear your TV—that's why you need to wear them."

"Maybe you're right. No. I got them in. My voice is so sharp. It has such . . . what do I call it?"

"Resonance?"

"No, it has kind of a, I don't know, what do I call it?"

"Resonance?"

"Maybe that's it."

"Good. All right, what else do you need?"

"Nothing. I got cookies, plenty of cookies, and, you know, a lot of nosh-y things."

* * *

26 December

Call One.

[Loud, piercing sound]

"Dad?"

"Hello."

"Dad?"

"Hello."

"Dad, it's Barry. Turn the TV down."

"It's not on."

"Yes, it is."

"Hold on."

"It's still on."

"It's not on."

"Dad."

"Okay, it's off now. There are too many people on the phone."

"Just you and me. Tell you what. Call me back. Maybe it's something with your hearing aids."

"I'm wearing them."

"Good. But call me back."

"I don't have your number."
"Yes, you do. It's on the automatic dialer. It says 'Barry.'"
"I see it. You want me to call you?"
"Yes."
"All right. I'm going to call you after I hang up."
Call Two.
My phone rings.
"Hello," I say.
The phone disconnects.
Call Three.
I call. His phone is busy.
Call Four.
I call. His phone is busy.
Call Five.
He calls.
"Hello," I say.
"Barry . . . "
He hangs up.
Call Six.
I call. His phone is busy.
Call Seven.
I call.
"Dad, don't hang up. Don't move. Don't do anything. Can you hear me?"
"Yeah, yeah. Fine. What was that noise before?"
"I don't know."
"But what was it?"
"I don't know."
"There was some kind of noise. Do you know what it was?"
"No."
"I wonder what it was."
"I don't know. But here's what I want you to do. Take your hearing aids out."
"I'm wearing them."

"Good. Now I want you to take them out and let's see if the noise is coming from them."

"You want me to take them out?"

"Yes."

"Okay, they're out."

"Do you hear any noise?"

"What?"

"Do you hear any noise?"

"What are you saying? I hear some words."

"Dad, there's a volume control on the phone. I think it's up too loud and it's interfering with the hearing aids. Can you hear me?"

"Yes. You mean the plugs?"

"Yes, the plugs."

"I took them out, you know."

"I know. And now you just can't hear."

"What?"

"Nothing. Before putting them back in, there's a volume control on the phone. Turn it down."

"On the phone?"

"On the phone."

"I see it."

"Push the lever."

"I'm pushing a button, but I don't know what the hell I'm pushing."

"I think it's working. There's no screeching."

"What?"

"I think it's working."

"Are you talking?"

"Yes. Now, put the hearing aids back in."

"In?"

"In."

"Okay, I'll put them back in. I had them out."

"I know. Now put them in again."

"They're in."

"Good. I'll call you back."
"Let me put them back in. Goodbye."
"Bye."
"What?"
"I'LL CALL YOU BACK!"
Call Seven.
I call. His phone is busy.
Call Eight.
He calls.
"Barry?"
"Yes. Can you hear me?"
He hangs up.
Call Nine.
I call. "Dad?"
"You know what I did," he says, "I took the plugs out and then I put them back in."
"Good idea. Okay, now that there's no noise, I want you to call me back."
"You want me to call you?"
"Yes."
"Do I have your number?"
"Yeah, you just called me."
Call Ten.
He calls.
"Barry?"
"Yes. Can you hear me?"
"Yes."
"Do you have the plugs in?"
"I hear you fine."
"Good. And the plugs are in?"
"They're in, they're in. I put them in."
"Maybe you had them in wrong before, and that was why there was so much interference."
"Maybe. They didn't feel right before. Now they feel perfect. I need to get used to them."

"Yeah."
"Do we have anything going on today? Any appointments?"
"No."
"All right. Everything is fine. I feel good. Keep in touch."

* * *

30 December

The call came in last night at 7 p.m.

"Fluids!" my father exclaimed. "I need fluids."

"Dad, I'm on the phone. Let me call you right back."

"Okay, but I need fluids. You know, the liquids."

"Dad, I know. I'll call you back, but don't worry."

"All right, call me back, but I need soda, milk, the cream. You know, the fluids."

"I know. Let me call you back, though."

"Okay, call me back. Just wanted you to know."

I head to the Hebrew Home.

"How's the money holding out?" he asks.

"The money's fine. No worries."

"You got?"

"I got."

Julie sent me a text late tonight: "Your dad as you were leaving said, 'That's my son. That's my son!' with an obvious pride in his voice and his big smile. 'Yes,' he said, 'I have children all over the world. I've had sex with so many women.'"

four
2021

AT THE START of this year, I moved my posts from Facebook to Substack. Looking back—and maybe it's because I wanted them to be—they felt more important, more purposeful.

JANUARY

2 January

We meet, as is our preference, in the front/back/other front entrance of the Hebrew Home.

I notice immediately.

"Whose glasses are they?"

"What do you mean?"

"They're not yours. Maybe you picked them up accidentally."

"I wear these to read."

"Not those you don't."

"Then which ones do I have upstairs?"

"The two new pairs we got you."

"Then which ones are these?"

"I don't know."

"Ach, I give up."

"No big deal, Dad. We'll figure it out."

"You know I have no hair."

"I do know."
"What do you want? I'm ninety-four."
"Exactly."
"What's in the bag, again?"
"Coffee."

As I was leaving, Julie told me he said to her, "'Two weeks ago I was a horny sixteen-year-old!' 'Well [she said], now you're a horny ninety-four-year-old. Some things never change.' When I was leaving his room, he thanked me and then realized he had taken off his mask. He said, 'Oh, no! I took my mask off. If we kiss, we could catch the virus.' I assured him I had us covered since I'm wearing two masks. He said, 'Well, first of all, I am old enough to be your father.' I told him, 'You're almost old enough to be my grandfather,' at which time he responded that I was under arrest."

* * *

12 January

If you can't surprise your ninety-four-year-old Jewish father with heavily discounted Christmas cookies, what the hell good are you? My father, I notice, has his hearing aids in backward, a situation carefully remedied by Carol, who tells me because of COVID I am not allowed to touch him.

"Why can't he touch me?" he asks Carol. "Because he's a foreigner, right?"

"Jack, you're impossible," she says, fixing the right hearing aid.

"Okay," he says, "now say something dirty so I can make sure they're working."

She walks away. He sits.

"Dad, how are you?"

"What's this?" he says, looking at the packages in front of him.

"Cereal, cookies, and an egg sandwich."

"Why did you buy such a small box?" he asks, picking up the cereal.

"Here's where 'Thank you' would go, but I bought a small box because you have three full and large boxes upstairs . . . somewhere."

"Where the hell are they?"

"I don't know that. I'm not allowed upstairs, but even though I'm sure you don't need any, I bought you more."

"What kind of cookies are these?" he asks, picking them up.

"They're cookies."

"Cookies? What kind of cookies?"

"What difference does it make? You like cookies, these are cookies."

"Cookies? What kind of cookies?"

"Christmas cookies."

"Christmas cookies?"

"You're killing me. They're fucking cookies."

"They don't look like the normal cookies you buy."

"They're not. I decided to branch out."

"And why did you buy such a small box of cereal?"

"We just went through this. Because—"

"—I know, I know. Barry, I'm bored."

"Yeah, I know you are."

"No, it's not that."

"I'm agreeing with you. What's not that?"

"No, it's nothing physical. It's emotional. You know I'm getting old?"

"I am aware of this, yes."

"Ninety-four? Ninety-four! Ach . . . anyway, what did you bring?"

"Cookies, cereal, and an egg sandwich."

"I'm fine, I'm fine. Again, it's . . . what do I say, not a physical pain, it's emotional, which is okay."

"Why is it okay?"

"Because if it's emotional, the blood starts flowing and that's a good thing."

* * *

16 January

I enter the Hebrew Home front (not side, back, other front, other front by the office, or other front by the cafe) entrance with two boxes of cereal to replace the two other boxes of cereals I brought my father last week that have since mysteriously disappeared.

"What's this?" he asks, holding a new box.

"Cereal."

"Cereal?"

"Cereal."

"What kind?"

"Read the box."

"I am, I am. It doesn't say."

"It doesn't?"

"Oh, wait, here it is," he says, reading the box. "Cheerios? What kind is it?"

"Chocolate Cheerios. It says on the box."

"Where?"

"There."

"Oh, yeah. And you got the flakes too, I see. You know I have this every morning."

"I know. And I also know you're not wearing your hearing aids."

"I just took them out."

"No, you didn't."

"I had them in all day."

"No, you didn't."

"I had them in yesterday."

"Today is today, yesterday is yesterday."

"You noticed that?"

"I'm good like that. Dad, you gotta wear them."

"I wear them, I wear them. But I don't need them. I hear fine. What if I walked out of here?"

"Where you going to go?"

"I have a lot of places I could go, don't worry."

"I'm not worried. Where, though?"

"A thousand places I could go."

"Name one."

"Massachusetts."

* * *

19 January

I call. "Dad, how are you?"

"Who are you?"

"Who am I? Your favorite son in Oklahoma."

"Who's my favorite son in Oklahoma?"

"Nice."

"I know it's you, Barry. What's up, sweetheart?"

"Not much. Listen, I'll see you tomorrow at eleven. Do you need anything?"

"Boy, did I take a fall today."

"What?"

"Yeah, I fell. I went down . . . boom! I don't know what the hell happened."

"Hold on—"

"—I'm fine, I'm fine, I'm fine. But I had a gash on my arm, I hit my head. Wow-wee-wow! But it's softening now."

"Why didn't you call?"

"Ach!"

"Do me a favor. I want you to go to the nurse's station and have her check you out."

"What is she going to do?"

"I don't know. Nurse things. Just let her check you out."

"Yeah?"

"Yeah."

"I'm fine, though."

"Dad, just go. Please. And then ask her to call me."

"All right, I'll go, I'll go. It's nothing, though. Was quite a gash, though. Seven inches."

"A seven-inch gash?"

"Maybe not seven."

* * *

24 January

I call. Worried about his fall. "Dad, how are you?"

"I got problems."

"The fall?"

"What fall?"

I guess he's fine. "Never mind. What's the matter?"

"There's a woman. She had a baby and she's in the desert and they don't know what they're going to feed her."

"You watching TV?"

"Yeah. Hey, Ba, you know I'm in my nineties?"

"I've been told."

"I mean, ninety-four, ninety-five, what am I?"

"Ninety-four."

"Well, I thought maybe ninety-four, because I'm going to be ninety-five. Can't I say I'm ninety-five?"

"If you want."

"Who knew I'd be living like this in my retiring years?"

"Best place for you. I'll let you go and deal with the mother and the baby."

"You're watching it, the movie?"

"No."

"It's a John Wayne movie. It's a jerky picture."

* * *

27 January

I call. "Dad, how are you?"

"Good, good. You know what's good about this place, this concentration camp I'm in?"

"'Concentration camp'?"

"Well, I don't mean concentration. I mean this place."

"Go ahead."

"Well, I'm not outside in the cold, so even though I'm bored, it's very comfortable. I got the food, plenty of food—the juice, the milk, the dinners . . . the TV."

"Yeah. How 'bout that?"

"Barry, I'm going to be ninety-five."

"I know."

"Wow-wee-wow! So what's new, sweetheart?"

I remember that our good friend Mayra Hudson wrote to me this morning to say she would stop by and say hello. "Hey, did Mayra come by?"

"Who?"

"Mayra. You remember Mayra? She said she knocked on your door."

"Oh, yeah, yeah."

"You remember, really?"

"Mayra? Who's Mayra? No, she wasn't here, I don't think, anyway. I'd remember if a woman knocked on my door."

* * *

28 January

I call. "Dad, it's Barry. What's new?"

"Well, I need the juice and the whatchamacallit."

"Milk?"

"No."

"No?"

"No . . . well, yeah. I'm out of the cream, but the milk I could use. You only brought a quart last time and I only have about a half left—well, maybe a little more, I don't know—so bring another quart, but bring a double quart, the big one. And the juice I can always use."

"You want some turkey, too?"

"It's good."

"So you want some, then?"

"Well, I'm out."

"So, yes?"

"Yeah. It's good for a nosh. I don't put it on bread. I roll it up."

"Great idea. All right, juice, milk, and turkey."

"Question: You call in for your messages?"

"In a sense."

"All right, but if I call and you're in a meeting or something, or out, I can leave the message and you'll get it?"

"I will."

"I don't think I'll need anything, though, but just in case."

"I'll alert my service you might call."

* * *

29 January

"Oy, Ba, I'm out of breath," he says in the Hebrew Home lobby, "you know?"

"Sit."

"I'm so out of breath. Why am I out of breath?"

"You're ninety-four."

"You noticed?"

"I noticed."

"Seriously, why am I out of breath?"

"Because you're ninety-four."

"Yeah?"

"Yeah."

"How come I didn't feel like this ten years ago?"

"Because you weren't ninety-four."

"Ach, Barry, what do they want from my life?" He sees the packages. "Oh, good, you brought the stuff. What did you bring?"

"Juice, milk, soda, turkey, cheese, and pineapple soda."

"Good, I needed that. But I'm out of breath, you know?"

"I know. Sit for a minute." I point to a chair.

"Nah, it's not that. It's just that I'm winded."

"So sit!"

"I don't want to sit."

"Okay, don't sit."

"Maybe I'll sit."

"Jack," Julie says from the desk, "you're doing well."

"Yeah," he says. "You ready to have sex?"

* * *

31 January

I call. "Dad, how are you?"

"Ba, I'm trying to decide how old I am."

"You're ninety-four."

"I know, I know, but am I ninety-four or ninety-five?"

"You're ninety-four."

"Wow-wee-wow! So, tell me, what happened to your mother?"

"She died of cancer."

"I know, but how did she get it?"

"Good question. Nobody knows about that."

"And me he didn't take? Nu? I'm still sitting here at ninety-four. You know I kissed her goodbye?"

"I do know that."

"Ach! Stupid cancer. So, what's new, sweetheart?"

"Doing fine, Dad. Oh, I'll see you Tuesday. Today's Sunday."

"That means there's a day in the middle. That would be Monday."

"Who says you're losing your mind?"

"There's a lot of that going around."

"Sure is."

"Listen, Barry, I'm so glad you're around. If you weren't here, I don't know what I'd do. I look at the furniture and I wonder how it got here and then I realize you got it here. I would be so lost without you. Look, I know you have a life and I want you to live it."

"That's very sweet—"

"—No, I'm very serious. If there's anything you need, you let me know. I don't know what the hell I can do, but, anything, you let me know. I'm so appreciative of you being around. I mean, Wayne calls once in a while, Susan does, but without you, I would be alone—well, not alone, there are people—but, you know, there would be nobody here. So anything I can do for you, you let me know. Anything you want me to do, I trust you completely. Just tell me."

"Dad, you want to do something for me?"

"Yeah."

"Stay alive."

"That's it?"

"That's it."

"All right, you got it. Just bring medicine."

FEBRUARY

2 February

I arrive at the Hebrew Home front (not real front/side/back/by the cafe and the girl/by the office) entrance. I watch my father shuffle to the table. He sits.

"Ach, Ba, I'm winded. You know, I'm ninety-four. I'm closer to ninety-five already than I was to ninety-four. Think I'll make one hundred?"

"I do."

"But how the hell did I get this old? Did they skip? Did they do two years at once?"

"Very funny, but no."

"Oh, I love these sandwiches so," he says, picking up the bag from Owl Head Bagels. "Did you make it?"

"No, the guys at Owl Head made it."

"'Owl Head'?"

"The bagel place. You called it 'Owl Head' for a while."

"I did?"

"You did."

"Oh, you mean the little guy? Did he make it?"

"Yeah, Aaron, but he didn't make it today."

"Who did?"

"I don't know who did. A little Latina woman, I think. What difference does it make? There it is." I point to it. "It was made. Listen, speaking of, how's your food holding up?"

"Food? What do you mean?"

"Food. Your food."

"What do you mean my food?"

"Your food."

"I get the dinners. I have a salad, the soup, the main course. It's very nice."

"I know you get the dinners. I mean the food I bring."

"The food you bring?"

"Yeah, the turkey, the cheese—"

"—Oh, I'm totally out."

"Really? I just brought you two packages last week."

"I'm out, no joke."

"Really?"

"What, you mean of the food?"

"Yeah."

"No, no, I got some left."

"You just said you didn't."

"I thought you meant something else."

"What about your pills?"

"What pills?"

"The pills."

"The pills?"

"The pills."

"Fine, fine. You mean the pills?"

* * *

3 February

The phone rings.

"Barry, it's Dad. I've got three empty pill trays. You want me to bring them over?"

"Tell you what. Just bring them down to the side entrance and leave them at the desk. I'll pick them up there today."

"When you say the side entrance, do you mean the back entrance?"

"Sure, why not?"

"I'm just saying because I got the three trays, they're empty. I got one I'm using and one is full, so I have three, but I have more upstairs."

"Just bring down the empty ones."

"The other trays have got pills in them."

"Then don't bring those down."

"That's what I'm saying. Do you want the empty trays, or what?"

"The empty trays. The ones without pills."

"Because two of the trays are not empty."

"Again, then don't bring those down."

"I wasn't going to. How do you know what pills to put in the trays?"

"I'm smart like that. Actually, I just do what the doctor prescribes and fill the trays."

"What doctor prescribes them? You mean the young guy?"

"Yeah, the young guy."

"Do I know him?"

"Yeah. You've seen him about a dozen times."

"What does he say about me?"

"He thinks you're incredibly healthy for a guy your age."

"He knows how old I am?"

"He knows."

"Who told him?"

"They know these things."

* * *

4 February

I call.

"Dad, it's Barry. Listen, I just filed your taxes for the year. For the first time in probably seventy-five years, you have no income. It's all Social Security. You can no longer tell people you're a semiretired accountant. You're now fully retired. You're a bum. A ward of the state. You suck society dry and give nothing back. You're a sponge, a leech. We support you. I support you. Where's our 'Thank you'?"

"Really? I made no income?"

"Nothing."
"All right, send me a copy of my return."
"You don't need a copy."
"What do you mean I 'don't need a copy'?"
"You don't need a copy."
"What if someone wants me to prove I filed my taxes and I don't have a copy?"
"Nobody talks to you. They talk to me."
"What if someone asks?"
"Who's going to ask?"
"I don't know—someone."
"Nobody's going to knock on your door and say, 'Jack, show us your tax return.' And if they do, which they won't—those people don't exist—tell them to call me."
"But what, I don't know, if you move to a foreign land and they can't find you?"
"All right, you have a good point, but I'm still not sending you a copy."
"You miserable . . . send me a goddamn copy, would you?"
"Fine. But only if I move to a foreign land."

* * *

10 February

I call. "Dad, how are you?"
"Do I have a car?"
"No."
"I didn't think so. Why not?"
"You kept getting into accidents."
"I did?"
"You did."
"What kind of accidents?"
"What kind? Accidents. For instance, you ran into someone who had the nerve to be making a left-hand turn."
"I don't remember that."

"Of course you don't. Hey, you really feel like driving anymore, anyway? Honestly?"

"No, you're right. Where the hell am I going?"

* * *

12 February

I call.

"Listen, I don't know if the blizzard is coming but we're supposed to get snow, so I'm going to bring some stuff by today. I'll meet you at the side entrance at noon."

"You mean the back?"

"Yeah."

"Where?"

"In the back, where you just said."

"Not the front?"

"Not the front."

"You mean—"

"—Right. The side, the back, the other entrance."

"Not where we usually meet?"

"Not where we usually meet."

"The other one?"

"Yes, the other one."

* * *

14 February

I call. "Dad, how are you?"

"I'm doing a crossword puzzle. These miserable bastards."

"So it's not going well?"

"Ach, it's all right. Stupid clues. So, what's new, sweetheart?"

"Cold as fuck out there."

"I noticed. The snow. Wow-wee-wow! I opened a window."

"Why did you open a window?"

"I was looking for something."

"What were you looking for?"

"I don't remember. I was looking for something. I think I wanted to see if it was as cold as it looked."

"You had reason to doubt it?"

"No, it's not that. You know what I mean."

"Actually, I do."

* * *

16 February

I call. "Dad, how are you? It's Barry."

"Who?"

"Barry."

"I know, I know."

"It's cold out there. Minus-six."

"You know, Ba, I notice when I take the plug out of the right ear, when I'm on the phone, I hear better, so I take it out. Otherwise I get interference. What is that called?"

"Interference."

* * *

18 February

Susan, the sister, calls with an update.

"Barry, I called Dad, and I have witnesses. He was on speaker. Noah and Emily were listening. And cracking up."

"Go ahead," I say.

She relays the conversation:

"Dad, hi, it's Susan."

"Who?"

"Your daughter in New York."

"Yeah? I have a daughter in New York. She lives in Montauk."

"Dad, I'm your daughter and I don't live in Montauk."

"So, how is Montauk? It's all the way out there."

"I know. It's fine. Montauk is fine. How are you?"

"It's cold. Lots of snow. But it's warm where you are."

"I'm in New York. It's cold here, too."

"You know I hear from Wayne. He calls every day and Barry calls to check on me and brings me food."

"Who are they?"

"They're my sons."

"I'm joking. I know. Hey, did Jesse {her son} call to tell you he's getting married? He told me he did."

"No, he didn't write me."

"No, did he call you?"

"Call me?"

"Yes, did he call you?"

"Jesse?"

"Yeah."

"Jesse? No, he didn't write."

"I know he didn't write you. Why do you keep saying he didn't write you when I'm telling you he called you? He said he called you. Did he call you?"

"Why would Jesse call you to tell you he's getting married?"

"Not me! You!"

"What about me?"

"Did he call you?"

"Who?"

"Jesse."

"I don't think so."

* * *

19 February

I call. "Dad, how are you?"

"I was watching a movie."

"Which movie?"

"I don't know. I went downstairs. They had a movie on. Did you call earlier?"

"Yes."
"Leave a message next time."
"I did."
"Yeah, I see you called."
"Was the movie good?"
"Was a jerky picture. The guy with the . . . and then the girl and he didn't know she was . . . and then something else. Ach! Who can remember? There are a lot of old-timers in this place, you know? I think there are people here over one hundred."
"There's nobody in the residence over one hundred."
"You know I'm ninety-four, Barry?"
"I do."

* * *

23 February

In the Hebrew Home lobby, Chelsea, the activities director, stops by.

"If you want children," my father says to her, before pointing to me, "he can give them to you."

* * *

27 February

Myra, restaurant manager extraordinaire, who has been wonderful to my father, is leaving Hebrew Home for greener pastures in the health-care arena.

She calls me:

"So they had a goodbye dinner for me last night and I told your dad I was leaving. So then he asked me, 'What do you mean?' and I said, 'After today, I'm not going to see you anymore.' He then asked me if they fired me, and I let him know that I was quitting."

"And then?" I wondered, sensing this was about to go off the rails.

"He asked, 'What is your business? What are you going to do? Are you going to be a hooker?'"

"I'm sorry. What did you say when he said that?"

"I just laughed. It's Jack."

* * *

28 February

I call him.

"Ba, how did Florence die?"

"Cancer. Mom died twenty-one years ago."

"Not Mom . . . Florence?"

"Your wife, Florence, is my mom."

"Oh, yeah, I knew that. She was with her mother, right, in Oklahoma?"

"No, she was back with you in Atlantic City. Jersey. You had fifteen years together after the separation before she died."

"So this was after we re-emerged?"

"Yes, after you got back together. Re-emerged? What a great way to describe it."

"What?"

"Nothing."

"Will I break one hundred?"

"Let's hope so."

"Yeah, well, no, it's not that. I'm very cautious these days. I don't want to extend myself because if you get sick at this age, it's not good, baby."

"No, it's not."

"But I feel good. I do. I just feel very age-y."

MARCH

1 March

"Dad, how are you?"

"You got work today?"

"Yeah, as a matter of fact, I do, but I'm coming to see you tomorrow."

"What's the occasion?"

"I need an occasion? A son wants to come see his father. It's a beautiful thing, actually."

"My son?"

"Yeah, your son—your favorite son, let me add, parenthetically. Is that all right?"

"Fine, fine."

"Good. I'll be there at eleven thirty, okay?"

"When?"

"Eleven thirty. Do you need anything?"

"No, I got the juice, the milk, the yogurt."

"Yogurt?"

"Not yogurt. You know, the salad."

"Potato salad?"

"Yeah, yeah, the potato salad. The last one you bought was delicious. The one before was the worst thing I ever ate."

"The worst thing you ever ate, really?"

"It was dry, what can I tell you?"

* * *

2 March

A robust-sounding Jack Friedman answers the phone. "Hello!"

"Dad, how are you?"

"I feel good, I do. I just saw a commercial for something where they said between a certain age and eighty-five, you could get something. 'Eighty-five,' I said. I'm ninety-four! I don't even qualify. How the hell did this happen? What were they advertising?"

"If I had to guess, I'd say insurance, and because you're ninety-four, they think you're going to die soon, so they're not going to sell you any."

"Yeah, well, I'm going to file a protest."

"Great idea. Let me know how that goes."

* * *

9 March

Bobby, the Hebrew Home's chief architect/carpenter/and all-around guy who does all the work that needs to be done (and who's new to our show) calls to tell me my father's bed frame had broken.

"How did it break?" I ask. "Or do I even want to know?"

"Your dad's a plopper, and after a couple of years of plopping on the bed, it just broke."

"How's he doing?"

"He's still a character but he's slipping."

My father and I meet outside the Hebrew Home.

"Dad, you doing all right?"

"Yeah, I don't know. I'm falling apart. I just got so scared last night that they were going to throw me out of here."

"Never going to happen. You will be here for as long as you like."

"What about the—"

"—It's all taken care of."

"You sure?"

"I'm sure."

"Yeah, but then Florence, your mother—"

"Mom's fine," I said, figuring this was not the time to remind him she had died twenty-one years ago.

"She went shopping?"

"Yeah, she went shopping. Come on, let's take a walk."

The man can still walk.

"Look at you—ninety-four! You're walking like an eighty-year-old."

"Ninety-five!"

"Ninety-four. You'll be ninety-five in October."

"I was born in 1926. What's it now?"

"2021."

"That's ninety-five years."

"But you weren't born until October, making you ninety-four."

"Well, I'm going by calendar years."

"Hey, I got a joke for you," I put in.

"Go ahead."

"A man gets hit by a car and he's lying in the street. A woman comes by, takes off her coat, and puts it under his head. She says, 'Don't worry, sir. The ambulance is on its way. Do you need anything? Are you comfortable?' Which is when the man looks up at her and says, 'Eh, I make a living.'"

My father laughs, a big belly laugh, and says, "That's funny. I heard that one a different way, though. So, nu, why is it so windy?"

***

10 March

Today, Dr. John Schumann asked my father to count backward from one hundred in increments of seven.

My father did.

John asked my father to tell him his birth day and year.

My father did.

John asked my father to name his children.

My father did (including naming his daughter, Susan, correctly).

John asked my father to draw a clock and draw hands on it that showed nine thirty.

My father did.

John said, "Hat, pocket, walking stick," and asked my father to repeat the words back to him a few minutes later.

My father didn't have a clue.

John pointed at me and asked if I was his son.

My father said, "Is the pope Catholic?"

John asked my father the name of the president of the United States.

My father said, "Irving Schlomowitz."

* * *

11 March

He calls.

"Barry, I need fluids—you know, the fluids. You know what I need? The fluids. I need the milk for the cereal. You brought a double quart and I'm down to the last quart—or maybe a little more. I need the juice, which I have every morning. I'm down to a little bit, and the Half and Half, which I have, but I use for the coffee. And the soda. I'm on the last bottle."

"That's a lot of information."

"The fluids. I need—"

"I know."

"Yeah, the fluids I use every day. There's the milk, the cream . . . you know, the fluids."

"You gotta stop saying 'fluids.'"

"What?"

"Nothing."

"Yeah, so I need, you know, the fluids: the milk, the juice—"

"I'm begging you, literally begging you, to stop saying 'fluids.'"

"Don't get so shook up. I'm just telling you."

* * *

12 March

I arrive at the Hebrew Home front (not side/back/other front near the cafe or the girls and by the office) entrance. I see Julie.

"I have to tell you a story," she says. "He hasn't hit on me all week."

"That must sting."

"Yeah, it does—no, wait, he did."

"Oh, good. Do tell."

"Well, he told me he was ninety-six, and pushing one hundred, and then asked how old I was."

"And?"

"I told him, 'Fifty.'"

"How did he respond?"

"He told me that some people would think he's too old for me."

* * *

16 March

Susan called today to tell me our father asked her where she lived.

"I told him New York," she said, "and he said he knew a woman from Long Island who lives there."

* * *

17 March

I arrive at the Hebrew Home front (not back/side/other front near the cafe and office where the girl is) entrance to see my dad waiting in the lobby. He enters the foyer, where we usually meet, and I slide an egg sandwich in a bag from Owl Head across the table.

"What's this?" he asks, looking in the bag. "Oh, yes, yes, the egg sandwich—I love it so. Really, a good sandwich. How do they make it?"

"I don't know. It's pretty simple, though."
"So how come they didn't cut it?"

* * *

23 March

I arrive at the Hebrew Home front (not side, or other front near the girls and the cafe, you know, in the back, by the office) entrance and see my father, along with our good friend Chelsea, activities director, approach. I also notice my father has his hearing aids in—a.k.a. "plugs," if you're just joining us—but, alas, they are in backward.

"Chelsea, would you help him with those?" I ask, pointing to the hearing aids.

"What, what?" my father asks. "They're in, they're in. I feel them."

"But they're in wrong," I say.

"What do you mean 'wrong'?"

"Not right. Incorrectly. Backward."

"Backward? They're not in backward."

"They're in backward."

"What do you mean 'backward'?"

"Backward."

"So, Dad, how you feeling?" I ask, handing him an egg sandwich—cut this time.

"Fine, fine. I have no physical ailments, you know. It's all psychological."

* * *

27 March

Good and gracious friend Walter Lipman sent my father an Avian Carrier hat—straight from a master Scottish hat maker.

"Dad, do you by any chance remember Walter Lipman?" I ask.

"Who?"

"You met him a few years ago. He joined us at the casino one night."

"What about him?"

"Well, he sent you a hat."

"Why?"

"He wanted to."

"Why didn't he send money?"

"Nice."

My father tries the hat on.

"You like?" I ask.

"Yeah, very nice. Why did he send a hat? I have hats."

"Because he sent you a hat! What do you want from me? He likes you."

"Yeah?"

"Yeah."

As I leave, I hear my father tell Julie, after she finished hugging him and telling him how good he looked in the hat, "If I get overexcited, it's your fault."

* * *

31 March

I enter the Hebrew Home side/back/other front (not to be confused with the actual front, though, in fact, it may not be the actual front, by the tables, downstairs, you know, by the door) entrance with a gallon of milk, cookies, cereal, moist potato salad, chicken, cheese, and pineapple soda, which is where we pick up the story.

"Dad, how are you?"

"What do you got there?" he says, seeing the cart filled with groceries.

"Fluids, cookies, you know, the usual."

He looks in the bags.

"Oh, good, you brought the double quart. Sometimes you

buy the smaller one, so it's good you got the full size. I was almost out. Well, not almost, but it was getting down because I eat it every day with the cereal"—boxes of which he then spies in the cart. "Oh, good—yes, yes! How did you know I needed this?"

"I figured."

"I forgot to tell you and I thought, 'Ach, I forgot to tell him' and 'What am I going to do because I don't have wheels to go shopping?' because I don't have a car anymore and you brought it anyway. This is exactly what I needed. Thank you."

"You're welcome."

"No, it's perfect. Perfect!"

APRIL

1 April

I call. "Dad, how are you?"

"Barry?"

"We don't have to meet downstairs any longer. We're both vaccinated. I'm coming up to your apartment."

"Did I get the shot?"

"Yeah."

"I don't remember. Yeah?"

"Yeah."

"Did I have any reaction?"

"No."

"You would think I would have had a reaction."

"Not everyone does."

"But if I didn't have a reaction, how do we know it's working?"

* * *

2 April

"How are you?" I ask, walking into his apartment. "I brought you a sandwich."

"Oh, it's you. What are you doing here?" he asks, getting out of his chair.

"Thought I'd come for a visit. You look good."

"Sure. But it's a rented body."

"Perfect."

He sits to eat. He takes two bites.

"It's a good sandwich. Your guy makes a good sandwich. Very good. But it's dry. I need some fluids. Get me something to drink. You didn't bring anything to drink?"

I bring him some orange juice.

"Why'd you fill it?" he asks, looking at how much I have put in the glass. "You don't use the big glass. Use the small one. Ach!"

* * *

7 April

I call. "Dad, how are you?"

"I gotta get out of here. Maybe I should move back to the Bronx."

"The Bronx? You never lived in the Bronx."

"You know what I mean. I'm bored. Where's Susan?"

"Long Island."

"What is she doing there?"

"She lives there."

"I know that. I don't know, Barry. You know I'm ninety-six."

"Ninety-four."

"I was born on October 14th, 1926."

"Right. That makes you ninety-four now, ninety-five in October."

"Oh, yeah, that's right. Ach, I give up! That's why I think I should move."

"Listen, Dad, I'll make you a deal. If I move, I'll take you with me. But if I don't move, you stay in Tulsa. Agreed?"

"All right, if you leave, you'll take me with you?"

"Yes."

"It's not that. It's just here, I don't know, I'm just not around my people."

"What people do you have?"

"You know, the cousins."

* * *

9 April

We arrive at Owl Head for the first time in weeks.

"You know they make good coffee here," he says.

"Yeah, I do."

"What is it? The coffee or the, you know, the . . ."

"It's the coffee."

"I know that."

"Then why did you ask?"

"Just wondering why the coffee is so good, that's all."

"The coffee comes out of a machine and the rest involves opening packs of sugar and plastic containers of Half and Half, pouring them in, and then stirring the contents. It's not that difficult. I have a college degree."

"Here, take some egg," he says, opening his sandwich and bringing it close to my salt bagel.

"I don't want egg."

"C'mon, you didn't get any."

"Right, because I didn't want."

"Oh, I just thought you wanted some."

"Why would you think that?"

"Because I have an egg and you don't."

"I don't."

"Your guy makes a good sandwich here, you know."

"I'll tell him. Listen, Jesse, your grandson, Susan's oldest boy, is getting married."

"Who?"

"Jesse, Susan's son. Remember, she has four children."

"Yeah, yeah, yeah, I know."

"Remember their names?"

"Yes, uh, there's Christopher and Noah and . . ."

"Close enough. And Jesse is getting married."

"What does he do?"

"He's a pastor."

"Where'd that come from?"

"He's a Methodist minister."

"I thought maybe Catholic."

"Then he'd be a priest and wouldn't be getting married."

"So he didn't get bar-mitzvahed?"

"No."

"Then the wedding is illegal."

"How do you figure?"

"Wait, he's a pastor? He's not Jewish."

"No."

"What happened? He woke up one day and decided he wanted to be a pastor?"

"That's probably exactly how it happened."

"Is the girl Jewish?"

"I doubt it."

"What does she do?"

"I don't know."

"Does she know?"

"Know what?"

"Jesse is, whatchamacallit, a pastor?"

"I'm sure it's come up in the conversation. Hey, you want more coffee?" I ask, getting up.

"Don't fill it, don't fill it. Half . . . half! Leave room for the cream."

* * *

10 April

"You gotta be crazy to get on these stupid animals," he says as I enter his apartment.

"What are you watching?"

"I don't know."

"It's rodeo, Dad."

"They ride these things and then they get thrown off. I don't know. What kind of stupid sport is this? Let me ask you something."

"Okay."

"How come every advertisement says 'eighty-five'? I think I lived too long."

"Nah. Don't let those rat bastards make you think that."

"And, you know, I'm winded. I just realized how old I am."

"'Just realized'?"

"Yeah. I'm going to be ninety-six."

"Ninety-five."

"What are you talking about? I was born in July 1926."

"You were born in October of 1926. And why would that matter, anyway? You'd still be ninety-four. What kind of accountant are you?"

"I didn't mean my birthday. I meant when I first got the horse."

"Horse? You didn't get a horse."

"No, I know that. I meant my birthday. How old am I going to be, again?"

"Ninety-five in October."

"But I look at the ads and they say 'eighty-five,' that's all."

"Ach!"

"Wayne is . . . what?"

"Seventy."

"How old are you?"

"Much younger."

* * *

13 April

I call. "Dad, how are you?"

"I'm good, I'm good. So, I was, what, thirty when I physically had you?"

"Technically, physically, you didn't have me. Mom did. But I get your point."

"So I was there when you were born?"

"I don't remember, but I would imagine you were."

"Just because I saw you as a baby doesn't mean I'm the father. Anyway, what's new, sweetheart?"

* * *

15 April

I arrive at my father's apartment at the Hebrew Home. Something seems to be bothering him.

"What's wrong?"

"Nothing. I feel good, no joke. My body's fine, but the mind —I don't remember things. You I remember. I mean, not from the younger years, but now. Are you married?"

"No. Got a girlfriend."

"Were you ever married?"

"Yeah, twice."

"Twice? What happened? They die?"

"No, they didn't die. Got divorced."

"What is it with you and marriages that don't work out?"

"Great question, that. What can I tell you? Things didn't work out."

"But you got a girlfriend now?"

"Yes."

"You going to get married again?"

"You want to come to the wedding?"

"If I'm alive, sure. This girl, does she know me?"

"Yes, she does."

"I mean, does she remember me?"

"She remembers you. Come with me."

We get up and go to the photos on the wall. I point out all the people in the pictures, including the one of Melissa. "That's the girlfriend. Melissa."

"I remember her. Very pretty. And next to her is . . ."

"Nina, my daughter, your granddaughter."

As we head back to the dining room table, he asks, "What do you do, by the way?"

"I'm a writer, a comedian."

"You can support yourself?"

"More or less."

"I just don't know what you do. What do you write?"

"Stuff. I write about you."

"Me? What do you say?"

"I'll let you read it someday. You have many fans, by the way, people all over the country know about you. I made you famous."

"Good you're here, Barry, because I don't remember things. I need you for history."

"All right, history it is. Who were you married to?"

"Ah, Florence. She died."

"Right. And your parents, what were their names?"

"Sam and Riva."

"Right."

"They died, too."

"Yes. And your children?"

"There's you, Susan in Long Island, and . . . and, uh, don't tell me . . . what's-his-name in California."

"I can't tell you how funny that is. Wayne."

"Yes, Wayne, Wayne. I knew that! You know—you make a good sandwich."

* * *

16 April

I arrive at my father's apartment, ostensibly to give him a haircut.

"Is my hair longer in the back or the front?" he asks as he sits down in the kitchen.

"You don't have any hair in the front."

"I had hair. What the hell happened to it?"

"You got old."

"Is it gray or white or what back there?"

"Yes to all three."

"Don't make it too short. Last time you made it too short."

"That was over a year ago and it wasn't too short."

"You know, I have a hairpiece somewhere I could put on."

"Nothing I will hear today will sound as frightening."

"What?"

"Nothing."

We go down to Doug's, the cafe at the Hebrew Home, for dinner.

I slide a chocolate muffin in front of my father and he starts to eat.

"What a great combination with the coffee. You know, Ba, I thank you for devoting time to me."

"You're welcome. But you don't have to thank me. I love you. My pleasure."

"The Big Guy" comes by and sits. "Hi, Jack."

"Who are you?" my father asks.

"That's Jim, Dad. You remember."

"You work here?"

"Yeah, Dad. He runs the place."

"I know, I know. How goes your life?"

"Good, Jack. You?"

"Fine, fine. This is my son"—my father points to me—"or am I the son and is he the father?"

"How about your son, huh, Jack?"

"Who, him? He's probably a Republican."

Jim laughs.

"No, no," my father says, "I'm just joking. He means well."

* * *

18 April

I arrive at the Hebrew Home to bring my father what's known in these parts as "the world," his specifically requested groceries. I enter his apartment. He's found a toupee and put it on.

"For the love of God," I say, "take that off."

"Why?"

"Have you seen yourself in it?"

"I just put it on, that's all. I didn't even know I had it, so I figured, 'What the hell?'"

"Dad, it looks, listen to me closely here, awful. You have to take it off."

"Why?"

"Everyone here knows you're bald. It's going to look strange if you come downstairs with a full head of hair."

"You know I have dinner every night at four thirty?"

"Yes, I'm aware. The point is, everyone will know something is up with you. Again, they know you have no hair."

Surprisingly, he took off the wig and put it on the bed, which is when I made my move. After unpacking the world, I rolled up some turkey, scooped out potato salad, added a bag of Chips Ahoy cookies, poured pineapple soda, and put it all in front of him for lunch. I went into the bedroom, while he finished the crossword puzzle, and placed the offending mane in my pocket—its hairs sticking out only slightly. Then I returned and joined him for lunch.

* * *

20 April

Tonight at the Hebrew Home: "Dad, how are you?"
"You had two marriages, right?"
"Yes."
"Two marriages? Wow-wee-wow! Are you here because I'm here?"
"You're here because I'm here."
"What do you mean?
"I brought you here from Vegas, remember?"
"That's right. You rent an apartment or what?"
"No, I own a house."
"You got an extra bedroom?"
"Yes . . . why?"
"Why don't I move in with you?"
"Not a good idea."
"Why not?"
"You're much more comfortable where you are."
"You're right. Besides, you'd have to supply meals."
"Exactly."
"Question: Do they charge me here for the meals?"
"It's included in the rent."
"What if I don't eat a meal? Do I get a credit?"
"No."
"Why not?"
"Are you planning to miss a meal?"
"That's not my point."
"No, you wouldn't get a credit."
"Why not?"
"How much do you want them to take off from your rent because you didn't have a chicken breast one night?"
"You know there are a lot of old-timers here?"
"I do know."
"Why are you in Oklahoma?"
"Went to college here."
"What did you major in?"

"English and theater."
"And what do you do now? I mean, generally."
"I'm a writer and a comedian."
"Do you rent?"
"I own a home."
"And the bank gave you a mortgage?"

MAY

1 May

"I missed you!" Sherman Ray bellows, smiling, on his walker, as he sees me exit my father's apartment. His arms are outstretched.

"Where you been?" I ask. We shake hands, hug.

"Me? I was sick, but now I'm better."

"Do you still eat downstairs?"

"How can you? The food? Ach! It's terrible. The concentration camp was better."

"I've heard."

"I eat in my room. If you could see my bloodwork—the doctor says I will live to be 110. It's unbelievable. How's the old man?" He points down the hall to my father's apartment.

"Good, good. The memory, eh, not so good, but he's hanging in there."

"He'll never be like you," he says, waving his finger in my face. "Your father, I like him, but he drives me crazy."

"As you do him."

"And you, you, look like you lost weight," he says. You must be, what, a 48-XL?"

"Now, probably a 46-XL."

"Yeah? No."

"I think. Anyway, I came by your shop a few weeks back to get my suit altered."

"I had to give it up. People still asking, though, 'Sherman, when are you coming back?' Where did you go for the suit?"

I tell him.

"No. No good."

"Why no good?"

"Let me tell you something: The Vietnamese are very good with pajamas, but not with suits."

* * *

2 May

I enter my father's apartment at the Hebrew Home with an egg sandwich from Owl Head, as usual.

"Barry, Barry," he says, coming to the door. "Who stole my jacket?"

"What jacket? What are you talking about? Here, sit down. I brought you a sandwich."

"They make a good sandwich, you know?" he says, taking a bite.

"Now what jacket are you talking about?"

"The one with the thing."

"What thing?"

"The thing in the front. You know, the . . . the . . . ach! What the hell do you call it?"

"The design?"

"Not the design. The lines, the . . . the colors . . . the stripe. It's right here." He motions to the area around his chest.

"That would be the design."

"Whatever it is. Someone stole my jacket. I wore the jacket all the time."

"Nobody stole your jacket."

"You don't know."

"This I know."

"That jacket is gone and there are other jackets in the closet," he says.

"Look at all these jackets." I show him.

"Mine?"

"Yours."

"What do you mean 'mine'?"

"Yours."

"Mine?"

"Yes."

"I don't remember buying them."

"I bought you one, Melissa bought you one, Susan bought you one. Others you had. They're all yours."

"This is a good sandwich, you know?" he says, taking another bite. "I had that jacket, like, a thousand years."

"So it was probably time to get rid of it."

"I wore it once. Ach! Here, you want some of this?"

"No. You know, my birthday's tomorrow," I say.

"How old?"

"Sixty-four."

"Yeah? You know I'm ninety-four?"

"Done with me so soon, are we?"

"What?"

"Nothing."

"I spoke to Wayne today."

"It was his birthday last week. And Susan's. All within eight days of each other."

"We did that on purpose, your mother and I."

* * *

5 May

I arrive at the Hebrew Home dining room. He is finishing dinner as I get to the table. We talk some about Susan and her kids. I mention again that Jesse, Susan's oldest son, pastor, is getting married.

"Is the girl a local girl?" he asks.

"I guess some people think so."

"So how much do we send for a gift? I mean, what, twenty-five dollars? Thirty?"

* * *

8 May

I arrive at my father's apartment with "the world" before taking him to Owl Head Bagels for our Saturday breakfast. He pulls out the bottle of Jarritos pineapple soda.

"What kind of soda is this?"

"I believe it comes from Mexico. Thought you might like the flavors."

"What do Mexicans know about soda? What do they put in there?"

"They don't tell us."

"Who doesn't?"

"The Mexicans."

"I know, I know."

At Owl Head, we take a seat outside.

"You know, Ba, I like the seashore," he says, taking a sip of his decaf that I have prepared, as always, with four Sweet'N Lows and five tiny containers of different-flavor Half and Half. "You don't have a seashore here. You got states surrounding you."

"You like the seashore? Since when?"

"Well, you know what I mean. Question: When did my father die?"

"1960."

"No."

"He did."

"And my mother?"

"1983."

"Couldn't have been that long ago."

"It was."

"How about my wife?"

"1999."
"Can't be."
"It is."
"How do you know all this?"
"I'm good like that."
"No, you're wrong. It can't be that long ago."
"What, am I going to lie about stuff like this?"
"You know they have good coffee here?"
"I do."
"Texas is right below Oklahoma, right?"
"Yes."
"It's the largest state."
"Actually, Alaska is bigger."
"But Alaska is colder."
"That it is."
"I wonder what kind of summers they get there. They must get summers."
"They do. I've been there. Alaska gets summers. They're mild, but it gets them."
"You've been there?"
"Yes."
"You know the coffee here is very good."
"I'm glad."
"You know, if I live to be one hundred, Oklahoma won't be a state. It will be its own country."
"You don't know how prescient that statement is."
"No, but the coffee here is very good. Excellent, in fact."

* * *

9 May

My father calls this morning. It is six thirty.
"Barry, Barry!"
"Dad, you okay?"
"Yeah. You're in the paper."

"What?"

"You're in the paper. What? You don't read the paper? Did I wake you? Let me read to you. It says . . . let me see. I had it at the . . . table. Ach, I can't hold the paper and talk on the phone. Something about Barry Friedman is speaking on . . . something. Let me read it to you. You don't get the paper? 'His books include'—what does it say here?—'*Road Comic* and *The Joke Was On*' . . . and, I don't know . . . 'the . . . the memoirs of . . . you know, I can't read. Let me read. I should have stayed at the table. The lighting's bad. Anyway, you're in the paper. It says he will be dealing with his father, Jack Friedman. That's me."

* * *

12 May

"So what happened to Molly Newman?" he asks at dinner. "Got an ice cube?"

"No."

"Coffee's too goddamn hot."

"No."

"C'mon."

"Dad, I'd give you an ice cube if I had one. I don't. Now, who's Molly Newman?"

"Molly Newman! You don't know Molly Newman?"

"No."

"How can you not know who Molly Newman is?"

"Why would I know who Molly Newman is?"

"Molly Newman! Bernie's mom."

"Why would I know Bernie Newman's mom?"

"He was my cousin."

"Your cousin, not my cousin. You were born thirty-one years before me."

"Oh, yeah, that's right. What happened to her? I wonder if she's still alive."

"Who? Molly Newman? I'm sure she's dead."

"How do you know?"

"She would have been over 120, that's how I know."

"How did she die?"

"Probably from being 120."

"Yeah?"

"Yeah. If Bernie, her son, was your age—"

"—He was a few months older. We ran together. What about Max's mother?"

"Max?"

"Max Mendelssohn."

"Of course. What about him?"

"His mom."

"Dad, long dead. Long, long, long dead."

"Yeah? You know, I was closer to Bernie than I was to Max."

"Yeah?"

"Yeah. Max was . . . you know. But then Bernie married a girl. I think she died, too. Ach!"

* * *

15 May

I enter my father's apartment at the Hebrew Home Hotel and notice he is wearing his hearing aids.

"You've got your hearing aids in?" I ask. "I'm impressed."

"Yeah. You know, I discovered that I hear better. You've been telling me that, and I think you're right. I don't wear them all the time, though."

On the drive to Owl Head:

"Ach, Barry, you know, I think I'm getting old."

"You are."

"Everything is fine, but there are certain parts of my body, like this one finger here, it doesn't work. The button right here"—he points to his knuckle. "Why is that?"

"You're ninety-four, that's why."

"It never hurt before."

"You've never been ninety-four before."

"You think that's it?"

"That's definitely it."

"When did Mom die?"

"1999."

"How much is gas in New York?" he asks after he sees the price at a gas pump near the bagel place.

"Don't know."

"Just wondering, that's all."

We arrive. He sees the table that includes the sign they put on it for me.

"'Bagel consultant,'" he says, reading the sign. "'Barry Friedman. Bagel Connoisseur.' That's you. Do they know you?"

"Yes. And 'consultant,' you say? I'm offended. I'm a connoisseur, damn it!"

"What?"

"Nothing."

"Say, Ba, why would anyone want to live in Oklahoma?"

"A great question, that."

* * *

16 May

My father and I are at Owl Head Bagels. I make and then bring him his coffee. He takes a sip.

"Anyway, how did you come to make such a good cup?"
"I went to college."
"Yeah?"
"Yeah. I'm very smart."
"I'm serious."
"Dad, it's decaf with a lot of Sweet'N Low and Half and Half. It's really not complicated."
"But how do you know how I like it?"
"Took a guess. How do I know? I've been doing it for years."
"But you don't drink coffee."
"Right."
"Why not?"
"Let me quote my first ex-wife on this one: 'Most people drink coffee because they have to get up and go somewhere—like work. But you, Barry, never have anywhere to go.'"
"But why don't you drink coffee?"
"Didn't we just cover this? I just don't. I don't like the taste and still don't have anywhere to go."
"Hey, what's that?" he asks, pointing to the "Pay It Forward" wall and all the five-dollar and ten-dollar notes people have left for others.
"That's something the Little Guy, his name is Aaron, and Joe, the other owner, do for people who may be short a little money. This way, people can come in and, if they need, they can take a five-dollar sticker off the wall and help pay for their meal."
"So could we use it?"
"Yeah, we could, but we don't, because we don't need to."
"But we could?"
"Yes, we could. But we're not going to."
"I'm not suggesting—no, it's a nice gesture."
"It is. Joe and Aaron are good people."
"I don't understand, though. Why would they do that?"

* * *

17 May

Facebook friends Opuchand Phillips-Renner and Bob Renner came to Tulsa this weekend. We ate dinner at Mondo's last night, and this morning, my father and I met them for breakfast at Owl Head Bagels.

He told them the "Purple Heart" story.

"I looked down and my arm was covered in blood."

"It wasn't your arm," I interrupted. "There was no blood on your arm. It was your toe. Your toenail was crushed from the piece of a bridge, remember?"

"That's what I meant. Not arm—toe."

Anyway, before my father and I arrived, there was a conversation in the car on the way from the Hebrew Home Hotel.

"So how many times were you married?" he asked.

"Twice."

"Twice? What happened? They both die?"

"Again with this. They didn't both die. Neither died. It just didn't work out."

"Two marriages? Wow-wee-wow! How many times was I married?"

"Once."

"I know, I know. So what happened to Bernie Newman?"

"He died, Dad."

"He died? What happened?"

"You're kidding me. You told me he died."

"I did? How did I find out?"

"I don't know."

"He was four months older than me. Yeah, I guess he got old. But he died? I'll be—"

"He did."

"But he died? I wonder who would know how he died."

"I don't know. Leo might know. Miltie, Bernie, George, Max might, too, but I think they're all dead, too. You're the last one left."

"These are the guys I ran with."

"I know."
"But Bernie Newman died? I wonder when he died?"
"I don't know."
"I should call someone."
"Good idea."
"What about his mother?"
"Dad—"
"Yeah, I guess she probably died, too. Ach, Barry, I give up!"

* * *

23 May

We're in New York for Jesse's wedding.

Today, Chris, the nephew, and Susan, the sister-daughter-woman on Long Island, and I went to New Montefiore Cemetery, along with my father, where, according to its website, there is room for more than 150,000 graves—information you must have, for Jack Friedman will allow no other discussion about any topic until he knows the precise number of bodies that are or can be buried there. Most of our dead relatives are buried at New Montefiore—it is, after all, the family cemetery, including my father's mother and father, brother, sister, cousins (no, I could not find Bernie Newman), Ida Meltzer, and, most important (certainly to me), his wife, my mother, Florence Friedman. I held my father's hand as we walked the plot of land. The upkeep family-circle fee notwithstanding, the place was overcome with dandelions, a development my sister said called for "giving an argument" to Ida Meltzer, who is president of the circle. My father pointed out the relatives, including the Rockaway guys, and, wait for it, Bernie Newman's parents.

At my mother's grave, my father, as custom dictates, placed a rock of remembrance on the stone, and saw where he will be buried: next to his wife, and two spots away from Betty Koralchek, of whom Chris, Susan, nor I have ever heard.

On the way back to the car, Susan noticed that Jerry Parker, one of my father's friends for more than 60 years, he with the foot who moved back to Nova Scotia or Newfoundland and married one of the Pitsys, had died in March of this year. Susan and I were not sure how my father would take the news, as Jerry was "one of the guys" he used to run with.

"Who's this?" my father asked, standing over Jerry's temporary marker.

"Jerry Parker."

My father was quiet for a moment.

"Jerry Parker?"

"Yeah. Sorry."

"How the hell did he get in here? He's not family."

"What?"

"Why is he here?"

"Isn't he your cousin?"

"No! He was a friend. He's not family."

"You sure?"

"He doesn't belong here. This must be another Jerry Parker."

"'Another Jerry Parker'? There are two?"

"Yeah! This must be the other one."

* * *

24 May

Osprey Park, Long Island.

Noah, Jesse, Chris, Emily, my father, and I are at lunch on the island's South Shore in a restaurant with a huge parking lot.

"This is very nice," my father says. "Question: How many cars does this parking lot hold?"

"I don't know," I say.

"But how many do you think?"

"Fifty? I don't know."

"Look how many spots are here, and what is that water out there?'

"It's the water between Long Island and Fire Island," Noah says.

"Yeah? So it's not a river or anything?"

"No," says Noah.

"I thought it was a river or, you know, some other water."

"No. It becomes the Atlantic."

"No."

"Yes."

"Yeah?"

"Yeah."

"I wonder how many boats could park there," my father wonders, pointing to some jagged rocks.

"None," I say.

"Is this where you bring the girl?" my father asks.

"Yes," Noah says, "you bring the girl here to make out."

"Yeah?"

"Yeah."

"It's a big parking lot, you know?" my father adds.

"Hey, Dad, let's go take a walk up the pier."

"I'm freezing, you know."

It's eighty-one degrees.

* * *

26 May

Susan, Chris, Noah, my father, and I went to the Airport Diner in Bohemia—yes, you heard right—last night to meet Dana Friedman, who's my cousin and my father's nephew, as well as Dana's son, Sean, and Sean's girlfriend, Matia, who (important to the story) is part Cuban.

"So," my father asked Matia, "are you married to him"—pointing to Sean—"or just rented?"

"What?" she asked, both horrified and perplexed.

"Where you from, dear?"

"Cuba."

"Cuba? I was in Cuba once. I was arrested."

"Really?"

"No, you weren't," I said.

"Well, I wasn't arrested, but the police asked what was in the package."

"What the hell are you talking about?" Susan asked.

"Bernie died, right?" I asked.

"Bernie Schechter died?" my father wondered. "When?"

"Wait. Who's Bernie Schechter?" Susan asked.

"A cousin," said my father.

"No. That was Bernie Newman," I replied.

"He was a cousin too," my father countered.

"You had two cousins named Bernie?" Susan asked.

"Yeah, Bernie Schecter and Bernie Newman."

"Wait," Susan said. "Is this the Bernie you played cards with?"

"That was Bernie Metz," he answered.

It hit me at this point: That was actually Bernie Metz, a non-cousin, with whom my father played pinochle.

For the love of the Wayans brothers, there was not one, not two, but THREE Bernies: Newman, Schechter, and Metz.

Ach!

And, and, and . . . two of the Bernies, Newman and Metz, had wives named Lylah.

To recap: All the Bernies are dead, all the Lylahs are dead, as are all the parents of all the Bernies and all the Lylahs. And we still don't know what was in that fucking package in Cuba.

* * *

29 May

Susan and I decide to take our father to 922 57th Street in Borough Park, Brooklyn, his childhood home. Because I thought, how to put this delicately, it would be the last chance my father would get to see where he grew up, if that would even matter to him. Somehow, it mattered to me, for I was hoping there might be one moment, one building, one street corner that would jog some memory in his mind, which is often elsewhere these days.

We drive by the town of Hempstead on the way, and he says, "Hempstead? Hempstead! My first tax client was there. West End Tavern. I think they're out of business now."

That alone is worth the trip.

Muscle memory is a funny thing, for my father remembers that the Belt Parkway is a mess. Has always been "impossible," will always be, he reminds us, especially on Sundays, even though today is Saturday.

"Why did you come this way? This is the long way," he says to Chris. "Hey," he adds, upon seeing the Verrazzano-Narrows Bridge, "is that London Bridge?"

He again brings up Pitsy, whose real name is Selma, Bernie Newman's sister.

"Dad, why did they call her Pitsy?" I ask.

"In Jewish," he replies (he means "in Yiddish"), "it's *pitseleh*, which means 'small.' She was small, that's all."

There was also some talk of Leo Meltzer, who lived in the Bronx, with Lou Meltzer, who lived in Far Rockaway. Max Meltzer, another of my father's uncles, was a good-looking man who married good-looking women, and Molly Meltzer, his aunt, married Harry Newman and together they "made" Bernie, who lived on 10th Street. Molly and Harry are probably dead too, I have concluded.

At 922 57th Street, my father comments about the surrounding homes: "They must have built the new ones later."

At the stoop, he says, "I was born in this house."

"You mean in the hospital when your family lived here?" Susan asks.

"No, I mean in the house."

We drive through the neighborhood, passing an inordinate number of Hasidic Jews, to which my father wonders, "Is this religion coming toward us?"

Then he notices a Mexican food truck: "How did the Spanish get here?"

There was a great moment in the film *Avalon* where the old man is taken through the old neighborhood and he can't remember any of it until he sees one place that reminds him of himself.

He says, "I was afraid I never was."

Jack Friedman was.

* * *

31 May

My father and I got back to Tulsa late last night.

The trip was too long. My father was exhausted, confused.

But we had surprised Jesse, who didn't think we were coming for his wedding; Noah helped his grandfather into the shower; Chris held his grandfather's hand and walked him into a diner; and there were occasions when Alyssa, the bride, called him "Grandpa" with sweetness and ease.

On the day we left, Susan and I decided to pack up all the clothes she had purchased for him through the years—and had kept in New York for trips just like this (she's like that, my sister)—so I could take them back to Tulsa. We both knew our father wouldn't be making another trip to New York.

JUNE

1 June

I decided on this, our second day back from New York, to take my father to Owl Head, figuring the quicker he resumed his normal activities at the Hebrew Home (it comes with meals, you know), the more recentered he'd feel in his life and surroundings.

"So you had two wives, yes?" he asks me as I bring him his coffee.

"Yes."

"And you got divorced twice?"

"Yes."

"What happened? Is it because the women tried to impose their will on you?"

"Yes! That's exactly what happened. Exactly! How did you know?"

"So what do you do for funds? Don't misunderstand me, but do you work during the week?"

"Sometimes."

"Ach, Barry, how did I get so old?"

Later, the egg sandwich and decaf with five Half and Halfs and four Sweet'N Lows finished, Aaron, the little guy, comes by to say hello.

"Hello, Mr. America!" my father says. "You got good coffee here, you know that? Are those your legs or did you rent them?"

* * *

4 June

"Dad, it's Barry."

"Hello, Barry! How goes your life?"

"Good, good. Listen, I got you out of jury duty."

"'Jury duty'?"

"Jury duty."

"What do you mean?"

"Jury duty. You had been summoned to perform your civic duty, to judge your peers on possible legal infractions, but now you don't have to do it."

"Why?"

"Because you're excused if you're over seventy."

"So what did you tell them?"

"That you're not of sound mind."

"Well, thank you very much. Does that mean I have to act crazy when I see them?"

"Yes."

"All right. Thank you again for the call. Have a good day."

* * *

6 June

I call. "Dad, how are you?"

"There's no one here. I'm the only one here. My son went out."

"Dad, I'm your son. I didn't go out. I'm here, you're there."

"Oh, that's right, you're my son. What was I thinking? What's new, sweetheart?"

"Nothing. Just calling to say hello. Hey, you want to go to breakfast tomorrow? I'll pick you up. I'll buy you an egg sandwich."

"You got a deal."

* * *

7 June

"So, Ba, what else is new?" he asks at Owl Head.

"You keep asking me that."

"This is the first time."

"You just asked me that two minutes ago."

"I asked what was new. Now I'm asking what else is new?"

"You're kidding me, right?"

"Okay, so what's old?"

"Nice."

"I'm just joking."

"Really?"

"How the hell did I get this old? Why am I out of breath?"

"Because you're ninety-four."

"I know that. But why?"

"Because you're ninety-four."

Moments pass.

"So what's new?"

"Nothing, Dad."

"Nothing? Is anything old?"

"You're killing me."

On the way back to the Hebrew Home: "You know, I feel better since I stopped smoking."

"You haven't smoked in forty-five years."

"What are you talking about?"

"You haven't smoked in forty-five years, since we lived in New York."

"It's only been a couple of weeks. Forty years—you don't know what you're talking about."

"You haven't been out to buy them, and I'm the only one who would bring you cigarettes, and I haven't. Believe me, you haven't smoked in decades."

"I just quit one day, you know. It was really easy. So what's new?"

"Nothing, Dad."

"Ah, Barry, what am I doing? I'm bored. I mean, when I say I'm bored, I don't mean I'm bored. I just don't have anything to do."

"That's pretty much the definition."

Just then we pass a house that has an entrance—not the only entrance to the structure, mind you—right off Riverside Drive, in Tulsa.

"Why would you put a door there?" he asks.

"Where?"

"There, on the side, right by the main drag. This is a main drag, right?"

"Right."

"So why would you put a door there? I don't understand that one."

"Why does this concern you?"

"I don't know. I might buy the house someday and I don't like the door there. People who would rob you would think, 'It's an easy house to rob.' But maybe they wouldn't because everyone would see them, since this is a main road, and decide not to rob you because they could be identified."

"So that means you would buy the house now?"

"Is the grass always green?"

"What grass?"

"The grass. I notice the grass is green. Is it always green? I mean, all the grass?"

"'All the grass'? Uh, in the spring and summer, yes, I guess it is. And then when it dies, it's not green anymore. Grass is funny like that."

"I was just wondering."

As we get close to Owl Head, we then pass Coney I-Lander®, a place specializing in hot dogs with all sorts of toppings, which, frankly speaking, do not need to be on top of a hot dog, but that's another matter.

"'Coney I-Lander'?" my father asks. "He came all the way down here? From Brooklyn?"

"The guy who owns that store? I doubt it. It's just a name. They make small hot dogs and put chili and stuff on top. I'm not sure you would like it."

"So did Coney Island, the real place, birth the hot dog or did it come from somewhere else?"

"Yes, it birthed the hot dog."

* * *

8 June

The phone rings.

"Barry, you called?"

"Yeah, how you doing?"

"I went to see a movie."

"I know. What did you think?"

"The movie? I don't know. The woman is trying to buy a house, but she can't buy a house, so she takes pictures of the boring parts of her life, and then she does . . . I don't know what she does. Was a nothing picture. So, what's new, sweetheart?"

* * *

10 June

Tonight, we go to Doug's, the cafe inside the Hebrew Home Hotel, for dinner. On the way down there, my father reminds me he needs a few things.

"Barry, I need the milk, the juice, turkey, the whatnot you get, and . . . uh, socks."

"'Socks'? You don't need socks."

"No?"

"I bought you socks last week."

"Oh, that's right. Wait! You bought me socks?"

"I did. You're not wearing them, though."

"No, it's not that, but I just don't have them on."

"So you're not wearing them."

"No, but I . . . you know, socks. I have socks."

"Glad we cleared that up. Hey, let me take your picture."

I take it.

"I still don't know how that thing works," he says. "You take the picture and it gets developed inside the phone?"

"Pretty much."

I show him the photo.

"It's too dark. You can't see my smile."

I take another one. I show him.

"You still can't see my smile."

"Is this important to you?"

"I mean, it's too dark, that's all."

"All right, I have a question for you. Grandma, your mother, Riva, she nearly married a rabbi, right after your father died, is that right?"

"Oh, yeah. Rabbi Shaw. She would have married him, too. Oh, he had a thing for her. When did she die?"

"Thirty-eight years ago."

"No."

"Yes."

"No!"

"What, I'm going to lie to you about this?"

"How long ago was that?"

"Thirty-eight years ago."

"And my father?"

"Sixty years ago."

"Wow-wee-wow! Time is moving faster, or is it just me?"

"It actually is. It's not you. You're an accountant, so you know percentages. When you're four and turn five, it's twenty percent of your life—that's a long time—but when you're ninety and turn ninety-one, it's a little over one percent, so it really does feel like it's moving faster. Hey, tell me, what do you want for your ninety-fifth birthday?"

"Ten thousand dollars."

"Why ten grand?"

"You know, for walking-around money. How do you know so much about the family?"

"How? I'm part of it. Okay, quiz time. Name your three children."

"Wayne, Barry, and Susan. But there was another one."

"No, that's it. No other children."

"What about Barry?"

"I'm Barry."

"Not you. The other Barry."

"There is no other Barry. I'm it."

"You're the Barry?"

"I'm the Barry."

"I didn't know that."

* * *

12 June

"Put some air on," he says on the way to Owl Head, "there's a terrible draft in here."

"You going to start with me? The AC is broken."

"What do you mean 'broken'?"

"Not working. It's broken."

"What do you mean?"

"The condenser, compressor . . . I don't know. Suffice to say, it's broken."

"What did you do to it?"

"I jumped up and down on it. What did I do? It broke. Things break."

"I don't understand."

"What's to understand?"

"It's working and now, all of a sudden, it's not?"

"Yes, that's how the whole breaking-down process works. Things break down as they get older. Look at you."

"Me? You know, I am feeling my age. It just happened when I turned ninety-six."

"You haven't turned ninety-six."

"It just happened last year. The legs."

"Really? Just last year?"

"Ach!"

"Ach!"

"Seriously, what happened to the air conditioner?" he asks. "Because there's a terrible draft in here."

"Again with the joke about the draft. It broke."

"Does it get very hot here?"

"Yes."

"I mean in Oklahoma?"

"Yes, it's hot now."

"Do you need the air conditioner?"

"Yes."

"I guess you mostly need it in the summer months."

We arrive at Owl Head and discover, once again, Joe and

Aaron are out of croissants so, once again, make my father's egg sandwich on King's Hawaiian Bread.

"Dad, is it okay?" I ask as I watch him eat.

"Oh, yeah, very good. The soft bread makes biting easier."

"Words to live by."

"What?"

"Nothing."

"So do you work at all?"

"I'm a writer, Dad."

"I know, but anything steady? What do you do for funds?"

"I get by."

"What happened to the house I grew up in?"

"I'm sure it sold."

"My parents?"

"Gone."

"How about Leo Meltzer?"

"Probably gone."

"They were all older than me."

"Yeah. Listen, you're probably the only one left from that group."

"Yeah?"

"Yeah."

"How is it I'm here and everyone else is gone?"

"Because you have a good son taking care of you."

"You know Molly Newman was the mother of Bernie?"

"I did."

"What happened to Bernie?"

"He's dead."

"When did he die?"

"I don't know. You told me he died."

"I told you?"

"Yes."

"I mean, that's what somebody told me, that's what I heard, but I don't know. So . . . Bernie's dead. I'll be a son of a gun. He was a cousin, you know."

Later . . .

He calls.

"Hey, Dad, what's up?"

"Barry, it's Dad. I just want you to know how thankful I am for all you do. I know I'm a burden—"

"You're not a burden."

"I'm not?"

"No. You're a pain in the ass, not a burden."

"That's better?"

"Much better."

"Anyway, the food, the coming over, the mornings we go out. I know I'm a burden—"

"You're really not."

"I don't know what I would do without you. I'm proud of you and I love you. Anything you need, you let me do it."

"I will."

"I'm serious."

"I will. Just stay alive. That's what you can do for me."

"Let me do something for you. It'll bring me joy. I know I'd be dead without you."

* * *

19 June

I call. "Dad, how are you?"

"Not good, not good at all."

"What's the matter?"

"My teeth. All of a sudden my gums hurt. Nu?"

"Your gums . . . ouch. I'll be over this afternoon. I'll bring you something. Remember Anbesol."

"What?"

"Never mind. It may not be a big deal. If the pain is still around on Monday, I'll call the dentist."

"The dentist. Why would you call a dentist?"

"Who should I call?"

"A dentist? I don't need a dentist."

"I could call a plumber, but a dentist, I'm thinking, would be more effective."

"Ach, why did he pull all of my teeth? I had them and he pulled them all."

"They were, I don't know, diseased or causing you problems, so he pulled them. And it wasn't just one dentist. A number of dentists pulled a number of teeth."

"They were fine. I go in, I sit down, and I come out with no teeth. Ach! And now this stupid razor."

"What's the matter?"

"It works, it doesn't work."

"I'll just pick you up a new one."

"What are they, like, a hundred bucks?"

"They can be. But no, I can get one for forty."

"Nah, they're a hundred. And what's with my finger?" he asks. "I bend it, it stays bent. I'm falling apart."

"You kidding me? You've got arthritis in one finger, and irritated gums. You're ninety-fucking-four and those are your problems? You should be dead at this age. You're playing with house money."

"Yeah, you're right. But why is my apartment so far away from the elevator? It's a long walk. They couldn't make it closer?"

"That's the spirit."

* * *

20 June

I check his thermostat. It is set at eighty-one degrees.

"Dad, it's eighty-on in here. Why do you have it set so high?"

"Me? I never touched it."

"The AC isn't even on."

"I don't know what the hell happened. I just checked it to see the temperature. I don't know how to work that stupid thing."

"You just said you didn't touch it."

"Well, I didn't touch it. I just wanted to turn it to, uh, you know."

"Yeah, I got it. I turned it down."

"Take it down, take it down," he says, all official-like. "It's hot in here. Make it seventy-nine."

"What if I make it seventy-six?"

"Yeah, yeah, I usually set it there."

"How are your teeth?"

"Fine, fine."

"Your gums?"

"My gums?"

"Your gums."

"What do you mean 'my gums'?"

"This is going to take a while—your GUMS!"

"Oh, my gums. You mean my gums? My gums are fine."

"And your razor?"

"My what?"

"Your razor?"

"Oh, yeah, that. I didn't use it."

"You didn't?"

"Well, I used it last night."

"So you used it?"

"Yeah, but I thought you meant did I use it this morning—that's all. No, it shaves good."

"C'mon, I'll take you to breakfast. It's Father's Day."

"That means I'm a father."

"Yes, it does."

We arrive at Owl Head and we run into Jim Jakubovitz, a.k.a. "the Big Guy," and Mimi Tarrasch, a dear friend. I invite them to join us for breakfast.

My father introduces himself to Jim, someone he's known for five years, and Mimi, whom he's never met.

"Is this your husband or just a friend?" he asks Mimi first thing.

Mimi had never heard the Purple Heart story—neither had I... Well, not this version, the one where he was standing next to a guy who just got shot before the bridge came down. My father did introduce me to Jim and Mimi, which I thought was gracious, and he did ask Mimi if she knew for whom her Cobb salad was named.

She did not.

Before I tell you how the morning ended, I must tell you that Mimi is an attractive, vivacious, hilarious woman, animated as well as (important to the story) toned and very much in shape. She and Jim had just finished a long walk, incidentally, and it was already, like, 4,000 degrees outside.

"So tell me," my father asks Mimi, "were you ever in your life thin?"

"For someone who has worried about this her whole life," Mimi says, cackling, "I will be in therapy tomorrow morning."

* * *

24 June

So that woman from Long Island, occasionally known as Jack Friedman's daughter, Susan, decided to play hardball in the intramural Father's Day greeting-card competition by sending the above.

"What is this?" my father asks when I hand it to him.

"Your daughter sent you a huge card in a transparent attempt to curry favor."

"What?"

"Nothing."

"Can I fold it?"

"Sure."

"Look at the postage she had to put on this thing. Wow-wee-wow!"

He sees the name on the card: "'Jack Friedman.' That's me."

"Yes, it is."

Joining my father and me at dinner tonight at Doug's, the restaurant downstairs in the front by the girl by the entrance—you know, in the back, at the Hebrew Home Hotel—was none other than Melissa, who handled the same 112 questions regarding her daughter, which she doesn't have, like a pro.

"So, what's your daughter's name, if I may ask?" my father asks.

"Dad, she has a son, not a daughter."

"That's what I meant. Does he work?"

"He's fourteen," she says.

"So she lives with you?"

"Dad, a son."

"That's what I meant. She's how old, again?"

"A son, Dad, a son."

"Oh, is she in school?"

"Melissa has a son, not a daughter."

"I know, I know."

"Okay, Dad," I say, "time for our quiz. What were your parents' names?"

"My parents or her parents?" he responds, pointing to Melissa.

"Why would I ask you her parents' names?"

"I don't know."

"Yours."

"Sam and Riva."

"Good."

"Your wife?"

"Florence."

"All right," I say, "now, who are your kids?"

"Do I get a prize if I get these right?"

"Yes, you do. I'll buy you dinner. Go."

"Let's see," my father answers, "there's you, Barry, and Susan and . . . oh, don't tell me, don't tell me. I know, I know. Ach . . . what's Wayne's name, again?"

* * *

26 June

As is our wont, we are this Saturday morning at Owl Head Bagels for my salt bagel with my usual side of mustard and a Diet Dr. Pepper, and his egg on a toasted croissant with decaf, Half and Half and four Sweet'N Lows. When he sees my "Old School Bagel Cafe" hat, the conversation immediately turns to said establishment.

"Why didn't you get an egg?"

"I didn't want an egg."

"Why didn't you want an egg?"

"Because I didn't want an egg."

"What's your girlfriend's name, again?"

"Melissa."

"Yes, yes, I knew that. She seems very nice."

"You've known her for ten years."

"I have?"

"Yeah."

"No, it's not that. She's just very nice."

"That she is."

"Listen, don't make the same mistake with this one you did with the others and marry her. You got two failed marriages, you know."

"Thanks for reminding me."

"Now, the wife I had. Why didn't she live longer?"

"A fabulous question, that."

* * *

27 June

"Ba," my father asks on the phone, "did Mom die?"

This is not good.

"Yeah."

"Someone asked me at dinner where she was, and I told them my wife doesn't eat with me. And I thought, 'Wait, did she die?'"

"She did, Dad."

"Oh, my God! Really? Why didn't I know?"

"You knew."

"I did?"

"Yeah."

His memory of this event, like many seminal moments in his life, is a bit fuzzy. He is often more upset that he can't remember the event than, say, devastated by the event itself, but there was something in his voice tonight that made me think this was more the latter than the former.

I go to his apartment. When I arrive, he is sitting on the sofa, not his chair, with the TV off.

"Dad, what's up?"

"Why can't I remember things?" he asks. "I mean, do I push things out of my mind and now they won't come back?"

"It's normal, Dad, for a man your age. You remember some things, but not others, like your phone number when you were growing up."

Which he recites for me.

"Like your address from the house you lived in."

Which he recites.

"See, the mind is just odd in what it remembers and what it forgets. You know the name of your family rabbi but can't remember your daughter's name."

"Cynthia?"

"Susan."

"That's what I meant."

"Happens, Dad. Don't feel bad."

"Listen, I don't have an estate to leave you."

"Yeah, I know," I say, suppressing a laugh. "You know why that is?"

"Why?"

"You lived too long. If you died twenty years ago, I'm getting about forty grand."

"Heh-heh, you're right. I want you to have the credenza. You're my link to the past. I connect with you."

"All right. Always loved this piece. You and Mom bought it more than fifty years ago."

"I mean, I have no money to give you, but I want you to have it."

"Thank you."

Just then Melissa calls on FaceTime.

"Say hello to my father," I say. I hand him the phone.

"Hi, Jack," I hear her say.

"I love you, sweetheart," he says to her. "I swear to God."

"I love you too, Jack."

"Is that your wife?" he asks after we hang up.

"My girlfriend."

"You got the good-looking one, you know?"

"I'll tell her you said so."

"Barry, where do I belong?"

"Here."

"Am I moving anywhere?"

"No."

"You sure?"

"Positive. Tell you what. If I move, you move. Otherwise, you stay here."

"You gotta deal. Ach, Barry, I give up. I lived too long."

"Not at all."

After a short review of the people in his life, living and dead, I ask if he wants to go out. He offers to buy me dinner.

"I already ate, thanks."

"C'mon, I'll buy."

"Tell you what. You want to go out for ice cream? I'll get you a chocolate cone."

"Ice cream?"

"Ice cream."

"Where?"

"Where they sell ice cream."

We head downstairs to the car.

(Ed. note: To Tulsa ice cream business owners—it would kill you to have soft-serve chocolate?)

"Look, Dad," I say after trying three places, "I can't get you chocolate. How about vanilla?"

"Fine, fine. Why don't they have chocolate?" he asks.

"I don't know."

We go to QuikTrip. I get two soft-serve vanilla cones. I come out to the car and hand him one.

"Why do they put so much ice cream on a short stick?"

"What?"

"I mean, the stick is short and the ice cream is big. Either get a bigger stick or a smaller amount of ice cream, that's all. And it melts. You gotta eat it fast."

"Anything else you want to complain about?"

Just then, as we sit in the car, we see a young woman, I'm thinking early twenties, enter the store. Black miniskirt, lime-green hair, heavily tattooed and pierced, leather necklace, embodying all that is goth. She is also wearing heels and knee socks, one black with white stripes, one red with black stripes.

"Her socks don't match," my father says.

"That's what you noticed?"

"You think she knows?"

"About her socks? Probably."

"Funny they don't match."

"Hilarious."

We head back to the Hebrew Home.

"Why does everyone have their lights on?" he asks. "Do they think the turn signals won't work unless their lights are on?"

"I don't think that's it. Some people say it's safer to drive with their lights on all the time."

"Yeah?"

"Yeah."

We arrive at the Hebrew Home.

"Barry, thank you for coming over."

"You're welcome."

"But call once in a while—just to bullshit around."

"I will."

"Come with your girlfriend sometime."

"I will."

"Tell her I'll be friendly."

* * *

29 June

It being Tuesday, I venture to the Hebrew Home Hotel to meet my father for our weekly dinner. Doug's Cafe being closed through July 5th, we head to the dining room . . . at 4:15. The conversation quickly turns to money, mortality, and meat.

"How much do I get a month from, you know, the retirement people?" he asks after we order.

I tell him.

"Yeah?"

"Yeah."

"Does that include meals?"

"That's something different. Has nothing to do with the Hebrew Home."

"So what if I moved?"

"You'd still get it. Again, dinner comes from the home, not the government."

"What do you mean?"

"The government doesn't care where you live, what you do. This place just happens to serve dinner and that's included in the rent."

"Can I get three meals here? You know, I only get the one?"

"You can."

"I can't eat that much!"

"Then why'd you ask?"

"I'm just curious, that's all. How much have I gotten total?"

"From Social Security? Well, you retired at sixty-two . . . you're ninety-four. It's more than half a million dollars, Dad. You want to know how much you paid in?"

"Yeah."

"Probably about forty grand."

"Yeah?"

"Yeah. You made out."

"I'm costing them money. You know, there are guys dropping in their seventies. I'm ninety-four. What if I live another twenty-five years?"

"You'll still get paid."

"Wow-wee-wow! Will I still get the meals?"

"Yes."

"How much, again?"

"Half a million. Yeah, you're the reason the country is going broke, so, on behalf of a grateful nation and a put-upon taxpayer for carrying you all these years, you're welcome."

Just then dinner arrives.

"I eat the fish now," he says, looking at his tilapia. "I like the fish. What are you eating?"

"Chicken."

"Chicken?"

"Chicken."

"It's not that. I eat the fish. I'm done with the meats."

"Chicken isn't a meat."

"No, but I'm done with the meats. The chicken, I eat the chicken, but I eat the fish, that's all. I fill up on soup, that's why I don't eat the soup. I mean, sometimes I get the soup. But I eat the fish now."

"Is it good?"

"What?"

"The fish?"

"What do you mean?"

"Is the fish good?"

"It's fish, you know. I eat the fish."
Just then the Big Guy comes by.
"Hi, Jack, how are you?"
"You know, the food here is usually pretty good," my father says. "So, how's business?"
"Good, Jack. As long as you're here, things are good."
"There's a guy who looks just like you who walks around. Do you have a twin?"
"Yes." Jim doesn't, but he's been down this rabbit hole before.
"You know my son?" my father asks, pointing to me.
"We're friends, Dad."
"Friends? What do you mean you're friends? You knew him before me?"

JULY

3 July

"How come some of the grass is green?" he asks on the way to breakfast at Owl Head, taking in the lawns and tracts of land.

"God," I answered.

"Yeah? Well, where does he get the water? Tell me, Ba," he adds, apparently done with questions about God and celestial irrigation, "this girl . . ."

"What girl?"

"You know."

"Melissa?"

"Yeah. You going to marry her, or what? Because does she know your two other marriages died?"

"'Died'?"

"You know what I mean. Done. Kaput."

We arrive.

"They got good coffee here, you know?"

"I am aware. Speaking of, do you need anything—coffee, potato salad? We can stop at the store on the way back."

"I don't know. Potato salad."

"Potato salad?"

"Yeah, yeah. It's a good nosh."

* * *

7 July

I call. "Dad, how are you?"

"Who is this?"

"Really?"

"Oh, it's you."

"It's Barry."

"Yeah, yeah, I know. Barry?"

"Barry. How do your feet feel today?"

"Ach, better. I don't know. Sometimes I look down and remember the pain but then it softens."

"What pain? From the pedicure?"

"No, from before—you know, the injury I had. Just something."

"The injury? You mean the war?"

"It bothers me, it doesn't bother me. But, no, there's no pain. I just feel it sometimes."

"Dad, you're not suffering from a toe wound from seventy years ago. Your nails were too long. You had them cut yesterday."

"Oh, that. Yeah, yeah, feels good. Much better. You can tell she did something. Cut the nail down. Did you tip her?"

"Yes."

"How much?"

"Don't worry."

"How much?"

"Christ, what are you worried about? I tipped her."

"I just want to make sure you tipped her."

"I've been tipping since I was in my thirties, don't worry about it."

"I'm not worried about it."

"You sound worried about it. I gave her ten."

"How much was the whole thing?"

"Thirty."

"Thirty?"

"Thirty. And you gave her ten?"

"Yes."

"So how goes your life?"

* * *

8 July

"What does your hat say?" he asks me, seeing the logo for Roswell, New Mexico.

"Roswell . . . New Mexico. It's where they keep the aliens who visit us."

"Yeah? Why'd they give it a Jewish name?"

"What?"

"Roswell. It's a Jewish name."

"Roswell is a Jewish name? You sure?"

"Well, you know what I mean."

* * *

10 July

"Why did the guy pull my teeth out?" my father asks on our way to Owl Head.

"You mean the dentist?"

"Yeah, there was nothing wrong with my teeth. He just pulled them."

" 'Cause he had nothing else to do. He didn't just pull them. They were falling out, full of cavities, and it didn't happen all at once. And, again, you have been to more than one dentist in your life."

"I don't remember."

"Trust me. They all needed to come out."

"Ach!"

At Owl Head, the egg sandwich is perfect, and as I bring him his second cup of coffee, filled with Half and Half and Sweet'N Low and even some coffee, he says, "Ba, this is nice. We go out, it's nice. We spend time. And if nothing else, the coffee's good."

* * *

14 July

I call. "Dad, how are you?"

"Feel good, really good."

"That's wonderful, because do you have any idea how old you are? You're pushing ninety-five."

"You know I'm pushing ninety-five."

"I knew I heard it somewhere. Anyway, how are you?"

"Everything is good. Nothing hurts. Oh, I mean, I wake up some mornings and the legs don't do what they used to, but otherwise I feel good. I keep waiting for something to happen—you know, for the whole thing to fall apart. Oh, listen, I'm out of sugar, the granular, the loose sugar. You know what I mean."

* * *

15 July

We're at the Hebrew Home Dining Room—we were supposed to meet at Doug's Cafe, but he didn't remember that I called to remind him.

He sees a number of residents enter the dining room.

"Look at the old-timers. They got a lot of 'em here."

"You're an old-timer."

"Yeah, but look at them crawl in."

"Lovely."

"No, this is a good place, Ba, I like it. I'd come back here someday."

"'Come back here'? Where you going?"

"You know, in case I go somewhere."

"Where you going?"

"I'm going."

"Where?"

"I may go away and then I may come back."

"You're not going anywhere."

"How do you know?"

"I know."

"What about heaven?"

"Heaven? What makes you think you're getting in?"

"I got a reserve."

* * *

19 July

Tonight, for dinner, my father and I head to Doug's Cafe, which, in case you're just joining us, is by the Hebrew Home Hotel's back entrance, by the side, where the girl sits, near the office. The Big Guy comes by to say hello.

"Here's trouble," Jim says, seeing us.

"You know him?" my father, pointing to me, asks Jim. "He's my son."

Chelsea, the activity director, comes by.

"Hello, Miss America," my father says. "You're looking very cosmetic today."

"'Cosmetic'?" Chelsea and I ask in unison.

"Yeah, you know, you look . . . what should I say? Your skin, I don't know. You hungry?" he asks her.

"No."

"So how goes your life?"

"Going well, Jack. How about yours?"

"Got a half hour, I'll tell you the whole story. You hungry?"

"No, thanks. I'm gaining weight. People always say my skin looks good when I gain weight."

"I thought maybe you were pregnant, the way you were holding your stomach. Anyway, you know my son?"

"We know each other, Dad."

"Yes, we do, Jack."

"Before I got here or after? You sure you're not hungry?"

"No. Before."

"How do you know each other?"

"We just do."

"You hungry?"

"DAD, SHE'S NOT HUNGRY!"

"All right, don't get so shook up. I just asked."

"Dad, believe me, she's not hungry."

"You sure," he asks her, quietly, "you're not hungry?"

"No, Jack, I'm not hungry."

* * *

21 July

My father is having a bad day. His memory is all over the place, his confusion rampant. He calls this morning wanting to know where his car is so he can go back to his parents' home in Brooklyn, a place he hasn't lived in seventy years. I head over to the Hebrew Home and—do what? I don't know. I decide to take him down to Doug's Cafe for coffee and a piece of cake.

I order him decaf and, because there is no cake, an orange poppy-seed muffin.

We sit.

"Dad, what's going on?" I ask, cutting the muffin into eight small pieces.

"Nah, it's not that. I'm not knocking the place, but I have no wheels. So I can't get out of here."

"Where do you want to go?"

"Where do I want to go? I want to go home."

"This is home."

He takes a bite of the muffin.

"This is good cake, you know? And the place is crowded. Doing good business."

"Yes, they are. Glad you like it."

"Where's my car?"

"You don't have a car."

"That's right. I don't have wheels. So how long am I going to stay here? When do I go back to New York?"

"You don't. This is home."

"I know, I know. Where do you live?"

"Tulsa."

"Coffee's good," he says, taking a sip.

"Good. Tell me, seriously, where do you want to go?"

"I thought I'd go home."

"You are home."

"I know, I know. This is really good cake," he adds as he takes another bite. "What kind is it?"

"Orange poppy seed."

"It's very good. And the coffee is good. Let me have some ice from your soda. It's too goddamn hot, though."

He dips his spoon in my cup of Diet Coke and removes some ice.

"My mother and father don't live there anymore, right?"

"Brooklyn? No. They died. And you haven't been there for seventy years."

"How many?"
"Seventy."
"Impossible."
"Really . . . seventy."
"Yeah? That long?"
"That long."
"This cake is delicious."
"Glad you like it."
"Why do I get so confused?"
"It comes with age, I think. Most of the time, things are okay with you but then you have days like today. That's why you can always call me. And here's the good news. As confusing as today has been, you knew enough to call me and how to call me."

"I nearly didn't. I couldn't remember your number, but you're on the automatic thing, so I pushed the button and, bingo! Plus, I thought maybe you were with the girlfriend. I didn't want to disturb you."

"You can always disturb me. The girlfriend's okay with you calling me."

"Yeah?"
"Yeah."
"Here," he says, cutting the last piece in half, "take the last piece. It's good cake. But I can't finish."
"I know. It is good."
"What kind is it?"
"Orange poppy seed."
"No joke, it's really good," he says, eating the piece he just gave me.

* * *

22 July

Today, I brought "the world" over to my father's apartment—milk, juice, Half and Half, potato salad, cookies, coffee, "the things, you know, the . . . things that go in the machine . . . the cups, the things, the pods," pineapple soda, orange soda, generic Neapolitan ice cream sandwiches, and chicken slices.

"What do you got there?" he asks, seeing the bags, "because I needed fluids. I forgot to tell you."

"I got you fluids."

"You mean the milk, juice . . . because I was out of almost all the fluids."

"I got you all the fluids, don't worry."

"Oh, good, good," he says, checking the bags. He points to the milk and juice: "Now that stuff goes in the refrigerator."

"Where all good fluids should go."

"What?"

"Nothing."

"Oh, good," he says, watching me place the new containers of milk, juice, Half and Half, pineapple and orange soda strategically behind the not-empty containers of milk, juice, Half and Half, pineapple and orange soda. "How did you know I needed the fluids?"

"I'm smart like that. Now stop saying 'fluids.'"

"So what's new, sweetheart?"

"I need to borrow your tool chest."

"I have a tool chest?"

"You do."

"What if I need it?"

"You won't need it."

"What if I have to fix something?"

"A frightening thought, that. You won't."

I head to the hall closet and see his Certified Public Accountant certificate—a flimsy photocopy, dated 1962—from the University of the State of New York Education Department. It is a complete and bad (and, frankly, hilarious) forgery. My father was a successful public accountant in New York for thirty years, but he was never a CPA, and he didn't graduate from any SUNY school. Most disturbing of all, his tool chest, which was inexplicably impressive and sophisticated, is nowhere to be found.

* * *

25 July

Doug's Cafe at the Hebrew Home Hotel is closed, so we head to the dining room on this Sunday evening for dinner.

"So, Ba, what's new?" my father asks.

"All right, let me ask: Your CPA certificate, it's fake, right?"

"What do you mean?"

"You're not a CPA."

"No."

"Then how did you get the certificate?"

"It was made available to me, so I took it."

"What do you mean 'made available'?"

"It was made available."

"You mean you photocopied someone else's, used Wite-Out on their names, and typed your name in."

"Something like that. But I don't remember. It was so long ago."

"'Made available'? That's hilarious. Was it Don's [his old partner]?"

"I think so."

"Now when did he die, again?"

"Don died?"

"You told me he did."

"I told you that?"

"You told me that."

"No, I heard he died, but then I heard he didn't die."

"I think he died, Dad."

"When did he die?"

"I don't know."

"Don died? When did Don die?"

"I don't even know when Bernie died."

"I didn't know Don died."

"Anyway, let's get back to the CPA. You went to school to be an accountant?"

"Yes, CCNY."

"And before that, North Georgia College, before the war?"

"Yes."

"You didn't graduate, though, right?"

"No, I did."

"You graduated from CCNY? I thought you didn't graduate."

"No, I didn't graduate. I took the accounting courses."

"But you just—never mind. So you never became a CPA, but you do have a certificate saying you are."

"Yeah, it looked better when I was competing for clients. Nobody ever asked me for it, but I had it."

"Even though you didn't really have it."

"No, I had it. It was good to have when you're going after clients."

"I'm sure it was."

"But I knew the work. I just didn't have the initials after my name."

* * *

27 July

The phone rings.

"Listen, I need the, you know, the whatchamacallit for the, uh . . ."

"Let me guess: paper products."

"No, no, I need the roll paper. I use it in the kitchen. You know, the paper."

"What do you mean 'no'? Paper products. We said the same thing. You couldn't give that to me?"

"What?"

"Nothing. I'll get you paper towels for the kitchen."

"Yeah, yeah, the roll paper. I cut them in half and then I use them for my face and hands."

"Why do you do that?"

"What do you mean?"

"Why do you cut them in half?"

"They're too big, so I cut them in half."

"Why don't I just buy you napkins?"

"What?"

"Napkins."

"What do you mean?"

"Paper napkins. That way you don't have to cut the big paper. Napkins are made for such use. And they're pre-cut."

"Yeah, I guess you could do that—or the roll paper, and I can cut them."

AUGUST

4 August

My father—who calls River Spirit Casino "River Stix" and Hard Rock Casino "Hot Rod" and Old School Bagel Cafe "Owl Head"—has just now called Broken Arrow, a suburb of Tulsa, "Buxom Whore."

* * *

5 August

Today, a meeting of the minds on the second floor of the

Hebrew Home.

I see Sherman near the elevators. "Would you two make up, for Chrissakes?" I say.

"You look familiar," my father says, approaching.

They shake hands.

"Wow-wee-wow," says my father. "What a grip. Where do I know you from?"

"You live next door to him," says I.

"I know, I know. I meant before."

"'Before'?"

"Yeah, I meant before."

"How you doing, Jack?" Sherman asks.

"Got a half hour, I'll tell you the whole story. Or wait for the movie, it's in color."

"The same jokes all the time," Sherman says.

"Dad, Sherman just turned 100. This is what 100 looks like."

"Yeah?"

"Yeah."

"I'm going to be ninety-five."

You have to admire a man who thinks turning ninety-five is going to impress a man who's 100.

"You look familiar," he again says to Sherman.

"He lives next door," I say, again.

"You called me a schlemiel last time," says Sherman.

"I did?"

"Yes."

"I don't remember."

"You did."

"I did?"

"You did. Why can't you be more like your son?" Sherman asks.

"Who? Him?" my father asks, pointing to me.

"Ach," says Sherman, smiling. "But you called me names last time."

"I don't remember. But how you doing?"

Sherman nods his head.

"All right, take care of yourself," my father says, "and if you can't, get a friend for me."

As we head down the hallway, my father says, "He looks familiar. Where do I know him from?"

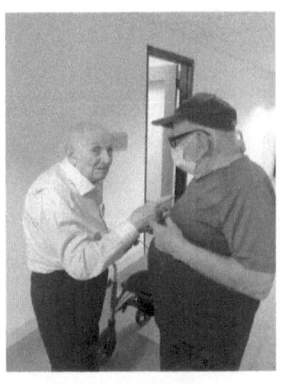

* * *

6 August

"You know, Ba," he says, looking at me across the table at Doug's, "that's a great shirt."

"Thanks."

"What kind is it?"

"I don't know."

"I mean, is it cotton?"

"I think so."

"No, that's not cotton. It shines."

"I think it's cotton."

"No! Cotton. It's not cotton."

"Okay, it's not cotton. I don't really know."

"Didn't you check?"

"No. I put it on."

"How come you didn't check?"

"Because it's a shirt. I didn't think about it."

"No, it's a good-looking shirt. It's like silk. The texture alone."

"It's not silk."

"How do you know?"

"That much I know. It's not silk."

"No. Look at the way it shines. It's so lustrous."

"'Lustrous'?"

"Yeah, you know, lustrous."

"I know what the word means. I don't know, Dad. It's a shirt."

"To talk to you is impossible. How can you not care?"

"What? It's a shirt. It's a T-shirt. I'm not emotionally involved with it."

"But it shines, it's crisp. It's not like the shirt I have on. This is cotton." He grabs his shirt. "Yours is not cotton. What kind of material is it?"

"I don't know! You want to touch it?"

He does.

"That's not cotton."

"Okay, it's not cotton."

"Good-looking, though."

"Would you like one?"

"You can get?"

"I can get."

"Because it's a great-looking shirt. That's not cotton, though. It shines. It's lustrous. Very lustrous."

"Again with the lustrous. Tell you what: I'll get you a shirt. They have it in black, green, and white."

"No, I like the white. But I like black. Green, yeah, you know, get the green."

"I'll get you all three."

"Because, again, it's a good-looking shirt. You don't know what the material is, though?"

"No."

"It's not cotton, though. It's shiny."

"Fine."
"This is a good cake, you know?"
"You mean the muffin?"

* * *

8 August

Owl Head is out of croissants, so I order my father the egg on toasted white bread instead.

"What is this?" my father asks as his sandwich is placed before him.

"They were out of croissants, so they put it on bread. Is that OK?"

"It's so long."

"'Long'?"

"Yeah, you know, it's not like the other one."

"Right. Different bread."

"No, but it's, just, I don't know, it's so much. I don't usually eat that much."

"It's the same amount of egg. Eat what you want."

"Yeah, but the bread, it's different."

"Right, it's toasted white bread."

"It's good, don't misunderstand me, but it's not the soft roll," he says, alluding to the croissant.

"No, it's not."

"Hey, Ba," he says, noticing there are people at my table, "why are there people at your table? Can we chase them?"

"Good idea."

Just then my father sees eight or nine teenage girls come in, all in shorts, making their way to the cash register.

"Look at all the bare legs," he says. "Wow-wee-wow."

"Easy, Pop. You're old enough to be their great-great-grandfather."

"Is that legal?" he asks, still looking.

"It is."

"They make good coffee here, you know?"

"I do."

"Is it you or is it the place?"

"Does it matter?"

"No, I'm just saying the coffee's good. But I don't usually have two cups."

"You always have two cups."

"I do?"

"You do."

"I don't remember. You know, you could come in here"—he motions toward the coffee station—"bring your own cup, you don't need their cup, you could fill up over there and they'd let you sit here all day."

"You sure about that?"

"Well, I don't know. Say, Ba, let me ask you something. What do you do during the week besides go to breakfast?"

"That's pretty much it."

"No, I'm very serious. Do you see clients?"

"'Clients'? Well, I'm a writer-comedian."

"But what do you do?

"Again with this. I work."

"I mean other than driving around. You got activities?"

* * *

11 August

"Ach, Barry, what am I doing here?" he asks at dinner.

"What do you mean 'here'?"

"I don't mean that, but what if I want to go to Europe? How do I go?"

"I'll get you on a plane and we'll go to Europe. You want to go to Europe?"

"I don't want to go to Europe, that's not my point."

"Sorry. It sounded like your point."

"I don't have wheels."

"You want wheels?"

"Nah. Where'm I going? Wheels? It's just that I'm winded. I think because I'm ninety-four."

"That's exactly why you're winded."

"You think that's why?"

"Yes, because you're ninety-four."

"Yeah, because I'm winded. That's a nice shirt, you know."

Yes, I wore the same shirt from days ago. The fuck was I thinking?

"Is that cotton?"

"It's polyester."

"What?"

"Not cotton."

"I didn't think it was cotton. It looks like silk. You said it was cotton. It's not cotton."

"You got me. It's not cotton."

The salads arrive.

"I'm not going to finish this deliberately," he says, pointing to the salad as he starts devouring it, "because I want to leave room for the chicken."

He proceeds to finish it.

"So why are you finishing it?" I ask.

"Because it's good. You got a girlfriend?"

"Yes. You've known her for ten years."

"I have?"

"You have."

"You've been married twice, don't forget."

"I won't."

"How does this one compare to the others?"

"Wow! Melissa's good, she's really, really good."

"You should invite her to dinner here."

"I will. I have, she's come, but I will again."

"What?"

"Nothing."

His chicken parmesan arrives.

"Look at the size of this. Ach, Ba, I'm so glad you're alive and here. Give me your hand, I want to thank you."

He turns to the food.

"Who the hell can eat all this? I'm up to here already," he says, his hand moving up to his neck.

* * *

15 August

We arrive at Owl Head and see David Blatt, Patty Hipsher, and her mom, Judy, heading out. Patty, once again, introduces herself and David to my father—that they have known my father for at least six years never doesn't make this hilarious.

David, because he loves torturing me, says to my father, "Nice to meet you. Are you the son?"

"Son? I'm the father!"

"You good on cereal?" I ask on the way back to the Hebrew Home.

"Yeah, though that cereal you bought last time, it's off."

"Off'?"

"I mean, it's good, don't misunderstand me, but it's so good, I enhance the other cereal with it, so I need more. It's very good. I eat more of that than I do the other kind."

"Did you like the soda I bought you?" I got him something called Tamarind.

"It's nowhere."

* * *

17 August

We're at Doug's Cafe.

"So, Ba, what happened to your two marriages? They went kaput."

"Yeah, good word for it."

"Seriously, what happened?"

"I don't know."

"So it was just the strangeness of love?"

* * *

18 August

The phone rings.

"Ba, it's Dad."

"How are you?"

"Listen, I need soap. You know, soap. The soap . . . bars of soap."

"Yeah. Got it. Bars of soap."

"You know what I'm talking about? I use the soap, the bars, and I'm down to my last bar. You know, for washing purposes."

* * *

20 August

"You know, Ba," he says to me, after we return from shopping, "there's a lot of old-timers in the place."

"That's because you live in a retirement community. Tell me something: Do you see a lot of their children come by?"

"What do you mean?"

"The people who live at the home—their kids?"

"No, I don't, as a matter of fact."

"Ah-ha! And why is that? Who has the best son?"

"You're right, you're right. I don't see a lot of their kids, but you come by. You bring the potato salad. It's very nice."

* * *

23 August

Tonight, my father forgot we had dinner planned at Doug's. I find him in the dining room.

"Ach, Barry, I am forgetting too many things. I'm sorry about dinner."

"Don't worry about it, Dad. The important thing is we're eating now. Doesn't matter where we eat."

"You know, I didn't even want this," he says, pointing to his beef taco. "I mean, it's good, don't misunderstand me. So what's new, sweetheart?"

"Nothing. Why did you order it if you didn't want it?"

"I thought it was something else."

"What did you think it was?"

"I didn't know. I mean, who knew they were going to give me two?"

"You want something else?"

"No, I'm up to here," he says, his hand to his chest. "Let me ask you: My children are Wayne, Barry, and Susan, right?"

"Right. I'm Barry."

"You're Barry. Are you a direct son?"

SEPTEMBER

5 September

"Ach, Barry. You know, I'm getting old," he says as we climb into the car for going to Owl Head.

"I know. Put your seat belt on. I'm a bad driver."

"I know, I know. How'd you get a license?"

"Bribed the guy."

"Say, Ba, what happened to Bernie Newman?"

"There's a name we haven't discussed in . . . a week."

"I heard he died."

"You told me he died."

"I said it?"

"Yes."

"No, no, I was talking to someone and they asked me if Bernie died and I said I heard he died."

"Who were you talking to?"

"I don't remember, but I heard he died."

"I know. That's what I'm saying. You told me he died after you heard he died."

"How did I hear it?"

"I don't know."

"No, I mean, I heard he died. But I don't know if he died. I just heard that. I wonder how he died."

"Dad, he died."

"Yeah?"

"Yeah."

"I wonder how he died."

"He was old."

"He was six months older than me."

"Well, you're old."

"And did Cynthia die?"

"Yes."

"Normie?"

"Yes."

"Did they die together?"

"At the same time? No."

"Were they divorced when they died?"

"I don't think so."

"But Normie was blind?"

"Yes."

"But they both died?"

"Yes."

"You know, everyone at the Hebrew Home knows me. I mean, how do they know me? They say 'Hi, Jack,' and I say 'Hi' back. Blah, blah, blah, bullshit, bullshit, bullshit. But it's very nice there."

We arrive.

"Say, Ba, what's the name of this place?"

"Owl Head."

"Owl Head? What kind of name is that?"

* * *

6 September

I stop by the Hebrew Home with frosted flakes from Trader Joe's. It's Rosh Hashanah.

"Why didn't they just change it to make it normal?" my father asks.

"Who? The Jews? The year? Change the calendar to make it normal? You wanted them to do that?"

"Yeah, make it like the one we have so we'd have one instead of two."

"Because the Jewish calendar is based on the rotation of the moon and the Christian calendar is based on the rotation of the sun. Plus, the Jewish calendar is thousands of years older than the Christian."

"Yeah, I know, I know."

"You knew all that?"

"Well, yeah, I mean the calendar, this one. I knew about the . . . uh, you know, the years, that's all. I know, I know. Anyway, you brought cereal, good. I was out. I mean, I wasn't out but I was getting low."

* * *

7 September

"So, Ba, let me ask you something," he says at lunch at the Hebrew Home. "If I go somewhere—I don't mean if I die—but if I go somewhere else, will the money hold out?"

"Yes. Social Security will follow you wherever you go."

"Oh, so if I leave here—"

"You're not leaving here."

"I know. But if I do?"

"You won't run out of money."

"Good. Because I don't know what I got. Do I have?"

"You got, trust me. You got enough."

Just then our old friend Marcel, a resident and world-class ophthalmologist, stops by.

"Marcel, how are you? You're looking good, my friend," I say.

"Hi, Jack," he says.

"I'm the father."

"He knows, Dad."

"So why does everyone ask if I'm the son?"

"Nobody asks that."

"You know what I mean."

"I'm ninety-four," he says to Marcel. "How old are you?"

"Eighty-eight."

"You're a youngster. Isn't anyone older than me?"
"I got a sister who's your age."
"Is she single?"

* * *

8 September

I forget to tell you. Yesterday, at lunch, as I was opening up packets of ketchup for his "French" and the ketchup accumulated close to the fries, he said, "Be careful. Don't flood them."

* * *

10 September

I arrive at the Hebrew Home.

"Before we go to lunch," I say, "let's get another shirt for you."

"Why?"

"This one is dirty," I say, pointing out the stains.

"'Dirty'?"

"Dirty."

"What do you mean 'dirty'?"

"Dirty. Stained, spots."

"'Dirty'? What kind of dirty?"

"What kind? It's just dirty."

"It's not dirty. It's got . . . uh, marks."

"Interesting distinction."

"How can it be dirty?"

"You must have spilled something on it."

"I just put it on."

"Something must have happened between putting it on and now."

"What? I had breakfast and I put it on."

"We're narrowing in on the cause, I can feel it."

He changes, and we head to the elevator.

"So glad you're here, Ba. Who knew I'd have such a rich son?"

"You mean Wayne?"

"Who?"

"Wayne."

"Wayne?"

"Your son."

There were others waiting for the elevator, a man and a woman, whom I can only assume have been following my father's exploits. The woman starts laughing: "Oh, oh, I want to hear this. Which one is the rich son, Jack?"

* * *

11 September

This from Julie at the Hebrew Home:

"During cocktail hour, I was talking to Jack and I had my arm around his waist. Chelsea [activities director extraordinaire] walked up and put her arm around him too and said, 'Be careful, now, Jack. You've got two women. Don't have a heart attack.'

"Jack responded, 'Two? Ach! I used to handle three!'"

* * *

13 September

Today, I decide to take my father to Owl Head for a special Monday breakfast. On the way, Susan, my sister, the girl from Long Island, my father's daughter, calls.

"Who do I got?" my father says, taking the call.

"Susan."

"Cynthia?"

"Susan."

"Hey, Sue, did Normie die?"

"Yes, so did Cynthia."

"She died?"

"Yes."

"How did she die?"

"I think cancer."

"And Normie was blind."

"Yes. And Cliff, their son, died, too."

"Wow-wee-wow! How come everyone's going and I'm still here?"

"Well—"

"My question's academic."

"Good. I don't have an answer for you anyway."

We arrive at Owl Head.

"Say, Ba, what's my state of residence?"

"Oklahoma."

"I mean realistically."

"Probably the same place."

"I so enjoy these mornings. I appreciate it so, you taking me. Let me ask, though: God forbid you die, what kind of money do I have? I mean, I have no idea."

* * *

16 September

I have brought with me a copy of my father's birth certificate. I thought he might like to see it. We're at Doug's Cafe—

and to review, it's located on the side of the building, in the back, near the girls in the front by the desk, and across from the office.

"Did you know," I say, handing him a copy, "your name is Jacob—not Jack?"

"No, it's Jack. They went with the Jewish name."

"Who went with the Jewish name?"

"The temple, I think, they did that. Wayne told me, so they went with Jacob, but they didn't call me Jacob."

"Wayne wasn't around then."

"That's right. Someone else told me."

"What name did they call you, if not Jacob?"

"Yankel."

"That's Yiddish for 'Jacob.'"

"Yeah?"

"Yeah. And it wasn't the temple, Dad, that did that. Your parents named you that."

"I don't remember."

"Of course not. You were . . . never mind. Who were you named after? Do you know?"

"Joe Meltzer, I think. He was a very close friend of the family. My mother's brother."

"So why didn't they name you Joe?"

"My mother didn't like the name."

"Of course not."

"How come you have this?" he asks, picking up the copy again.

"I made a copy."

"When?"

"When did I make a copy? Before."

"'Before'?"

"I don't know when I made a copy—I made a copy!"

"And they spelled my name wrong on this thing—'ee' of 'Friedman' instead of 'ie.'"

"I noticed that. How does something like that happen?"

"Well, back then, the doctor didn't always fill out the forms. They had a guy do it."

* * *

18 September

On the way to Owl Head:
"Did you say Bernie Newman died?"
Unbelievable.
"Not recently, why?"
"I heard he died."
"You said he died. We're having the conversation about the conversation again."
"He died?"
"YOU said he died."
"I said he died? How do I know? I was talking to someone who said he died."
"There you go, then."
"Well, I wasn't talking to them, I just heard."

* * *

21 September

Around 11 p.m. on Monday, I saw my father was calling. Never a good sign—he's usually asleep by this time. So, either he was up and confused, or someone was in his apartment calling to let me know he was in trouble.

It was the former.
"Ba, it's Dad," he said. "What did I do with the gun?"
Oh, boy.
"Dad, there's no gun."
"What do you mean 'there's no gun'?"
"You don't have a gun."
"I don't have a gun?"
"No, you don't have a gun."

"I just had the gun in my hands."

"You didn't have the gun in your hands."

"I didn't?"

"No. You were probably watching TV, some cop show, you fell asleep, slept hard, and woke up confused."

"Maybe so. Do you have a gun?"

"I don't have a gun."

"Then who has the gun?"

"Nobody has the gun. Not you, not I. Nobody we know has the gun."

"I could have sworn I had the gun. They said I had the gun and they were coming for it."

"That was probably someone on *Law & Order* who said that someone else had the gun and they were coming for it. You don't have the gun."

"I didn't stash it in the sofa?"

"No," I said," stifling a laugh, "you didn't stash it in the sofa. And if you did, that would be the first place they'd look."

He laughed.

"Yeah, you're right. So . . . no gun?"

"No gun. Why don't you go to bed, Dad? It's late."

"Good idea. I could have sworn I had a gun. I was looking high and low. I just had it in my hand."

"You didn't."

"You're right. What a dream I had! What would I be doing with a gun?"

"My thoughts exactly."

* * *

25 September

"You know who that is?" I ask him at Owl Head, pointing to Gregory, who's standing near the table. "It's Gregory."

"Who?"

"Gregory, Melissa's son."

"I know, I know. He got so tall."

"He did."

"Who is he, again?"

"Melissa's son."

"Oh, your girl."

"Yeah."

"How does he know me?"

"You've known him for more than ten years."

"Yeah?"

"Yeah."

"They got good coffee here, you know," he says, sticking his fork in my Diet Dr. Pepper to get an ice cube. He then guides the cube, which he has balanced on the fork, to his cup and pushes it in with his finger. "I'm trying to cool it down, that's all."

"Dad, I put five different flavors of Half and Half and four packets of Sweet'N Low in there. That's what you're tasting—not the coffee."

"You don't know what you're talking about. This is the way coffee is supposed to taste."

"Some people like it black. They like the taste of actual coffee."

"They're wrong."

* * *

27 September

I got a call from the Veterans Administration.

"Hi, this is Tonya from the VA, calling for Jack Friedman, to confirm his checkup tomorrow."

"This is Barry Friedman. Can I help you?"

"Are you related?"

"I'm the son!"

(Of course she didn't get the joke.)

"Are you authorized to make his decisions?"

"Is the pope Catholic?"

"Sir?"

"I'm sorry, I'll stop. It's an inside joke. Yes, I am."

* * *

29 September

Before heading to the VA yesterday, my father and I had lunch at Doug's Cafe.

"Ah, Ba, how much longer I got?"

"Six and a half years. That way you'll make it to 100."

"And if I make it longer?'"

"I'm sending you to Wayne."

"How old are you?"

"Sixty-four."

"I'm thirty years older than you?"

"Yes."

"I'm more educated than you."

"Where the hell did that come from?"

"And all this is paid for? The meals, the room charges?"

"It's not a hotel . . . Yes. All paid for."

"Why?"

"Because you got old and you served this nation. Social Security, Medicare, the VA. It's our way of saying, 'Thank you.'"

"Do they know I have a Purple Heart?"

"Yes, everyone knows you have one."

"So what's new, sweetheart?"

"Well, Dad, interestingly enough, a writer from *The New Yorker* got in touch with me—"

"Who . . . what?"

"*New Yorker* magazine. Remember that, when we lived in New York?"

"Yeah, yeah."

"Anyway, someone wrote to say he enjoyed reading my stuff."

"Yeah?"

"Yeah."

"Why would someone from *The New Yorker* read you?"

OCTOBER

2 October

I'm with my father. It's raining.

"Was this in the forecast?" he asks.

"I don't know."

"Why don't you know?"

"Why? I don't know why I don't know."

"You mean you don't know?"

"I don't know."

"Why don't you know?"

"It's not important for me to know."

"Don't you care if it's raining?"

"No."

"Why not?"

"It's not going to change my life."

"But was it in the forecast?"

"I don't know."

"I wonder if it's going to rain all day."

"That would be in the forecast I don't care about. It might, but it might not. Rain's funny like that."

"Why do I talk to you?"

"Because I'm the only one who will talk to you. Listen, Susan is coming next week with your grandchildren. Do you know how many she has?"

"No."

"She has four."

"I thought she only had three, but I can't remember either of their names."

"Well, three are coming."

"Is she paying their carfare?"

"I don't think so."

"You're right, she doesn't have to. You know, they all work."

"I'm aware."

"Are they bringing gifts?"

"I doubt it."

"Why not?"

"I'm joking. They're bringing gifts. So what do you want for your birthday?"

"Another fifty years."

"Nice."

"Ach, Ba, how did I get this old? But I have to tell you: I enjoy these lunches, breakfasts, whatever they are with you. They brighten up the day."

* * *

6 October

"Bless you, my dear," my father says to Rosa, the pregnant woman who brings him dinner at the Hebrew Home. "May you never know the horrors of stretch marks."

She laughs like she's never heard it before.

"Mr. Jack, do you want a salad?"

"Is the pope Catholic?"

"Yes, he is," she says without missing a beat. "Do you want dressing?"

"No. Dressing? I don't know. Dressing? Maybe. No, give it to me stark naked. Hey, you're pregnant," he adds.

"Yes," she says with a giggle.

"Science knows what causes that."

The Big Guy comes by.

"Hey, Jim, how are you?" I say. "I was just thinking about you."

"What are you thinking about him for?" my father asks. "You

should be thinking about a woman. You don't get out much, do you?"

"Yeah," Jim says, laughing. "Hi, Jack."

"Do you know my son?" my father asks.

"Yes, we've met."

"Oh, I didn't know."

Jim leaves.

"Who was that?" my father asks.

"Jim, the Big Guy, he runs the place. You know him. He's the reason you're here."

"Him?"

"Yes, him."

"I know, I know. I've seen him around. But this is a Jewish place."

"Yeah, so?"

"And they let him run it?"

"Why wouldn't they?"

"He's not a Jew."

"Yes, he is."

"Jim's a Jewish name?"

"Again with that? Yes."

"No. Jim's not a Jewish name. Jews don't name their sons Jim."

Just then Rosa brings the salad, stark naked, as requested. My father starts eating. He doesn't seem to be enjoying it.

"It's dry, Ba, you know."

"You want dressing?"

"Yeah, yeah. It's too dry. Usually the cheese softens it, but it's dry."

* * *

9 October

We are joined in the elevator by one of the nurses at the Hebrew Home.

"How are you, Jack?" she asks.

"Got a half hour, I'll tell you the whole story. Better yet, wait for the movie. It's in color."

The nurse laughs.

"But now," he says, "you're our prisoner. Before we let you go, we'll need $150."

"How long have I lived here?" he asks me.

"About four years."

"And before this?"

"Another place in Tulsa."

"And before that?"

"Las Vegas."

"Las Vegas?"

"You remember the house on Tumble Brook Drive?"

"Oh, yeah, that's right."

"You went bowling twice a week."

"Yeah, yeah, I had a fantastic average. Say, Ba, what happened to your women?"

"My women? A fabulous question, that."

* * *

12 October

"Look," my father says, seeing the Target banner, "they're hiring. Fifteen bucks an hour. What do you think? Should I go back to work?"

"What could go wrong?"

* * *

14 October

(Front row: the woman from Long Island, the man himself, and Wayne. Back row: yours truly)

Jack Friedman turned ninety-five today, and we had a little party for him in the library at the Hebrew Home (which inexplicably has a disturbing number of books from the Bill O'Reilly *Killing* series). Some dear friends and other family members stopped by as well, and my father "met" them all again for the first time. He told everyone he was now ninety-five and then asked everyone how that was possible because he "was sixteen two weeks ago."

The repetition of this and so much of his "act" is like a song you come to love and can't get out of your head. Earlier today, Wayne and I went to Walgreens to buy our father an electric razor because the one that replaced the one that replaced the one that replaced the one that my father tried to fix broke. A man goes through a lot of electric razors between sixteen and ninety-five.

I can't imagine ever getting tired of buying him a new one.

He's pushing 100, you know.

* * *

17 October

"Who are you?" my father asks Chris, Susan's second-oldest son, he who makes the big bucks.

"I'm Chris. I'm your grandson."

"I know that. But what function do you serve?"

"I am here to take you to IHOP."

"Are we going to hop?"

"You want to hop?"

"I'm just joking. How long have you been a person?"

On the way back to the Hebrew Home, after IHOP, we pass a billboard for Israeli Diamond Supply.

"Israel diamonds?" my father asks. "Are we in the Jewish section of town?"

* * *

21 October

"This is a good combination, you know," he says as I make him lunch, "the chicken and potato salad, but I'm getting fat from the potato salad. I got a gut. And the cookie's cold."

"You want another kind of cookie?"

"Yeah."

I bring him an Oreo. He bites into it.

"Much better. Why was the other one so cold?"

"I put it in the fridge."

"Why?"

"An error in judgment."

"Yeah?"

"Yeah."

"I like them softer. And why can't I get them all like this?" He studies the Oreo. "Just chocolate. Some are with the vanilla on top."

"Those are the vanilla Oreos. I'll get you all chocolate from now on."

He then reaches across the table and grabs a Hebrew Home flyer.

"What is this?" he asks, reading, "'The crisis and future with American refrigeration?' What's that?"

"Can't tell you how funny that is. It's not 'refrigeration'—it's 'education.'"

"Oh. Anyway, what's the problem with it?"

Later, I head to the Hebrew Home office and see Pam, who works with the Big Guy.

"How's your dad?" she asks.

"Not bad. Short-term memory shot, as you know."

"He's a sweetie. And he hasn't said anything icky to me since I let my hair go gray. He's not interested anymore. I must be too old for him, but when my hair was reddish-brown, look out."

* * *

25 October

I call. "Dad, you know what day this is?"

"What's today?"

"Your anniversary. You and Mom got married sixty-eight years ago."

"Sixty-eight years ago! I totally forgot. I mean, I knew it was around this day."

"Mom was born on October 7th, you October 14th, and the anniversary is the 25th. I guess you decided it would be good to celebrate all in the same month."

My father then told me that his father, Sam, his mother's first husband, gave him a check for $500 that day sixty-eight years ago. This was 1953. Reason I bring that up? In 2003, fifty years later, on my second wedding day, my father handed me a check. He had typed in the amount, $500, using a Prestige Elite Selectric II typing ball.

NOVEMBER

5 November

Rosa, who's working at Doug's Cafe today, and still pregnant, comes by and brings my father his usual cup of decaf and a glass of cranberry juice.

"Does it come with a nipple?" my father asks, pointing to the juice glass.

Rosa laughs.

"C'mon," my father says, pointing to her pregnancy signs, "feed me! It'll be good practice for when you have to do it."

Rosa walks away smiling and/or to give her notice.

"I'm going to order the fish, Ba, because it's digestible."

"A fine choice. I'm going to have the burger."

"Why a burger?"

"I want a burger."

"A human-type burger?"

"Yeah."

Just then the Big Guy, now with a goatee, comes by.

"You look a lot like that other guy," my father says, pointing to somewhere.

"We're twins," says Jim.

"Good idea," I say to Jim. "Start with him on this. He doesn't know who you are, so by all means, let there be two of you he doesn't know when he sees one of you, both being you."

Jim laughs because he knows I will get the fallout from his short visit.

"Let me ask you something," my father says to me. "What if I get married again?"

"You're not getting married again."

"Why not?"

"You're ninety-five. Who would marry you?"

"Yeah, that's true. But what if I did get married? Just saying. Would she be allowed to live with me? Because, you know, I got a big place."

"Yeah, she would, but you're not getting married again."

"Why not?"

"Because nobody wants you."

"But what if the girl needed a place to stay?"

"And that's why she'll want to marry you?"

"Yeah."

"In that case, you have my blessing."

"Ach, Ba, it's not that I feel bad, except for the age number."

* * *

6 November

Today at Owl Head: "All right, Dad, tell me about Bernie Newman."

"You know they got good coffee here?"

"I know. Tell me about Bernie."

"He died, you know. I mean, I heard that. Someone told me."

"I know. Go 'head. Bernie. Was he a relative?"

"Bernie Newman was my first cousin. We ran together. His mother, Molly Newman, and my mother were sisters. Molly married Max Newman, who was a painter." He mimes a painter with a brush. "A housepainter—not, you know, a *painter* painter."

"Got that. Now, who was Bernie Schechter?"

"Bernie Schechter was my second cousin because his mother, also named Molly, was Dora's daughter. Dora was my mother's sister."

"So there are two Mollys?"

"Three."

"Three?"

"There was also a great-grandmother named Molly too."

"Were there no other names?"

"What do you want me to tell you?"

"You were closer with Bernie Newman than Bernie Schechter, though, right?"

"Oh, yeah. Bernie Newman was a first cousin. Bernie Schechter was much younger and lived in the Bronx, but he was named for Bernie Newman."

"What do you mean?"

"Molly Schechter . . . well, she married a Schechter, a doctor [here my father didn't mime anything]—named him Bernie because her aunt Molly Newman—"

"—who married the painter?"

"Right. Anyway, she named her son Bernie because she so respected that Molly had a son Bernie."

"Were they close, the two Bernies?"

"Not really."

"Dad, are you sure this is the story? Because I'm writing a book about you and I want to get it right. Two Bernies, both related, and at least three Mollys?"

"A book? What kind of book?"

"A book-book."

"What's this book about?"

"You."

"Just make sure you tell people I'm the father."

* * *

10 November

"Say, Ba, what happened to my mother's house?" my father asks at dinner.

"In Brooklyn? It was sold . . . forty years ago."

"I grew up in that house."

"I know."

"Who was the broker?"

"The broker? How would I know that?"

"You know, the guy who handled the transaction."

"Yes, I know what a broker does, but it was, as I say, forty years ago. I have no idea. Who knows if he's even alive."

"It probably sold for $200,000."

"Probably."

"Can I call him?"

"The broker? No."

"Why not?"

"He's probably dead, Jack," says Melissa.

"Dead?"

"Dead."

"What do you mean 'dead'?"

"Dead."

"So what happened to the money?"

"What money?" I ask.

"From the proceeds of the house. When you sell a house, you pay off the mortgage, and the rest gets—"

"—I'm familiar with the concept. But I don't know."

"You know what it was worth?"

"Probably 200,000."

"How do I get hold of the broker?"

"You can't. Again, he's dead."

"Well, who's still alive from back then? Who can I talk to? Someone must know."

"Nobody. He's dead, your brothers are dead, your mom, dad, sister. You're the last one remaining. The house sold, I'm sure some of the money went to pay off the mortgage, and the rest, who knows."

"What about Molly Newman, my mother's sister?"

"Bernie's mom? What about her?"

"She'd know."

"She'd know?"

"Yes."

"She died, Dad."

"She died?"

"She'd be about 125 right now."

"Yeah, you're probably right."

"Yeah, Bernie died, too."

"Bernie Newman died? When?"

"I don't know. You told me he died."

Melissa starts laughing.

"Oh, my God!" she says, nearly choking on her chicken nachos.

"Told you, honey," I say. "I don't make this stuff up."

"So what happened to the money?" my father asks.

"I'm sure Hy got some, Leo, you, and Mom."

"I didn't get a dime. Who was the lawyer involved?"

"Probably your brother."

"Yeah, he was an attorney. But who was the broker?"

"WE DON'T KNOW!" Melissa and I say, maybe a tad too loudly.

"So where are my millions?"

"Millions? That was quick," says Melissa.

"Inflation, babe," I say.

"Ach, this is terrible," my father says. "I'm going to be thinking about this now. This is going to be bothering me. I'm never going to be able to sleep again, ever."

"That's a bit harsh, don't you think?" I ask.

"Jack, let it go," says Melissa. "It's not important. It was forty years ago."

"Ach, I give up! What does your shirt say?" he asks her.

"You wore a shirt with words on it?" I ask. "What were you thinking? What's the first rule of dining with my father?"

"'Don't wear a shirt that says anything.' I'm sorry, I forgot."

"Well, he's all yours now."

"It says 'Be kind,' Jack," she tells him.

"'Be kind'?"

"Be kind."

"What do you mean 'Be kind'?"

"Be kind. Don't be mean," she says.

"Be kind?"

"Be kind."

"Oh, I thought it said 'Behind' and you were wearing it backward."

* * *

11 November, Veterans Day

I found this picture of my father. Showed it to him.

"Imagine," he says. "This is who they sent to win the war?"

I told that story to my friend Charlie Pierce of *Esquire*. No doubt thinking about his father on a Liberty ship in the North Atlantic as a naval armed-guard gunnery officer during those years, he wrote back, "They all felt like that. And did it anyway."

As Charlie writes on his blog every year—and I find it impossible to improve upon—"Thanks, Dad, for saving the whole damn thing."

"You know I tell people I was in Europe," says my father.

"You weren't in Europe."

"I know, I know. We won that war, you know?"

"So I hear."

"I was there when we made the French march in Yokohama."

"The French marched in Yokohama?"

"They didn't march in Yokohama?"

"I don't think so."

"Maybe it was Tokyo."

"I'm sure that was it."

* * *

17 November

Last night I went to the Hebrew Home Hotel to see my father for our regular Tuesday-night dinner. We decided to eat in the dining room because Doug's Cafe was, we concluded, too far a walk. We sat and ordered, and then our good friend Chelsea, activities director extraordinaire, came by, which is where we pick up the story.

"Look who it is, Dad."

"Hello, Miss America. How goes your life?"

"Good."

"I want to talk to you about bra sizes," my father says. "Because you're busting out."

Chelsea leaves, smiling.

"Dad, you really have to watch what you say."

"What did I say? I was just joking. I know she's not that big."

"That's not the point—ahhh, forget it. Let's change the subject. Oh, yeah—and I'm going to regret bringing this up, why am I doing this?—I have a book coming out in February."

"A book?"

"A book."

"You?"

"Me."

"You wrote a book?"

"Yes, it's my fifth . . . never mind. Yeah, I wrote a book."

"What kind?"

"It's a novel."

"A Western?"

"A Western? Now, why would I have written a Western?"

"I don't know. They make good stories. I thought you wrote a Western."

"A Western?"

"Yeah, you know, cowboys and Indians—"

"—I'm familiar with the concept. But, no, it's not a Western. A fucking Western?"

"Don't get so shook up. I thought it was a Western."

* * *

19 November

One thing I fear, as I imagine anyone with a nonagenarian parent fears (or a parent of any age, or a child, or, or, or), is the late-night/early-morning phone call. Nothing good happens at those hours. Well, at precisely, 4:39 a.m., my father called.

"Ba, I'm out of soup. You know what I mean: soup."

* * *

21 November

I call.

"Where are my tax returns?" he wants to know.

"I have them."

"Why do you have them?"

"What are you going to do with them?"

"What about my clients?"

"You don't have any clients. You're retired, remember?"

"Oh, yeah, that's right. I don't feel like doing it anymore, anyway."

"Right. And you don't need to do them anymore."

"Am I a resident of Oklahoma?"

"You are."

"Do they know that?"

"The state? Yes. They're aware."
"What do they say?"
"They're overjoyed."
"Let me ask: this girl you live with—"
"Melissa."
"Is she easy to live with?"
"Yeah."
"Does she take care of things?"
"'Take care of things'? Yeah, why?"
"I'm just curious."
"She does."
"As long as she takes care of things."
"Is she just after the funds?"
"The funds? I'll ask her."

* * *

23 November

We are heading to see Dr. John Schumann.
"Do I know this doctor?"
"Oh, yeah, John Schumann. You've known him a long time. He's been your doctor for years."
"Yeah?"
"Yeah."
"Jewish?"
"Yeah."
"No."
"What 'no'? Yeah."
"Yeah?"
"Yeah."
"John is not a Jewish name."
"Nevertheless, he's Jewish."
"Why did his parents name him John?"
"I don't know. I'll ask, should I ever meet them—or you can ask him."

"But he's a medical man?"
"Yes, he's a medical man."
"Does he know I'm ninety-five?"
"Yeah."
"Did you tell him?"
"I did."
"When did you tell him?"
"When? I don't know. He probably did the math on his own."
"What am I going for?"
"General health stuff."
"Is anything wrong with me?"
"Yeah, you're losing your mind."
"Then you need a mentalist. Is this guy a mentalist?"
"No."
"But he's Jewish?"
"Yeah."
"He doesn't sound Jewish."
"He's Jewish!"
"What's his name, again—Johnson? Because that's not a Jewish name."
"Schumann."
"And he knows me?"
We arrive. The nurse enters.
"Hi, Mr. Friedman."
"Good morning. It is morning, isn't it? Are you going to take pictures of my nudity?"
She runs screaming from the office.
I kid, of course. She walks briskly.

* * *

24 November
"So what did he tell you?" my father asks.
"The doctor? That you're in fabulous shape, especially for ninety-five."

"I feel good, I do, except parts of me. But I weigh . . . what do I weigh?"

"195."

"195? I used to be 150."

"You haven't been 150 in forty years."

"What are you talking about?"

"You haven't been 150 since the early eighties."

"160, then."

"Whatever. Just enjoy yourself, eat what you want. Why are you worried about your weight?"

"Enjoy myself? What if I find myself in a strange bedroom?"

"Call me. I'll come get you."

"So I'm really all right?"

"Swear to you, Dad. You know how many men your age wish they had your health? You know how many men hope to get to your age? You read the paper, the obituaries, you see how many people are dying younger than you."

"You know, you're right. I noticed that eighty-two is a big number."

"For those who die?"

"Yeah, eighty-two's a big number."

"You crunched those numbers, did you?"

"What?"

"Nothing."

"So did they know about the war injury?"

"The nurses? Yeah. Well, you told them about the grenade."

"What grenade?"

"I don't know. You mentioned a grenade went off."

"I mentioned that?"

"Well, I didn't mention it."

"I got a Purple Heart, you know."

"Yes, but not from the grenade."

"I'm not suggesting it was."

"That's exactly what you were suggesting. I was there."

"Ba, let me ask you something. Let's say a rich woman with

an apartment in New York City wants me to move in with her. What then?"

"That's not going to happen."

"I'm not suggesting it will, but if it does—"

"Yeah."

"My question's academic, but what about my furniture? Do I leave it at the home or take it with me?"

"That's what you're worried about?"

* * *

25 November

"Look at that guy sitting over there," my father says during Thanksgiving dinner at the Hebrew Home, pointing over my shoulder.

"What?" I say, looking.

"That's where the women sit, and when they come down and see this guy, it's not going to be good."

"Can't they sit somewhere else? It's open seating today."

"It's their table. They're not going to be happy."

"Can't they sit with him? There's plenty of room."

"He doesn't belong."

"I see."

Minutes later, the women from that table walk into the dining room. Jack Friedman is right. They're not happy.

* * *

27 November

"So, Ba, let me ask you," my father says as we approach my table at Owl Head. "Years from now, when you're gone, what happens to your table?"

"What do you mean 'what happens'?"

"When you die, I mean, what are they going to do with it?"

"When I die? I don't know. You want it?"

"I'm just asking. Are they going to sell it?"

"Yeah, I'm sure they're going to sell it. Let's try to keep the nameplate in the family, though, for future generations of Friedmans to enjoy."

On the way home: "Ba, you know I'm ninety-five."

"Yeah."

"But at least it's under 100."

"That it is."

"So why does everything hurt?"

"Dad, look at it this way: You're like a car. A brand-new one has no problems, right?"

"Right."

"But one with 100,000 miles starts to break down. You are a 100,000-mile car."

"Then I want to be a motorcycle."

We pass a Braum's Ice Cream billboard advertising "Basket of Burgers $5.95."

"How many burgers in a basket?" my father asks.

"Five."

"That's seventy cents a burger," he says, without missing a beat.

"Close enough."

* * *

28 November

I return to my father's apartment this morning to give him yet another tutorial on the use of the new coffeemaker. I notice a tube of Elmer's Glue in with the plates.

"Dad, why is there glue in with your plates?"

"Glue?" he says from the next room.

"Glue."

"Glue?"

"Glue."

"What kind of glue?"

"Glue-glue. What kind? White glue."
"Glue? I don't know. I must need it for something."
"Like what?"
"I don't know. It was here when I moved in. I think the last guy must have left it here."
"The last guy left his glue?"
"It was here when I moved in. He must have left it."
"Dad, no guy left his glue."
"Well, I thought he did."

DECEMBER

10 December

It's been years since my daughter, Nina, saw her grandfather, and Dave, her boyfriend, has never met him. My father is watching *Baywatch* when we come in.

"So, Nina, you're his daughter?" he asks, pointing to me.

"Yes, I am."

"So what are you to me?"

"Well, I'm his daughter and he's your son, so you're my grandfather."

"My son?"

"Yeah, he's your son. You're the father!" she says, laughing.

"Well," he says to Nina, "I'm his father by label only."

"'By label only'?" Nina asks.

"I haven't seen him in years," he says, pointing to me, "and then he comes into my life all of a sudden for my estate."

He turns to Dave. "And what do you do?"

Dave explains he works in farming and owns his own wire-sealing company.

"So she's your girlfriend, or are you going to marry her?" my father asks.

"Depends if she'll have me."

"You know, if you invite me to the wedding, I got fifty or sixty bucks I can give you. Nina, are you married?"

"Yes, Grandpa. Yes, I've been married three times."

"Three times? What happened?" my father asks.

"They all died in the war."

"Lovely, honey," I say.

"You know I have a Purple Heart?" he asks.

"I do," says Nina.

"Let me go get it," I say.

"You know where it is?" my father asks.

"Yeah, it's in the drawer in the bedroom."

"No, you'll never find it. It's in the drawer in the bedroom."

I bring it back and pin it on him.

"Ouch, ouch," he says. "You're putting it right through my chest."

"I am not."

"I'm just joking . . . Yeah," he tells Dave and Nina, "I stepped on a bomb."

"You didn't step on a bomb," I say. "You dropped a piece of a bridge on your toe."

"Anyway, I was in the hospital and I said, 'Where's my medal?'"

"You demanded a medal?" I ask.

"Yeah, it got me out of the war early."

"You didn't get out of the war early."

"I know, but my mother told me, 'You'll get out of the war early if you have the medal,' so I made up a story."

"Did they believe you?"

"No, I don't think so. I was in the First Cavalry Division. No horses, just infantry. We won that war, I think. You know, I'm going to be ninety-five. In five or six years, I'll be 100. So, Nina, did you come here"—he points at me—"to put a stamp on his wealth?"

"Yes, that's exactly why I came."

* * *

14 December

"Let me ask you something," he asks me at dinner. "If you die, God forbid, do I have to move from here?"

"No, you can stay."

"Oh, good," he says. "'cause that's the important thing."

* * *

17 December

I called my father today. I can't be certain, but I think I woke him from a nap, which may or may not explain the following. I could hear the television. I think maybe you could hear the television.

"Hey, Dad."

"Who do I got?"

"Barry."

"Yeah, yeah, I know. Hey, Ba. What are we doing?"

"What do you mean?"

"Why are we shooting at each other?"

"Shooting at each other? Who's shooting at us?"

"What the hell's going on? And we're shooting at each other

and breaking in and telling people to get out. And some leave, some don't. Ah, it's a mess. And then with the bombs. I think someday I'm going to go to the bathroom and then someone's going to break into the apartment and . . . I'm going to be in the bathroom."

"You're going to be in the bathroom when someone breaks in?"

"I don't know," he says, laughing. "How am I supposed to know?"

"You're right. Who knows? Look, I don't think that's going to happen. Nobody's going to be breaking into your apartment and then shooting. You're safe, Dad."

"Ach! I don't know what the hell's going on half the time."

"Nobody does."

"I mean, what do we want from each other?"

"Good question."

* * *

19 December

"How you doing, Dad?" I ask, walking in. He hasn't been himself lately. Lethargic, not hungry.

"Fine, fine," he says from the sofa. "You know, I think I'm getting old."

"Really?"

"There's nothing left," he says, laughing.

"You hungry?"

"For what?"

"Lunch."

"Yeah, I could go for some lunch. How the hell did I get to be ninety-five?"

I make him lunch.

"You make good coffee, though, I'll give you that. So, tell me," he adds, cutting turkey slices into sections. "You live with the cleaning lady, right?"

"What?"

"The girl. She's the cleaning lady, right?" he asks, as he starts eating chips.

"Well, Melissa, yeah, she cleans houses, but she's not the cleaning lady."

I decide to draw a rudimentary family tree on the back of a piece of mail. He sees the name of his brother, Hy.

"Hy, he was my brother. He was married to Shirley?" he asks.

"Right."

"What happened to her?"

"She died."

"But she was from England."

"She still died."

Then he sees his immediate-family breakdown.

"Okay, so Florence is what relation to you?" he asks.

"She's my mother. Your wife . . . my mother."

"No."

"Yeah."

"Oh, I thought—"

"—my mother, Dad."

"I thought . . . wait, you're my blood son? I thought you were someone else's and they gave you to me to raise."

* * *

21 December

Today we're at the Veterans Administration to get his hearing aids checked.

As we were leaving the Hebrew Home, in the elevator were three women, each wearing a "What a friend we have in Jesus" T-shirt. Before the door has closed, my father, in full stride, says, "You're in the wrong place."

At the VA, the audiologist takes out my father's hearing aids, cleans them, and puts them back in his ear.

"Can you hear a difference?" she asks.

"Tell me a dirty joke and I'll let you know."

* * *

26 December

"So what excites you, Ba?" he asks me at Owl Head.

"What excites me?"

"Yeah—your girl, your work, your lifestyle? What excites you?"

"Great question. Pretty much all those things."

"Say, Ba, tell me, what the hell are we doing in Tulsa? Oklahoma! That's not a state, that's a condition. How much longer I got, Ba? How much longer?"

... to be continued

about the author

Barry is the author of eight books—*Road Comic, Funny You Should Mention It, Four Days and a Year Later, The Joke Was on Me,* and *Jacob Fishman's Marriages*—as well as the Jack Sh*t trilogy. He is a standup comedian, political columnist, and reporter, and his work has appeared *The New Yorker, Esquire, The Progressive Populist, MediaPost, The Las Vegas Review-Journal,* and *AAPG Explorer,* a magazine for petroleum geologists, which is noteworthy, considering how little Barry know about petroleum geology and how he usually hurts himself filling his car with gas. Barry was also in *UHF* with "Weird Al" Yankovic, setting a cinematic high water mark for those who have since played (or dream one day of playing) "Crony #2" in a major motion picture. The movie still provides him with $3.76 residual checks every time it plays at a Lithuanian drive-in or some lost soul downloads it. Barry now lives in Portugal and hates referring to himself in the third person.

also by barry friedman

Jack Sh*t Volume One: Voluptuous Bagels and Other Concerns of Jack Friedman

Jack Sh*t Volume Two: Wait for the Movie. It's in Color

Jacob Fishman's Marriages

Four Days and a Year Later

The Joke Was on Me

Road Comic

Funny You Should Mention It

www.ingramcontent.com/pod-product-compliance
Lightning Source LLC
Chambersburg PA
CBHW022026050526
44107CB00118B/1291/J